Moving On

Moving On:
The Heroines of Shirley Ann Grau, Anne Tyler, and Gail Godwin

Susan S. Kissel

Bowling Green State University Popular Press
Bowling Green, OH 43403

Copyright © 1996 Bowling Green State University Popular Press

Library of Congress Cataloging-in-Publication Data
Kissel, Susan S.
    Moving on : the heroines of Shirley Ann Grau, Anne Tyler, and
Gail Godwin / Susan S. Kissel.
        p.   cm.
    Includes bibliographical references (p.   ) and index.
    ISBN 0-87972-711-X. -- ISBN 0-87972-712-8 (pbk.)
    1. American fiction--Women authors--History and criticism.
2. Heroines in literature. 3. Women and literature--Southern States--
History--20th century. 4. American fiction--Southern States--History
and criticism. 5. American fiction--White authors--History and criti-
cism. 6. American fiction--20th century--History and criticism. 7. Grau,
Shirley Ann--Characters--Heroines. 8. Tyler, Anne--Characters--
Heroines. 9. Godwin, Gail--Characters--Heroines. 10. Southern States--
In literature. 11. Women in literature. I. Title.
PS374.H47K57   1996
813'.54099287'0975--dc20   96-23213
                                                                CIP

Cover design by Laura Darnell Dumm

To my mother, Viola Predmore Steves, and to
the memory of my father, Mervin Franklin Steves,
for their liberating influence

Contents

Preface and Acknowledgments

In 1979, I was one of twenty-five faculty who participated in a Modern Language Association and National Endowment for the Humanities joint-sponsored summer course on "Nontraditional Women's Literature" at the University of Alabama. As a result of that experience, I developed a course on southern women writers that I have continued to teach (in various forms) for more than fifteen years, along with other courses on the American South and specific southern authors.

As a result of teaching these courses, I have become aware of distinct traditions of southern writing: in particular, of differences between white and black, male and female, modern and contemporary, writers of the twentieth century American South. In this book, after a brief introduction in the first chapter, I attempt to deal with only one segment of southern writing of this century—and with only one aspect of contemporary southern women's writing, in particular. I have concentrated in this study on only a small part of the whole southern literary picture: on novels by contemporary southern white women. In doing so, I attempt to show that white southern women are, at last, "moving on" in their fiction, that their heroines are not only continuing to renounce southern patriarchal tradition (in the manner of Kate Chopin's or Ellen Glasgow's protagonists) but moving beyond to establish independent lives and caring communities in American society. In other words, I endeavor to show how white southern women writers and their protagonists are beginning to close the gap that has existed for a long time between themselves and black southern women authors (whose protagonists have long shown that strength and independence can coexist with feminine softness and love for others, that female maturity must be synonymous with complex character development).

After looking at the history of white southern women's writing in the twentieth century, I concentrate on three contemporary southern white female authors, in particular. Shirley Ann Grau, Anne Tyler, and Gail Godwin, I believe, are representative of the changes taking place today in the novels of white southern women writers. In addition, I consider a number of their white southern contemporaries in a later chapter both to broaden my study and strengthen my case that white southern women novelists and their heroines are, indeed, "moving on" in their writing.

Although this book deals only with the novel, a traditional form of female writing, I remain indebted to the many scholars who took part in the 1979 "Nontraditional Women's Literature" seminar—especially Leonore Hoffman (who directed it), and Elizabeth Meese, Ellen DuBois, and Margaret Culley (who served as core faculty throughout the entire five weeks). I am also indebted to the hundreds of students who have taken my courses on the American South and shared their ideas with me over the years. They have helped me consolidate the ideas about southern women writers that I present here.

This book would not have been possible without the support of Northern Kentucky University in granting me two sabbatical leaves, one to conduct research and a second to write several chapters of my manuscript. I am also grateful to my department chair, Paul Reichardt, for his support through reassigned time and his continuing interest in my research. Sharon Taylor, of Steely Library's Interlibrary Loan department, has also provided considerable service by obtaining materials from libraries throughout the country. In addition, I would like to thank a number of my colleagues for reading and commenting on portions of my manuscript: John Alberti, Paige Byam, Conrad Carroll, Steve Gores, Sally Jacobsen, Hilary Landwehr, Tom Leech, Gisele Loriot-Raymer, Danny Miller, Andrew Taylor, and Robert Wallace—whose time and feedback I greatly appreciate.

Finally, I am grateful, as always, to my husband and colleague, Michael C.C. Adams, for reading the manuscript, sharing ideas with me, and giving me his unfailing support throughout the many phases of this project.

1

Introduction

When we think of contemporary American fiction, we think of characters cut off from the past and from the present; men and women leading frenzied, yet aimless lives; individuals who find they have lost their faith—and feel helpless on that account—while being aware, at the same time, that they never had much faith in the first place. As Fred Hobson explains in *The Southern Writer in the Postmodern World*, contemporary writing explores the "post-modern world, a world in which order, structure, and meaning—are constantly called into question" (9). Many contemporary authors invite us to query the purpose and meaning of their characters and their fiction, their own authorial credibility. Contemporary literary critics such as Michel Foucault, Roland Barthes, and Jacques Derrida further encourage us to "question the whole notion of the unified subject, the center, the self" in authors, characters, texts, readers, and life itself (Cheryl Walker 552).

At the heart of this cultural and literary upheaval lies a sense of great loss. As Patricia Drechsel Tobin concludes in *Time and the Novel: The Genealogical Imperative*, "the disappearance of god, the end of history, the demise of man, the death of the novel, the murder of the father—these are the apocalyptic phrases by which we now measure the passage of our culture through time" (192). Gone is the "conceptualization of human life as purposeful and therefore imbued with meaning" (Tobin 5); gone is the sense of "causality. . . . [of] familial significance. . . . [whereby the father] extend[ed] the paternal promise of purpose throughout his progeny, bestowing upon them a legacy that contain[ed] within this structural unity an entire history of meaning" (Tobin 7). With the death of god as father and the death of the father as god came the birth of contemporary authorship. Tobin explains that today's author (whom she characterizes in the midst of the dissolution of traditional culture, ironically, as male) can no longer be seen as

the good father who dutifully holds together his novelistic family, nor the superego or reality principle functioning under the aspect of rationality and causality, nor the ironic consciousness that revises the dream upwards for our waking acceptability. Instead, he is a Fancy man . . . [who] subvert[s] both sequence

1

expectation and symbolic interpretation—that is, life and meaning as determined by the father. (206-07)

Many contemporary authors, thus, call into question "an entire history of meaning extending from the family into the world" (Tobin 7), refusing to imbue their texts with an ultimate authority and significance they can no longer find in the external world. As Tobin has concluded, with "[the] desymbolization of the father" in Western history and literature has come "a general postmodern tendency to demetaphorize, demythologize, deconstruct our thinking about people and objects and events" (210).

The death of the father as patriarchal authority has been cause for much celebration in contemporary literature, yet there has also been bewilderment, fear, and regret. For we have become accustomed to looking at time as linear and progressive, leading from generation to generation, stretching from father to son, at life as having a significance extending beyond immediate deeds and lives. There can be little wonder that twentieth-century Western literature has revealed a "double movement of desire and repulsion for the world of the fathers" it has repudiated (Tobin 12). Sandra Gilbert and Susan Gubar, in Volume 2 of their encyclopedic critical study, *No Man's Land: The Place of the Woman Writer in the Twentieth Century,* depict the literary battles between the sexes that have resulted from "the radical sex changes, generated by the Great War of 1918 . . . the metamorphosis of sexuality and sex roles . . . the gender transformations connected with the decline of faith in a white male supremacist empire" (258-59). Women felt newly threatened by men, men by women, as they altered their traditional roles or engaged in struggles for power within the patriarchal void. Post World War I authors reflected the confusion and disorder they saw everywhere around them—as well as the nostalgia they felt for a past that no longer existed, one that had seemed whole and significant (even while fraught with its own terrors and battles). In the modern void, Gilbert and Gubar found "women oscillating between their matrilineage and their patrilineage in an arduous process of self-definition" (*No Man's Land* 1: 169).

In recent decades, as women have continued to struggle to define themselves as writers and as readers, they have discovered themselves doing so while the very concept of the "self" is being deconstructed. Further, as Cheryl Walker has pointed out in "Feminist Criticism and the Author," contemporary literary theorists who have proclaimed the death of the author and the fluidity of the self have done so at the very moment in history when women have embraced their literary identity and the potential of their powers of authorship. However, as the psychological research of Nancy Chodorow and others suggests, "female identity is a process, and primary identity for women is more flexible and relational than for men" (Gardiner 354). In addition, as Joanne Frye points out, the postmodern "emphasis on process, on constant construction and reconstruction of individual identity, opens the possibility of a female character *not* constrained by assumptions of essential femininity but rather definitional of a new complexity embracing both autonomy and femaleness" (42-43). Thus, contemporary women writers and their readers have continued undaunted and, in fact, aided by prevailing postmodern and deconstructionist theoretical winds, in following heroines through various stages of development as they search for new (yet ever changeable, adaptable) "selves."

Contemporary women writers and their readers begin with different concepts of the self, different legacies from their fathers, and different responses to twentieth-century change than those of their male counterparts. Once defined largely as the wives, daughters, and sisters of men, occupying the small and peripheral places of history and literature, women have felt newly empowered to proclaim authorship of both their lives and their texts in the twentieth century. As Carolyn Heilbrun asserts in *Writing a Woman's Life,* "What became essential was for women to see themselves collectively, not individually, not caught in some individual erotic and familial plots and, inevitably, found wanting" (46). Rejecting the old "erotic plots" that always ended with obeisance to the impossible ideals of "wifedom and motherhood" (Heilbrun 48, 58), women began to create fictional alter egos who dared to embark on their own heroic plots of adventure. As Carolyn Heilbrun has shown, in writing new lives for their characters, women authors set out to reshape and restructure new lives for themselves and for their contemporary female readers.

In fashioning new journeys and new "selves," contemporary heroines have faced many setbacks. The shadows both of past experience and present uncertainty have continued to darken their way. As Dana Heller explains in *The Feminization of Quest-Romance: Radical Departures,*

the young woman's call to adventure must somehow transcend the limits of an enclosed space: a house, a garden, an institution, an introspective mind. Her call to adventure often becomes, in Susan J. Rosowski's words, "an awakening to limitation" . . . . The tragic illnesses, suicides, and mental deterioration [of women's fiction] speak of a culture, as well as a male-dominant tradition of literary forms and themes, that has privileged the might of male flight and denied female protagonists the experience of "lighting out" for feminized territory of self-creation and social fulfillment. (10-11)

In other words, the heroine often has ended up right back where she began: "Women's quests that seek resolution through marriage often signal the female protagonist's recognition that individual aspirations and desires are impossible to achieve outside the institutions which she had once hoped to transcend" (Heller 11). When the contemporary heroine does succeed in her escape, she can find herself in yet another trap. As John Aldridge comments in *The American Novel and the Way We Live Now,* "It is not surprising that the picaresque journey [for the contemporary female protagonist] . . . often ends in the discovery that the state of freedom has become as oppressive a tyranny as the tyrannies left behind" (18). The contemporary American heroine may "find nothing to which she is willing to give herself and in the giving achieve the meaning of her freedom" (Aldridge 18). According to Aldridge, she may end up asking, "Am I freeing myself or becoming imprisoned in my search for freedom? . . . What am I freeing myself for and from? Am I freeing myself from all those things that in the past limited my freedom, but gave me limits in which to define my function, only to find myself without a means of defining a function in a freedom at least theoretically without limits?" (Aldridge 17-18). Bereft of the certainties, albeit limiting certainties, of the past, the contemporary American heroine may end up as distraught and disillusioned as the contemporary American hero often seems to be.

I believe, however, that the contemporary white southern heroine is less likely to be at such loose ends—or, at least, finds herself at different loose ends. Her past and her tradition have been, paradoxically, both more sustaining and more burdensome than her northern counterpart's. As Fred Hobson reveals in *The Southern Writer in the Postmodern World,* southern writers, male and female, have remained concerned "with place, family, community, and religion . . . with history, with the southern past" of a structured and continually restructured tradition until as recently as the 1970s (4). Even now, Hobson argues,

the southern writer in a postmodern world is not necessarily, is not usually, a postmodern *writer.* That is to say, the contemporary southern writer . . . essentially *accepts,* rather than invents, his world, is not given to fantasy, does not *in his fiction* question the whole assumed relationship between narrator and narrative, does not question the nature of fiction itself. The contemporary southern fiction writer, although he or she may experiment with time sequence and point of view (as the great southern modernist Faulkner did, after all), in more basic respects usually plays by the old rules of the game. (9)

While the southern writer certainly has reflected the New South and its multiple changes in work after work, seldom has there been in southern fiction what Lewis Lawson has called "the nameless anxiety concomitant with urban, industrialized existence, the anxiety that drained off all vitality and love of life, the anxiety that compelled people to live frantically, yet fruitlessly" (15). The traditions of southern life have changed and are changing, but the storyteller, the story, a sense of meaning and purpose, a strong sense of time, place, character and plot have, for the most part, remained for both male and female writers. This is not despite, but because of, the separate tradition and the devastating history of the South.

For at least a century, the story of the American South was one of loss and disintegration. The end of the Civil War in 1865 had brought the painful loss of thousands of white southern husbands and fathers who had not returned from battle; of those who had, many came back maimed, traumatized, and broken. So massive had been the human, physical and cultural losses of the white South in the Civil War that their reality could not be endured. The white South's response was denial of the present coupled with nostalgia for the past, nostalgia for the lost, romanticized world of the fathers that had ceased to exist. As Richard King explains in *A Southern Renaissance: The Cultural Awakening of the American South, 1930-1955*, there developed a "historical consciousness" in the post-Civil War white South that fixated on the lost father as mythical hero; in the ensuing tradition, the "essential figures were the father and the grandfather and . . . [the] essential structure was the literal and symbolic family . . . what I call the 'Southern family romance'" (7). In such a tradition, the present could never measure up to the past; the truth could not erase the lie; the most courageous of women, the most promising of children, could never hope to equal the vanquished—yet triumphant—father. As King explains,

In defeat, in the memory of the common struggle against the Yankee and the Freedman, the white South became united as it rarely had been before the War. . . . The father came to be the gracious, courteous, but tough planter of the pre-war years who had led the heroic and collective struggle against the Yankees. He was the "presiding presence" in the [Southern family] romance; and, as he faded from the scene, the grandsons in the early years of the century idealized the great hero of the romance even more. Measured against the heroic generations of the grandfathers, the fathers seemed rather unheroic and prosaic to their sons. (21, 34-35)

6 Moving On

The mythic fathers and their stories lived on; all else could be understood and measured in their light.

The battlefields of World War I were to offer the grandsons of the white South hope—a chance, "as Allen Tate put it, to rejoin the world . . . to demonstrate the heroism which had been drummed into them as one of the transcendent virtues of the Southern tradition" (King 13-14). Will Percy, uncle of contemporary author Walker Percy and author of *Lanterns on the Levee*, serves as a case in point. As Richard King reports,

All his life he felt small and physically unprepossessing beside his virile father and grandfather. . . . Only with the onset of WWI and his service in combat did Will Percy for a time feel necessary. . . . Thus the war had great meaning for Percy and many Southern young men, for it represented a chance to prove themselves the equal of their heroic grandfathers and fathers—real and symbolic—who had risked their lives in the only war that had really counted. (92-93)

The grandsons found themselves caught up in the desire to relive the heroic quest of a mythological southern past.

The prominent male writers of the Southern Renaissance that Richard King considers in his study, covering twenty-five years of literary history in the South, from 1930 to 1955, fixated on the heroic white father and the myth of the transcendent experience of his Civil War sacrifice. King considers the writings of Allen Tate, Robert Penn Warren, Cleanth Brooks, Will Percy, John Crowe Ransom, Thomas Wolfe, James Agee, W.J. Cash, C. Vann Woodward, and especially William Faulkner (Lillian Smith is the only woman author discussed)—writers who were engaged in perpetual dialogue with the lost fathers of the past.[1] Their struggle was defined by the southern myth, "the family romance—which was the burden to be thrown off. But for some of the same writers, especially the Faulkner of 'The Bear' and Will Percy and perhaps even C. Vann Woodward, it was historical consciousness itself that was burdensome" (288).

In Faulkner's "Barn Burning" we see how the burden of the father, of blood ties, of the past, becomes intertwined with an opposing theme, that of the romance of the father and his courageous heroism. Sarty feels "the old fierce pull of blood" (419); protests, *"He's my father!"*; and defends his father, "He was brave! . . . He was in the war! He was in Colonel Sartoris' cav'ry!" (436). But even without knowing the full story of his father's corruption, he feels humiliated by their relationship, by "the old blood which he had not been permitted to choose for himself, which had been bequeathed him willy nilly" (433). Sarty's is a shameful heritage similar to that passed on to many sons and daughters of southern Civil War "heroes" whose cause was repudiated and whose "virtue" came to be branded selfish, racist, and sinful. Love and grief, attraction and repulsion, vie within Sarty even as he acts to renounce his father and warn Major De Spain in time, he hopes, to save another barn from burning.

Similarly, throughout the literature of the white South's twentieth-century male writers, the conflict between love and hate, past and present, pride and shame has persisted. White southern male literature has become a complex interchange between father and son, one in which Randolph Runyon, in *The Taciturn Text: The Fiction of Robert Penn Warren*, contends,

the father wrote for the son to read, a text the father should have written but someone else wrote but the father came to possess and passes on to the son, a text . . . whose existence the father refuses to acknowledge in the very moment he transmits it to the son, a text the father wants the son to write for him, or a text the son inherits from the father and rewrites to his own advantage. (2)

Only recently, King explains, has the white southern male writer found this extended and all-absorbing, if convoluted, "conversation" at an end and the burden lifted from his shoulders:

But the South, and the modern world which it has finally, albeit reluctantly, joined, must now deal with a new cultural situation. The value of the work of a contemporary southern writer such as Walker Percy is that he recognizes that the tradition of the fathers is gone forever, as are the heady days of the Southern Renaissance. The fathers and Faulkner must both be transcended. (292)

The son's dialogue with the sinful, yet heroic, white father seems, at last, to have come to an end.

Only recently, as well, have women writers of the white South begun to throw off the tradition of the heroic fathers of white southern mythology. Certainly, it would seem that they had little to gain from validating the romantic myths in the first place, for, as Richard King points out, "The family romance was built around the fundamental valorization of difference and hierarchy. Past was superior to present; parents to children; male to female; white to black; rich to poor" (290). Yet, as Gerda Lerner has argued, the system of patriarchy can function only with the cooperation of women. This cooperation is secured by a variety of means: gender indoctrination; education deprivation; the denial to women of knowledge of their history; the dividing of women, one from the other, by defining "respectability" and "deviance" according to women's sexual activities; by restraints and outright coercion; by discrimination in access to economic resources and political power; and by awarding class privileges to conforming women. (217)

All of these were widely practiced in the American South where white women were "condemned to hearing, accepting, and living by the self-destructive myths of the nature and role of women as passive, submissive, obedient, compliant, pious" (Joan Schulz 93).

While Anne Firor Scott believes that Ellen Glasgow's generation of white southern women writers, born in the 1880s, was the last "expected to bow entirely to the father's will" (214), and Joan Schulz speaks of women writers of the Southern Renaissance who "establish[ed] an alternative tradition of dissent respecting the values and virtues of family" (92), the struggle for the liberation of even the white South's most outspoken women—its writers—has been prolonged and difficult. Lucinda MacKethan in *Daughters of Time: Creating Woman's Voice in Southern Story*, in discussing the works of more recent writers such as Eudora Welty and Lee Smith, speaks of their

concern [with] a culture that remained patriarchal even longer than other regions of America; thus, the women who tell them begin with the voices, the identities, the constraints of daughterhood. Southern daughters were the creations and inheritors of a culture which in part defined and perpetuated itself by their silence. . . . [There exists] conclusive evidence that women's right to growth into autonomous selfhood was delayed even more strenuously in the South than in other regions. (5)

After the Civil War, white southern women, in the face of their returning, vanquished men, worked hard to bolster injured bodies and damaged pride, repair and revive fallen structures—and myths, and erect memorials to the Civil War dead—and to a "heroic" fallen past. They fulfilled their traditional female role as conservators of the culture (all the more desperately because the culture barely remained) and directed their strength and energy into tasks of subservience and self-sacrifice, much as they had done before the war. Catherine Clinton, in *The Plantation Mistress*, explains that "feminist ideology, nascent in the post-Revolutionary North and destined to emerge vigorously at mid-century, lay dormant throughout most of the nineteenth century in the South" (205).

That this pattern would continue into the twentieth century in women's struggle for the vote and in later struggles in the 1940s and into the 1980s for passage of the Equal Rights Amendment, seems attributable not only to the loss of the Civil War and the demands of its heroic mythology, but to what Jean Friedman in *The Enclosed Garden* identifies as the South's "older agrarian and family-oriented structural pattern . . . [which strengthened] patriarchal boundaries" long ago weakened in the industrial, urban North (7). And so, even in recent works by southern women writers (both white and black), Lucinda MacKethan finds these characteristics:

first, respect for family as the heart of social order; next, the symbolization of the home as the locus of all inheritable values; third, the tension between hate and love for the father, who in the culture holds the power to define, to validate, to circumscribe, and to disinherit; and finally, acceptance of memory as the primary means of knowing and conscious selection of what Lewis Simpson has called a "southern aesthetic of memory" as a means of organizing perception. (10)

The struggle between respect and contempt, love and hate, worship of and revulsion for the patriarchal tradition of the white South has continued for women writers—as it did for male writers—until the last decades of the twentieth century.

Family defined the role of the southern white woman and afforded structure and salvation to her shattered culture. Yet, at the same time, we find that the white southern family subordinated and degraded those very women who struggled to anchor and uphold it. As Richard King explains, "Powerful though the [white] Southern woman might be in fact, she was distinctly subordinate in the romance to the powerful and heroic father" (34). This was especially true as she was not only placed under the control of the male in the southern hierarchy, but as she also experienced erosion of her own domestic sphere. She found her female roles as mother and wife diluted, largely given over to southern black women who existed as caretakers of white children, cooks, housekeepers, maids, and secret concubines within her own household. What was left to her was the paradoxical role of "the asexual mother" (King 35). She was most often seen as merely a child woman: dependent, weak, and innocent herself. As Richard King explains, "Since white women in a patriarchal society were seen as children of sorts, it was customary for the male-female relationship to include a defused component of the parent-child relationship" (128). Lillian Smith had revealed that the South's "real [black] mothers could never be acknowledged publicly.

This was the ultimate denial at the heart of Southern culture" (189). Black women, empowered sexually and maternally, were denied social, political, and familial status by the dominant white society. Yet they knew they were needed and valued (if secretly)—leading, as we shall see at the end of this chapter, to a different literary tradition (one that I will not be considering in this work) from that of their white female counterparts. White southern women, however, while ostensibly idealized as being at the very heart of the culture, were, in reality, marginalized (as well as infantilized). Anne Goodwyn Jones argues in *Tomorrow Is Another Day: The Woman Writer in the South, 1859-1936* that "in general, historians agree that the function of [white] southern womanhood has been to justify the perpetuation of the hegemony of the male sex, the upper and middle classes, and the white race" (10). The white southern woman was not important for herself but for her function in legitimizing class, race, and gender privilege for her protection. Jones continues that "such a system reveres the white mother yet deprives her of her sexual and maternal identity, leaving her a child-wife, and forces the black woman into a paradoxical position, strong and dependent, responsible and subservient" (*Tomorrow* 29). Nothing proved more necessary for the perpetuation of the "family romance . . . [with its] history of domination" (King 133) than white female silence and passivity, white womanly collusion and cooperation, in the process of her own marginalization.

By their very acts of authorship, white women writers threatened the social system of the South. Merely to claim an identity, a self, was to shatter the symbol of white southern womanhood—especially since the symbol was one of ultimate selflessness and acquiescent silence (as the black woman writer of the South was also to give voice to her *real* strength and power, long hidden in the white kitchen and nursery). Nor did the white southern woman writer simply give voice to her own being, her own consciousness, and that of her heroines. In writing, as Anne Goodwyn Jones reveals, she rebelled against the patriarchal tradition, the family romance, the heroic father of southern history, in order to "criticize the ideal of [white] southern womanhood" (Jones, *Tomorrow* xii)—as the black woman writer was to expose her own personhood and cultural value, as well. Through her works, the white woman writer of the South began to "resist, refuse, or reject the kind of family identity, family roles, and family ties with the past or the present considered so vital to the Southern way of life, sought after or lamented with such vigor and obsessiveness by male figures in Southern literature" (Joan Schulz 92). In doing so, nevertheless, the white woman writer of the South followed the Faulknerian pattern of love and hate, defiance and compliance. For much of the twentieth century, white southern daughters wrote, as did their Southern Renaissance brothers, ultimately validating patriarchal power and authority even while rejecting the "voicelessness, passivity, [and] ignorance" required by the ideal of southern womanhood (Jones, *Tomorrow*, 40).

With Elizabeth Madox Roberts's heroine in *The Time of Man* (1926), white southern women writers rejoiced to discover, "Here I am! . . . I'm Ellen Chesser! I'm here!" (81). Accompanying that self-discovery usually came both gender self-hatred and the rejection of negative patterns of white female lives: "When they say, 'Come see the bride,' I always say, 'I'd rather see her in ten year' "; if she's not careful, she'll "look like a buzzard. Up by sunup to cook for Tom and up till midnight with the youngones" (*TM* 147). Yet Ellen Chesser and other white southern heroines most often find themselves fulfilling the traditional female pattern of wifedom and motherhood they fear and despise, trapped in the ongoing struggle of life as a part of the nuclear, patriarchal family, the most impoverished of them such as Ellen Chesser bearing children only to watch them struggle, "hollow-eyed and thin, their beings waiting upon the hazards of the seasons" (*TM* 319). Despite extensive hardship and personal suffering, they most often continue, too, to feel sympathy for their beleaguered husbands, working to protect them, even through failure and betrayal, standing by them and following along wherever the male journey takes them. If Ellen Chesser longs for "some better country. . . . Our own place maybe" (*TM* 380) where she can feel more in control, more at home, the life she finds herself accepting is the one she has always known in patriarchal society—"a hard country, not gentle like you'd want" (*TM* 380). Rebellion and submission go hand in hand, even in the most ostensibly subversive works by white women authors of the twentieth-century South.

From Kate Chopin to Ellen Glasgow to Harriette Arnow, southern white women writers have spoken out to attack the concept of female subservience and self-sacrifice for husband and family, revealing its destructiveness not only for adult women themselves but often for the very children, husbands and society these women have served. Nevertheless, as Anne Goodwyn Jones has shown in *Tomorrow Is Another Day*, their fiction has been either evasive about, or despairing of, lasting changes in the lives, relationships, and communities of southern women and men. In Kate Chopin's *The Awakening* (1899), Edna Pontellier commits suicide, defeated by a system that denies her selfhood in favor of sacrificial wifehood and motherhood, instead. In rebellion against the anonymity of daughterhood in the home of an authoritarian father, Edna has fled his house only to enter another state of female invisibility in the home of her husband, Leónce Pontellier. Too late, Edna protests merely playing out familial roles and satisfying oppressive cultural requirements; "I'm not going to be forced into doing things" (*TA* 132), she cries—but she has long since been caught in society's trap, snared, as Dr. Mandelet declares, by the "illusions [of youth]. It seems to be a provision of Nature; a decoy to secure mothers for the race. And Nature takes no account of moral consequences, of arbitrary conditions which we create, and which we feel obliged to maintain at any cost" (*TA* 132). Edna rejects the "arbitrary" demands of southern culture that she sacrifice herself for others and seeks her own identity, her own life—by developing her artistic talents, by establishing her own life apart from Leónce in her "pigeon-house," and by acquiring her own set of friends.

But Edna has children—and their very existence threatens the personhood she has rejoiced to begin discovering. Edna protests to Adèle Ratignolle at the outset of her "awakening," "I would give up the unessential; I would give my money; I would give my life for my children; but I wouldn't give myself" (*TA* 67). Ironically, Edna finds that the only way she can retain her selfhood is by giving up her life. Suicide will be her final protest, her ultimate escape from society's demands, and her last tribute to their power. At the moment of her decision, her children "appeared before her like antagonists who had overcome her; who had overpowered and sought to drag her into the soul's slavery for the rest of her days. But she knew a way to elude them" (*TA* 136). To preserve her selfhood from defeat and enslavement on land, Edna swims out into the sea until "the shore was far behind her, and her strength was gone" (*TA* 137).

Even there, as Elaine Showalter reveals, she is pursued by the sound of her father's voice, the barking of a dog chained to a tree, the clanging of the cavalry officer's spurs, and the hum of bees extracting pollen from the pinks in the garden—"the 'humming' life of creation and achievement" which both attracts Edna to desire it for herself and finally silences her with its insistence on its own enduring history and logic (Showalter 187). Awakened into desire for independence by discovering her sexuality, Edna finds that same sexuality connected to what Anne Goodwyn Jones calls her "bondage—to men, as possessors (Robert) and masters (Alcée), and ultimately, through childbirth, into bondage to nature itself" (Jones, *Tomorrow* 160). Edna can find no way to live apart from the female body and the female roles which continue to chain her to nature and to society in painful and demeaning ways (as Mademoiselle Reisz and Madame Ratignolle remain chained in their own ways, as well). Anne Goodwyn Jones asks, "Why couldn't [Edna] have gone, like Huck Finn, into the *territory* ahead of the rest?" and answers, "I think . . . because Edna has been unable to find, on the land, any image of freedom that is not derived from an essentially masculine and capitalistic value system and thus can serve as a satisfactory model for her growth into womanhood" (*Tomorrow* 158). John Carlos Rowe agrees, arguing that Kate Chopin understood that "woman's rebellion [would] involve much more . . . than merely the assertion of her naked self; that rebellion [would] require thorough transvaluation of the modes of production that govern[ed] both the psyche and the economy of late-nineteenth-century capitalism" (121). The enormity of the task of rebellion and recreation of southern culture defeated Edna Pontellier—and Kate Chopin's imagination, as well.

Even when the white southern heroine's adventure ends in her apparent triumph, we find, upon closer inspection, the same signs of her entrapment that prevail in *The Awakening*. In *Barren Ground* (1925), Ellen Glasgow's protagonist, Dorinda Oakley, continues to validate most of the cultural givens of her time and place in the South, even as she seems to subvert them. Dorinda turns her back on men and on her female sexuality after being jilted by the fickle Jason Greylock, determined now to remain independent and free: "She had finished with romance, as she had finished with Jason, for ever" (*BG* 144). Yet in her rebellion, Dorinda embraces the very essence of what Anne Goodwyn Jones has called the South's "essentially masculine and capitalistic value system" (*Tomorrow* 158) which had defined her and reduced her to insignificance in the first place (so insignificant that Jason has not had to concern himself with her feelings and her fate at the outset of the novel). Dorinda's rebellion stems from her anger that men have failed her—her ineffectual father and her alcoholic lover Jason—*by not being manly enough*. Dorinda sets out to succeed where they have failed, turning "barren ground" into fertile soil, making a good profit on her farm, hardening herself against life's difficulties (and her own female softness). After the pain of being jilted and her subsequent miscarriage in New York, Dorinda begins, as Lucinda MacKethan explains, to "chart [her] determined movement away from the [feminine] fate that would be considered natural for her" (69) and becomes, according to Elizabeth Jane Harrison, "her own rescuer" (34) in "a female-centered quest for heroism . . . a radical plot for southern women authors of this era" (29).

Dorinda's female-centered quest, however, seems very familiar: a carbon copy of the traditional male plot. Dorinda returns to Pedlar's Mill, rejoicing to be "caught again in the tide of material things" (*BG* 407), to find her strength in "the land [that unlike human beings] would stay by her" (*BG* 408), to look to "the future . . . [in her] search for buried treasure and the possibilities of high adventure" (*BG* 408)— heretofore an essentially masculine and materialistic quest. Having married Nathan Pedlar in a loveless business arrangement planned to allow her to acquire more land and a competent manager for her property, both at one time, Dorinda can complete her adventure in traditional, patriarchal fashion, passing on her property to the male child (although a daughter, Minnie May, is the eldest of Nathan's children). At the end of *Barren Ground*, she proudly tells her beloved John Abner (Nathan's son and hers now by marriage), "When I am gone, both farms will be yours" (*BG* 409). Through her actions, Dorinda has paradoxically taken upon herself the male role, unexamined and unchanged—endorsing its traditional values, preserving the patriarchal system, and passing it along intact in her will.

At the same time, she continues to embody the unfulfilled, unhappy, enslaved womanhood of the South she has sought to avoid. Unconsciously, she has become almost a mirror image of the very mother she pitied and despised—the pathetic Mrs. Oakley, who admits, "I can't stop. . . . I can't see things going to rack and ruin and not try to prevent it. . . . It rests me to work" (*BG* 36). Dorinda has asked of her mother, "Was this life?" (*BG* 39), yet her own adult life in Pedlar's Mill has also been one of ceaseless toil, constant drudgery, and strict asexuality, a life without joy, requiring "Endurance. Fortitude" (*BG* 408). If it is a life more successful economically than her mother's, it is also one closer to the white aristocratic ideal of southern womanhood: the white mistress overseeing the work of slaves on her plantation. Dorinda condescends to her employee, Fluvanna—her only intimate female friend from whom she, yet, remains estranged by color (Elizabeth Schultz 70-71)—and the black farm laborers who assist her in her struggle with the land.

Ostensibly turning her back on the romance of white southern womanhood, "dismant[ling]" and "revis[ing] the heroic order" of the South as Michael Kreyling sees Ellen Glasgow attempting to do through heroines who wrest plots away from failed southern heroes (93), Dorinda Oakley acts most often to perpetuate the values and behaviors of a racist, sexist, materialistic, hierarchical system long associated with southern history. She has become a successful farm owner with little time for her own sex, or for sex itself, a woman dedicated to making a profit through the use of the latest scientific methods, as well as historically exploited black labor. And, traditional as she is, Dorinda must nevertheless be punished for "steal[ing] the role of hero from the male characters . . . she must 'atone' for this sin" (Harrison 32). Elizabeth Jane Harrison shows how Glasgow requires Dorinda's acts of female courage to be overshadowed by Nathan's life-giving chivalry near the end of *Barren Ground* and how Glasgow portrays Dorinda as paying tribute to the other rightful male hero of the novel, Jason Greylock, when Dorinda nurses at his deathbed to make amends for her earlier acts of harshness towards him (32).[2]

Similarly, *Gone with the Wind* (1936) by Margaret Mitchell paradoxically "articulates, challenges, and finally confirms the traditional view of the nature and roles of the sexes" (Jones, *Tomorrow* 349) in the post-Civil War South it portrays. Like Dorinda, Scarlett O'Hara is simultaneously a complex and rebellious, yet submissive and conventional, southern heroine. Too, she proves to be an excellent businesswoman, a hard worker, ambitious, and strong. She also follows her father's advice to place her faith in the land, returning to Tara in times of crisis, as Dorinda Oakley follows her father in putting her faith in the land, first at Old Farm and later at Five Oaks, as well. In *Gone with the Wind*, Scarlett saves Tara following her father's breakdown after the war, her mother's death, and the destruction of her beloved Ashley Wilkes's Twelve Oaks plantation—working to create a future for all of them. Scarlett has the competence, energy, and vision to take advantage of the post-Civil War South's new industrialization, as well, beginning her own lumber business in Atlanta, again being strong when all the men around her appear as weak and ineffectual as had those around Ellen Glasgow's Dorinda Oakley. But we find that Scarlett O'Hara, too, upholds the patriarchal tradition, that she actually longs for a Rhett Butler to overpower, dominate, punish, and reject her.

Anne Goodwyn Jones explains that Margaret Mitchell's view of southern womanhood was so complex that she needed two heroines in *Gone with the Wind*, Scarlett O'Hara and Melanie Wilkes, finding "it imaginatively impossible to unify her conception of woman. . . . she had meant for Melanie, the ideal Southern woman, to be the leading character, but . . . somehow Scarlett had simply taken over" (*Tomorrow* 333). Margaret Mitchell used Rhett Butler to control Scarlett, punish and defeat her, in order to redeem herself imaginatively and validate Melanie Wilkes as the truly good southern heroine, "the oxymoronic ideal of the woman made of steel yet masked in fragility . . . [exerting her] strength . . . only within the home and only to serve the husband, the family, and the South" (Jones, *Tomorrow* 13).

Darden Asbury Pyron's biography of Margaret Mitchell, *Southern Daughter: The Life of Margaret Mitchell*, suggests that the rebellious Scarlett and the submissive Melanie represent two sides of the struggle going on inside Mitchell herself. If Mitchell had been raised to fulfill the ideal of southern womanhood, *Gone with the Wind* revealed that she saw that very "womanhood [as] the burden. Sex, reproduction, pregnancy, motherhood, babies, children, domesticity—that whole set of values associated with home and the woman's sphere became the load to carry"

(Pyron 282). Clearly, Scarlett O'Hara had set out in the novel to escape that burden, becoming "a bad girl and a worse daughter who lives all her life in constant revolt against her mother's precepts . . . repudiat[ing] feminine virtue and her mother's and Mammy's code of self-abnegation, devotion, and family" (Pyron 275). However, Pyron reveals that the character of Scarlett O'Hara had, in all probability, been based on Mitchell's grandmother, Annie Elizabeth Fitzgerald Stephens, a woman Mitchell had been raised to "hate" (253) as "vulgar and mercenary; full of splurge and swagger" (251). Pyron writes that Mitchell "expressed the most radically divided mind about her protagonist. Thus, despite the character's power and popularity and the energy with which she was created, the author herself repudiated the character, or otherwise evinced the most consistent ambivalence about her creation" (253).

Rhett Butler resolves the conflict (at least within the confines of *Gone with the Wind*) when he tells Scarlett, "I wish I could care what you do or where you go, but I can't." He drew a short breath and said lightly but softly: "My dear, I don't give a damn" (*GWW* 732). Scarlett has failed Rhett by being the wrong kind of woman while "in him [she now found] something strong, unyielding, implacable—all the qualities she had looked for in Ashley and never found" (*GWW* 732). He was the right kind of man, a truly *manly* man; she had failed to be what Melanie Wilkes symbolized for Rhett, "[a] very great lady," "the only completely kind person I ever knew" (*GWW* 724). Melanie was the *womanly* woman who could win the true man's love and respect:

Scarlett shivered and the glow went from her heart, the fine warmth, the splendor which had sent her home on winged feet. She half-grasped what was in Rhett's mind as he said farewell to the only person in the world he respected and she was desolate again with a terrible sense of loss that was no longer personal. . . . She was seeing through Rhett's eyes the passing, not of a woman but a legend—the gentle, self-effacing but steel-spined women on whom the South had built its house in war and to whose proud and loving arms it had returned in defeat. (*GWW* 725)

Rhett's vision is the true one: the fate of the South depended on its truly self-sacrificing women, its courageous, heroic men. Margaret Mitchell endorses the superiority of that vision; restores the patriarchal order once more; punishes the rebellious Scarlett and sends her back to Tara, alone and unloved; then puts down her transgressing pen. Margaret Mitchell had conceded, "too much independent action would threaten the institutions created to preserve race, class, and sex hierarchy" (Harrison 64). (And yet, the main text is subverted again by the novel's last rebellious line, "tomorrow is another day" (*GWW* 733); Scarlett's female self remains flexible, resilient, capable of another reconstruction, and the South she is in the process of rebuilding *could* still be revolutionized and reshaped through her potential, if unfulfilled, difference.)

In *The Dollmaker* (1954), Harriette Arnow's protagonist gives up her own dreams and abandons her rebellion early in the novel—by chapter 9 of 39 chapters. By that stage of Arnow's work, Gertie Nevels has fulfilled Rhett Butler's dream of the legendary, virtuous southern woman sacrificing herself for her husband and children, becoming the true southern daughter Scarlett O'Hara was not—although Gertie is big, strong, plain, and poor, an unlikely southern heroine. Gertie's selflessness is unquestionable, however. Lewis Lawson has called Gertie Nevels a "woman who, like Christ, accepts sacrifice as her life" (18) and Dorothy Lee, too, calls Gertie's sacrifice for others Christ-like. But the South is not saved through Gertie's actions—nor are her husband, her children, her community, or her world. What *The Dollmaker* reveals, perhaps unintentionally, is the destructiveness of such sacrifice as Gertie's for all concerned.[3]

Like Scarlett O'Hara and Dorinda Oakley before her, Gertie has set out to buy the Tipton Place, to have a farm of her own and provide for the needs of her family through her own hard work and skill on land she loves. But her mother shames her into following her husband to Detroit where he has gone to work in the factories during World War II:

Oh, Lord, she's turned her own children against their father. She's never taught them th Bible where it says, "Leave all else an cleave to thy husband." She's never read to them th words writ by Paul, "Wives, be in subjection unto your husbands, as unto th Lord." (*TD* 141)

John Tipton must agree that Gertie's mother is right as he calls an end to the sale of his farm, "Yer youngens does need schools, an when Clovis is a maken you a good liven you ought to go to him if he wants it thataway" (*TD* 146). But Clovis does not make good money; the family gets deeper and deeper into debt in Detroit; and Gertie's family grows more and more troubled, more and more apart from one another, in Merry Hill.

One by one, Gertie loses her family. Her eldest son, Reuben, is unable to forgive Gertie from the moment she gives in to her mother:

The trouble grew in his eyes, but still he waited, watching Gertie, hopeful, unwilling to believe she would not speak up for their farm. She continued silent. Gradually the hope in his eyes died. His glance, fixed on his mother's face, was filled with the contempt of the strong for the weak. (*TD* 143)

18 Moving On

Reuben leaves Detroit and returns home to Kentucky, away from his mother's failures and the misery of urban life in Merry Hill. Cassie, too, is lost even more irrevocably, struck and killed by a train when she has been denied the pleasure of playing at home with her imaginary playmate Callie Lou. Again, Gertie is well aware that it is her own weakness that is responsible, that she has succumbed to the will of Cassie's teacher, of Clovis, of her neighbors, of others who "know best." She alone understood, and she alone could have defended, Cassie's individuality and creativity, saving her life. Too late she admits, "All this business of doing away with Callie Lou had been a mistake. . . . Cassie could have Callie Lou at home. She, Gertie, couldn't kill her when already she lived in the alley" (*TD* 401). But Cassie is destroyed as surely as Callie Lou has been denied a place in the Nevels's home. While Gertie's other children are more fortunate, adjusting smoothly to their new school and neighborhood, Gertie must watch as they learn to look down on "hillbillies," people such as herself and her relatives. When Enoch shows her a "funny picture," she strikes back instinctively to protect herself from his laughter:

Gertie knew, even as her palm shot out, it wasn't Enoch she wanted to slap; he was a good boy—everybody said he was good. Her palm came against his cheek, but not too hard; and he, used now to the falls and blows in the alley, was more angry and startled than hurt, yelling at her, "Mom, cain't a guy laugh at a funny picture?" "It made me think a yer Granma Kate," she said. She wanted to apologize for the slap, but was unable to make her voice kind as she said, "It wasn't funny." (*TD* 523)

Enoch and his sister Clytie both have come to accept acts of cruelty, violence, greed, and hatred as commonplace: "She shook her head over the strangeness of her children" (*TD* 443). Further, she must watch as her husband turns into a murderer in the midst of a labor dispute. Afraid to confront him with her unbearable knowledge, Gertie thinks, "She wouldn't say it. No, she couldn't—tongue-tied she was by him as by her mother. Would she in time feel toward him as toward her mother? She couldn't live with him and feel that way" (*TD* 571).

When the break-up of her family seems almost assured, the war is over. Two atom bombs have been dropped on Japan, burning human bodies like "tater bugs" destroyed in the garden (Enoch recalls with his mother how she "allus wanted u big fire an burn em all up right quick; but no matter how big a fire we'd have they'd be some that'd jist git scorched, an they'd crawl like crazy ever which away till they died" [*TD* 494]). With the killing and maiming of World War II over now, Clovis will be out of work permanently—not just on strike. Gertie thinks,

If only she had stayed and held out against her mother for these few months only, Clovis would be coming back to them—back to all of them—Cassie maybe the first to go running to meet him, with Reuben as always lagging behind, but even he, hurrying a little, to see the new truck, a good secondhand truck, paid for with all the money they'd saved; and the farm all their own. (*TD* 495)

Too late, Gertie discovers that Clovis would actually have supported her plan to buy a farm and remain in Kentucky if she had spoken up and confided in him about her intentions. Clovis complains,

Cain't a body think about how nice it ud be if'n you'd bought that Tipton Place an I'd a cleared out a this town soon as V-J Day come an put my car in on a pretty good truck. Then I'd a come rollen home in it —had a good truck might nigh paid fer by now—an you . . . . (*TD* 541)

Clovis blames Gertie, as she blames herself, for the deterioration of their family life and their economic independence. She has become a burden, not a help, by subordinating herself to Clovis and following along in his footsteps, as her mother has reminded her she is supposed to do. Gertie's devastation seems complete, a harsh penalty for playing out the role of the virtuous southern woman—a submissive, silent, cooperative child-mother and wife who has denied her own strength, wisdom, and needs in order to "serve" others.

But Arnow demands even further sacrifice of her protagonist. Gertie must destroy the block of cherry wood that has been her cherished companion and her artistic masterpiece, both. Through it Gertie has tried to express the essence of her life experience, her innermost soul. This, too, must be forsaken, "sawed into boards fer whittling," to provide for her family's needs (*TD* 598), and Gertie once more is asked to perform the destructive act herself:

She stood above it, the ax lifted. . . . She hit it . . . . and it sank into the wood straight across the top of the head; . . . then slowly the face fell forward toward the ground, but stopped trembling and swaying, held up by the two hands. (*TD* 599)

Gertie has found the answer to her own destiny, and to that of millions of others, in the bent and ravaged figure, its silent supplication, and its final destruction.

But is it—are they—is she—Judas or Christ? This remains the novel's ultimate question—and Harriette Arnow continues to be as ambivalent in her answer as was Margaret Mitchell about her rebellious heroine Scarlett. Through her last sacrifice, Gertie once more, like Judas, betrays her self, her art, her values—and, thereby, further injures her family through her weak example and her self-betrayal. At the same time, however, she becomes even more Christ-like, more of a martyr, in her willingness to give of herself for the sake of the family she loves. Critics remain divided in their interpretation of Gertie's actions, but whatever their views of Gertie's self-sacrifice, it seems clear that "an essentially masculine and capitalistic value system" has won out and co-opted the white southern female heroine once more (Jones, *Tomorrow* 158). At the end of *The Dollmaker*, Gertie gives up her creativity and individuality in order to begin mass producing Appalachian crafts for the modern, urban market. If it seems that Gertie has formed a sisterhood with other women in Merry Hill that "constitutes a potential alternative to the competition and aggression of capitalism and war, even while emerging from within those systems" (White 137), as Elizabeth Jane Harrison explains,

The Dollmaker demonstrates that, despite the cooperation among the women in the housing project, communal values are ultimately ineffective in a capitalistic world which favors bitter rivalry over compassion. . . . the women in the alley will support one another as long as they can circumvent their husband's authority, but their ultimate loyalty still rests with the official unit of patriarchal control: the nuclear family. (94)

Gertie continues to remain loyal to the family, and to the southern ethic of feminine virtue, even as she prepares to enter the materialistic, competitive, male world of business—which Dorinda Oakley and Scarlett O'Hara have passed on to her, unchanged, intact, as ruthless and hard as ever.

The message of *The Dollmaker* is a familiar one in white southern women writers' works: social change would seem impossible. The atom bomb becomes a fitting symbol not only for "all the planned killing and wounding of men" (*TD* 495) in World War II but for all the unplanned skirmishes, fractures, and fatalities that characterize modern life in Detroit's Merry Hill. There will be no end to violence and destruction. "Gertie could hear no rejoicing, no lifting of the heart [at the end of the war]. . . . Rather it was as if the people had lived on blood, and now that the bleeding was ended, they were worried about their future" (*TD* 495). Her neighbors have become as accustomed to the slaughter of war as to their own suffering—suffering which Gertie discovers on "millions and millions a faces" (*TD* 599) throughout the world. Both Gertie and the reader know that her great physical strength, her kind and gentle ways, her creativity and wisdom, have proved even more ineffectual and defenseless in the North than in the South, in the urban world than in the rural one she has left behind, in modern life than in the traditional one from which it stemmed. As Kathleen Walsh has concluded, "one carries away from *The Dollmaker* a sense of the awful cost of such passivity [as Gertie's and her neighbors']. . . . Gertie's acquiescence in her victimization is the trait by which her heroic qualities are reduced, betrayed" (104-05).

Gertie Nevels joins Dorinda Oakley and Scarlett O'Hara in endorsing and participating in the dominant culture she had once opposed. All three female protagonists acknowledge a deep sympathy for their defeated fathers and work to redeem the failed lives of these same fathers—or of their husbands and lovers—even at the height of their resistance to their own traditional female destinies. When the white southern heroine has pursued her rebellion further, ultimately renouncing the control of her father or husband, as does Edna Pontellier in *The Awakening*, we have seen that she can find no alternative life to sustain her.

Other fiction by the most important white southern women writers of the post-World War II period, Carson McCullers, Flannery O'Connor, and Eudora Welty, continues to question the status quo while ultimately confirming its practice. All three writers persist in fantasizing female defeat, punishment, and self-punishment (Eudora Welty less so than the others), even as they challenge the tradition of the patriarchal southern culture their fiction portrays. As Louise Westling has shown in *Sacred Groves and Ravaged Gardens*, Carson McCullers and Flannery O'Connor finally affirm the father's rule and the mother-woman's subordination as inevitable, perhaps even necessary, in the structuring of society. McCullers's young heroines, from "Bienchen" in "Wunderkind," to Frankie Addams in *The Member of the Wedding*, to Mick Kelly in *The Heart Is a Lonely Hunter*, find themselves confronted and trapped by their female destiny as soon as they reach puberty. They soon submit, as Louise Westling has shown:

In McCullers's case, we find again and again the tomboy heroine suddenly confronted by society's demands that she subdue her behavior, accept the facts of adult sexuality that she has tried to deny, and start acting ladylike. . . . Entrapment seems to be the preoccupation of the one writer who appeared to have escaped both her region and the restrictions of her gender. McCullers's heroines in *The Heart Is a Lonely Hunter*, *The Ballad of the Sad Cafe*, and *The Member of the Wedding* are all ultimately defeated, forced to accept imprisonment by the sexual conventions of their world. Thus Carson McCullers, who left the South and lived a sexually unconventional life among artists and intellectuals in New York and Paris, wrote stories of tomboys who failed or were punished. (*Sacred* 5-6)

As with Margaret Mitchell, so Carson McCullers, too, seems to have found a kind of psychic relief in punishing her heroines for crimes she herself had committed (either imaginatively or in fact).

In "Wunderkind" (1951), McCullers's "Bienchen" gives up her dream of becoming a talented concert pianist, whispering "I can't. . . . I don't know why, but I just can't—can't any more" (*The Ballad of the Sad Cafe and Other Stories* 89). She flees her beloved teacher, Mister Bilderbach, "stumbled down the stone steps, turned in the wrong direction, and hurried down the street that had become confused with noise and bicycles and the games of *other children* [my emphasis]" (*Ballad* 89). McCullers, too, had forfeited her career as a concert pianist while still a teenager, but "Bienchen" must make more sacrifices than did her successful creator. At the end of "Wunderkind," "Bienchen" remains childishly female; she fails to master her own destiny in any way; and she surrenders her adulthood to her male competition (represented by her talented peer Heime Israelsky). Mister Bilderbach has made it clear that her female identity requires her to look "blank and immature" (*Ballad* 83) while wearing pink dresses accented by ruffles—hardly the appearance of an accomplished concert pianist or successful woman of any sort. "Bienchen" finds she must move backwards, not forwards, to fulfill her destiny as a female in her society.

Similarly, Mick Kelly in *The Heart Is a Lonely Hunter* (1940) discovers her sexuality in the arms of Harry Minowitz, fantasizes with him about "plot[ting] to kill Hitler" and becoming a great hero: "To be a hero was almost like being a great musician" (*HLH* 209). Before the afternoon is over, however, Mick must confront the reality of her sexuality and of her adult destiny. Not only will Mick never realize her heroic fantasies, she acknowledges to Harry, "A boy has a better advantage . . . than a girl. I mean a boy can usually get some part-time job that don't take him out of school and leaves him time for other things. But there's not jobs like that for girls. When a girl wants a job she has to quit school and work full time" (*HLH* 210). We are not surprised to find Mick at the end of the novel, her dreams cast aside, employed full time at Woolworth's: "But now no music was in her mind. . . . it was like the store took all her energy and time. . . . now she was always tired. . . . That was the way things were. . . . It was like she was cheated. Only nobody had cheated her. So there was nobody to take it out on" (*HLH* 301-02).

Mick's sexual initiation with Harry Minowitz would be her one adventure—a disillusioning and frightening one, at that. It is followed by "a kind of paralysis. . . . At fourteen she is a grown woman whose life seems to have reached a dead end" (Westling, *Sacred* 118).

Unlike Mick Kelly, Frankie Addams at the end of *The Member of the Wedding* (1946) still retains a few dreams. She plans to travel around the world someday with her new friend Mary Littlejohn, "Mary was going to be a great painter and Frances a great poet—or else the foremost authority on radar" (*MW* 150). Nevertheless, the reader understands that, in a few more years, Frankie will have given up these grandiose aspirations even as she was forced to give up her desire to join her brother Jarvis and his new bride as they start out on their honeymoon from Winter Hill. Louise Westling points out that "this absurd fantasy is a denial of the adult sexuality which Frankie cannot bear to acknowledge, but her attraction to it is obvious in her infatuation with the engaged couple. . . . ultimately . . . [she will] accept the limitations of her sex" (*Sacred* 129-30). Frankie's immediate destiny is her aunt and uncle's new home in the suburbs, with its own basement and laundry room, far from the "Luxembourg" of her dreams. The message of *The Member of the Wedding* is clear: Frankie will remain trapped in her southern female identity as the housekeeper Berenice Sadie Brown will remain trapped in the segregated South, even more bound by the "extra bonds around all colored people" (*MW* 98) than by those that bind both Frankie and herself to conventional female roles and female sexuality. Louise Westling points out that "McCullers is making a traditional association between the oppression of women and that of blacks in *The Member of the Wedding*" (*Sacred* 130), as she does in the earlier *The Heart Is a Lonely Hunter*, as well. Neither southern black nor southern white women can free themselves from the label of "inferiority" that white patriarchal society has imposed upon them.

McCullers's white female protagonists find they are trapped forever both in their female bodies and in the small southern towns of their youth. Even the strongest and eldest of them, Miss Amelia Evans of "The Ballad of the Sad Cafe," never leaves the "dreary," "lonesome," "sad," cotton-mill town in which she grew up (3). By the age of thirty, however, Miss Amelia Evans seems to have out-maneuvered her traditional female fate. She has become "the richest woman for miles around" due to an inheritance from her father; her thriving liquor business; and her many other business endeavors:

With all things which could be made by the hands Miss Amelia prospered. She sold chitterlins and sausage in the town near-by. On fine autumn days, she ground sorgham, and the syrup from her vats was dark golden and delicately flavored. She built the brick privy behind her store in only two weeks and was skilled in carpentering. It was only with people that Miss Amelia was not at ease. . . . the only use that Miss Amelia had for other people was to make money out of them. And in this she succeeded. Mortgages on crops and property, a sawmill, money in the bank. . . . She would have been rich as a congressman if it were not for her one great failing, and that was her passion for lawsuits and the courts. She would involve herself in long and bitter litigation over just a trifle. (*Ballad* 5)

Miss Amelia has shown herself as skilled at playing a man's game in a man's world as other white southern heroines we have discussed—and, in addition, she has proven adept even at physical combat with male partners.

However, Gilbert and Gubar in *No Man's Land* (Vol. 1) reveal how

McCullers shows in her dreamlike mystic narrative of "The Ballad of the Sad Cafe" the culturally determined psychic logic that condemns the autonomous woman as a freak who must necessarily be sentenced to the defeat that is femininity. . . . Specifically, she dramatizes the punishment meted out to a woman who has arrogantly supposed that she could live in a no man's land—first without a real man, and then with a dwarfish no-man. (104-05)

McCullers's narrative reveals how "Cousin Lymon becomes the 'false phallus' that [Miss Amelia] can control, [but] the true phallus will eventually repossess her and all her worldly goods in an ultimate act of masculinist retribution" (Gilbert and Gubar 1: 108). After Marvin Macy and Cousin Lymon join forces to defeat her,

at the conclusion of "Ballad" Miss Amelia has been metamorphosed from a woman warrior to a helpless madwoman. Her very body has shriveled. . . . Bereft of her once legendary physical strength, she has also lost her social, intellectual, and economic authority; her cafe is closed; her house is boarded up; and all her "wise doctoring" is over. (Gilbert and Gubar 1: 111)

McCullers's "Ballad of the Sad Cafe" serves as a cautionary tale about deviant, ambitious womanhood in a male-dominated, traditional culture. As Louise Westling points out, Miss Amelia Evans would seem to have brought about her own "ultimate destruction from a punishing male alliance [by having become] . . . a grotesquely mannish Amazon [insisting on her] . . . solitary authority [and] . . . refus[ing] to play even the physical part of a woman in her brief marriage to Marvin Macy" (*Sacred* 176).

In the fictional world of Flannery O'Connor, as well, female protagonists are punished for getting above themselves, as McCullers's Miss Amelia Evans has done. They are women who have managed farms, raised children, earned advanced degrees, and held their own in a man's world, all on their own. But, one by one, they are defeated:

In fully half the stories published in *A Good Man Is Hard to Find* and the posthumous *Everything That Rises Must Converge*, widowed or divorced mothers are central characters who are tricked, deluded, or violently chastened. These stranded women have been left to raise bad-tempered sons or, more often, daughters, but they prove tough and resourceful in their dealings with the outside world and thus create modest little matriarchies where their sour children can lead comfortable lives. . . . In most of these stories the mother's pride is ultimately smashed by a vindictive male force, perhaps most extremely in "Greenleaf," "The Comforts of Home," and "Everything That Rises Must Converge," where she dies under assault. (Westling, *Sacred* 145)

In *Southern Honor: Ethics and Behavior in the Old South*, Bertram Wyatt-Brown shows that O'Connor is reflecting a cultural reality of the South's legal, business, and social traditions whereby "the widow had to struggle keenly against the presumption that she would be the loser in any sort of transaction" (240). But O'Connor's Mrs. May, Mrs. Cope, Mrs. Turpin, Mrs. Hopewell, Mrs. Crater, and Mrs. McIntyre are undaunted. They seem to persevere and prosper, despite the odds against them.

Then retribution descends, usually in male form. In O'Connor's fiction, Louise Westling contends,

Almost every son wants to punish his mother or "teach her a lesson." Two actually kill their mothers, and the Misfit of "A Good Man Is Hard to Find" could be said to have the same instinctive reaction in shooting the grandmother when she reaches out to him saying, "Why, you're one of my babies!" Daughters, on the other hand, usually end up as allies of their mothers, forced by male deceit and violence into humiliating defeat. (*Sacred* 145)

O'Connor's solitary, adult women are punished for their presumption as independent land-owners and businesswomen set on controlling their own lives. When their destiny overtakes them, their sexual identity and vulnerability are reaffirmed at the same time. Mrs. May, in "Greenleaf,"

remained perfectly still, not in fright, but in a freezing unbelief. She stared at the violent black streak bounding toward her as if she had no sense of distance, as if she could not decide at once what his intention was, and the bull had buried his head in her lap, like a wild, tormented lover, before her expression changed. One of his horns sank until it pierced her heart and the other curved around her side and held her in an unbreakable grip. (O'Connor, *Complete Stories* 333)

In "The Displaced Person," the resourceful Mrs. McIntyre proves vulnerable to male forces, as well, finding herself incapable of dealing with her masculine farmhands or the moral and spiritual challenge the Polish Mr. Guizac presents her heretofore impervious world. At the end of the story, she admits her feminine weakness, develops "a nervous affliction," and acknowledges "that the place would be too much for her to run now . . . eventually she had to stay in bed all the time with only a colored woman to wait on her. Her eyesight grew steadily worse and she lost her voice altogether" (*Complete Stories* 235). Mrs. McIntyre has been as effectively silenced and eliminated from the male-dominant world of southern culture as the brutally gored Mrs. May at the end of "Greenleaf" (or the withered Miss Amelia Evans in McCullers's "The Ballad of the Sad Cafe").

O'Connor's rebellious daughters fare little better than their mothers. Louise Westling illustrates their plight:

In her complex and troubling presentation of mothers and daughters in the farm stories, Flannery O'Connor has inadvertently presented a poignant and often excruciating picture of the problems these women have in living together, of female self-loathing, powerlessness, and justified fear of masculine attack. She presents fictional doubles of herself, as Sandra Gilbert and Susan Gubar have shown so many women writers to have done, doubles who express the rage and frustration which is too dangerous for women to admit in ordinary life. O'Connor allows these dopplegängers to act their defiance . . . but then . . . she punishes them with a finality which restores a balance with the dominant values of the world in which we all must live. (*Sacred* 174)

O'Connor's daughters are, with the notable exception of the retarded young Lucynell Crater in "The Life You Save May Be Your Own," belligerently defiant, "one by seeking to escape her mother's fate of childbearing and others by deliberately wearing ugly clothes and acting rude. One twelve-year-old girl escapes the whole issue of sex-differences and adolescent courtship by identifying herself with a hermaphrodite" (Westling, *Sacred* 5).

O'Connor's rebellious daughters dress in male attire—as does Sally Virginia Cope in "A Circle in the Fire." They scoff at feminine flounces and male courtship patterns, along with the twelve-year-old protagonist of "A Temple of the Holy Ghost." And they rage against good country women such as Mrs. Turpin in "Revelation" who smugly accept stereotypical gender roles, religious conventions, and moral precepts. O'Connor's daughters are determined to avoid traditional femininity at any cost but are no more successful in their attempts to remain free of gender restrictions than are Carson McCullers's protagonists before them.

In "Good Country People," we see how Flannery O'Connor punishes one fictional daughter's deviance from traditional femininity:

Like [McCullers's] Miss Amelia, [Joy-Hulga], the weak-hearted, wooden-legged, atheistical Ph.D., is punished for unfeminine arrogance when a seemingly stupid Bible salesman outwits her, teaches her not to judge a book by its cover (he keeps whisky, dirty playing cards, and condoms in a hollowed-out Bible), and absconds with her leg. (Gilbert and Gubar 1: 112)

In the character of Joy-Hulga, with whom Flannery O'Connor acknowledged a shared identity,[4] O'Connor has shown the paradoxical nature of the daughter's rebellion against female sexuality. The more Joy-Hulga denies her female self, wearing her "yellow sweat-shirt with a faded cowboy on a horse embossed on it" ("Good Country People," *Complete Stories* 276), the more central it becomes in the drama that befalls her. Louise Westling explains,

Joy-Hulga's sexuality is essential to her identity, though she is completely unaware of it. The part of her personality which the Bible salesman takes away by stealing her wooden leg is her sour independence as a female who refuses to accept the submissive role her Southern world has dictated for her. In trying to live an independent intellectual life, Joy-Hulga fails to realize the power of sexual differences and her needs as a woman. Thus her apparent toughness is brittle and her wooden leg an apt symbol for her independence. (*Sacred* 152)

Ignorant of her own sexual nature, she becomes immediately vulnerable to Manley Pointer's advances: "The girl at first did not return any of the kisses but presently she began to and after she had put several on his cheek, she reached his lips and remained there, kissing him again and again as if she were trying to draw all the breath out of him" ("Good" 287). When Pointer removes her leg, "She was thinking that she would run away with him and that every night he would take the leg off and every morning put it back on again" ("Good" 289). Having coldbloodedly determined to seduce him, she is betrayed by her own unexpected passion: "Her brain seemed to have stopped thinking altogether and to be about some other function that it was not very good at" ("Good" 289).

By the end of "Good Country People," Manley Pointer has rendered Joy-Hulga helpless, robbed her of her delusions about her female independence, and reasserted the principle of male superiority among "good country people." As Louise Westling concludes, "O'Connor has taken the significance of rape to a symbolic extreme in the picture of this man who preys sexually on women and literally leaves them crippled" (*Sacred* 153). The more free Joy-Hulga has felt from her female destiny, the more defeated she must be by it. The elder Mrs. May in "Greenleaf" and the younger Joy-Hulga in "Good Country People" meet their fate in the form of demon-lovers who violate, enlighten, and chasten them at the end of O'Connor's works.

Eudora Welty's fiction has been acclaimed by many recent scholars as being much less punishing, much more supportive of its female protagonists than that of McCullers and O'Connor (or of the earlier twentieth-century women writers of the white South we have discussed). Louise Westling has labeled Welty's "fictional world . . . matriarchal in its source of power," one that "celebrate[s] the land and the fecundity and independence of the world of nature" (*Sacred* 5, 7). Westling shows that Eudora Welty in *Delta Wedding* (1946) has created a fertile world that "really belongs to the women. To a degree unusual in fiction, Welty's women move freely and comfortably across the landscape, at the center of a world which affirms them and denies male pretensions of control" (*Sacred* 179). Michael Kreyling agrees that the novel "focuses on the trials of the heroic figure—George Fairchild—as seen through the eyes of various women who maintain the culture by different but no less effective means. . . . [that Welty in *Delta Wedding* is portraying] the end of the southern heroic paradigm" (185). Yet, if Welty rejoices in her female characters, "see[ing] the world through their eyes, lovingly, reaffirming the old female powers of the land as she reaffirms the fruitful alliance of male and female humans and celebrates their domestic arrangements" (Westling, *Sacred* 183), portraying her father figures as "vulnerable" (Westling, "Fathers and Daughters," 111), there are uncertainties and shadows that intrude upon her female-centered fiction. Louise Westling qualifies her vision of Welty's "matriarchal" world in this way:

the gracious Southern life celebrated in *Delta Wedding* and wistfully reexamined in *The Optimist's Daughter* is dying. The New Women of the South are already emerging in *Delta Wedding*, impatient of their mothers' heritage and searching for wider and more active destinies. Virgie Rainey of *The Golden Apples* and Laurel Hand of *The Optimist's Daughter* have forged independent, clearly feminine identities, but they are rendered exiles and solitary wanderers by their choices. No community sustains them; no comrades share their new worlds. In fact, Welty does not seem able to dramatize their independent life at all. (*Sacred* 175)

If female independence is good, it is also costly. While Lucinda MacKethan believes that Welty's *The Ponder Heart* (1954) reveals "the creative function of authorship for woman in a society that traditionally denied her a story of her own" (3), she admits that

part of [Edna Earle Ponder's] story is her silence concerning her lack of status in that place. Yes, she steals Uncle Daniel's show, but the costs are the dark side of this comedy. What Edna Earle wants, she cannot say: a home of her own, a story that does not have to be stolen, a creative life that does not depend on menfolk for its validity. (4)

The same could be said for other Welty stories in which women steal the show from men—albeit temporarily. In "Why I Live at the P.O.," Papa-Daddy still retains the power to disinherit his granddaughter (as he had the power to set her up as local postmistress in the first place) despite her defiant five-day rebellion against her family, and in "Petrified Man," the women may complain all they wish and lash out at the hapless young Billy Boy at the story's conclusion, but their anger at their husbands— Leota's for not working while she slaves away in the beauty parlor and Mrs. Fletcher's for getting her pregnant, and thereby limiting her freedom in another way—can be neither acknowledged nor acted upon.

In fact, Eudora Welty most affirms her female characters when they accept their feminine roles and use their power in traditional ways connected with domestic duties or the natural world. She is not unlike the authors Anne Goodwyn Jones discusses in *Tomorrow Is Another Day* who admire female strength when it has been "exerted . . . within the home and only to serve the husband, the family, and the South" (13). When Welty's women exhibit power outside the traditional domestic sphere, as does the piano teacher Miss Eckhart in *The Golden Apples*, they are often punished—snubbed by their best pupils (Virgie Rainey) and made to die pitifully and pennilessly in a county home. It is her spinster schoolteachers such as Miss Eckhart with whom Eudora Welty most identified, saying that "they are to a great extent my heroines. . . . What animates and possesses me is what drives Miss Eckhart, the love of her art and the love of giving it, the desire to give it until there is no more left" (*One Writer's Beginnings* 82, 101). And it is these characters (as we have seen with other white southern women authors we have discussed) whom Welty punishes most.

Miss Julia Mortimer in *Losing Battles* (1970) is one of Eudora Welty's most important schoolteacher heroines. She is a courageous woman who has engaged in a lifelong battle to educate the children of Banner, Mississippi, and elevate the civilization she finds in this impoverished, hilltop, southern community. Her victories have been few, a fact she acknowledges in a final letter to her former pupil Judge Moody:

All my life I've fought a hard war with ignorance. Except in those cases that you can count off on your fingers, I lost every battle. Year in, year out, my children at Banner School took up the cause of the other side and held the fort against me. We both fought faithfully and singlemindedly, bravely, maybe even fairly. Mostly I lost, they won. But as long as I was still young, I always thought if I could marshal strength enough of body and spirit and push with it, every ounce, I could change the future. (*LB* 287)

Now Miss Julia is old and dying, but she continues to relish the struggle, admitting, "From flat on your back you may not be able to lick the world, but at least you can keep the world from licking you. I haven't spent a lifetime fighting my battle to give up now. I'm ready for all they send me. There's a measure of enjoyment in it" (*LB* 288). Yet the story that unfolds in *Losing Battles* reveals the high price Miss Julia Mortimer must pay for deviating from community standards. The more she fights, the more she loses. Her most caring students eventually betray her. In her last letter, she warns her admiring pupil, Judge Oscar Moody, "Watch out for innocence. Could *you* be tempted by it, Oscar—to your own mortification—and conspire with the ignorant and the lawless and the foolish and even the wicked, *to hold your tongue?*" (*LB* 289). The answer is "yes," as Judge Moody looks at Julia Mortimer's last star pupil, Gloria Short Renfro, her husband Jack (an escaped prisoner whom he has sentenced to jail earlier and Gloria's possible cousin, besides), and their little child, Lady May Renfro, and concludes "in a heavy voice,"

It's that baby. I think we'll have to close one eye over that everlasting baby. . . . You end up doing yourself the thing you hate most, the thing you've deplored the loudest and longest. . . . Here I am taking the law into my own hands. . . . I think we'll have to leave it that what's done is done. That there was no prior knowledge between the partners. And no crime. (*LB* 312)

Judge Moody gives in to "innocence" and "conspire[s] with the ignorant and the lawless" (*LB* 289) in Banner, Mississippi, just as Julia Mortimer feared he might, and as Miss Julia's last protégé, Gloria Renfro, has, as well.

Much as Gloria resists becoming a Renfro in more than just name, her love for Jack has caused her to quit teaching school and enter into the midst of the Beecham Renfro family's ignorance and foolishness. The women of the family wash Gloria's face in watermelon juice to punish her for her standoffishness and, when she complains to Jack, "They all banded together against me!" he consoles her by saying, "Anyway, they've quit making company out of you, Possum," he said softly. "You're one of the family now" (*LB* 301). Gloria's worst fears are coming true. In addition, Jack's pleadings are designed to wear down Gloria's resistance to Beecham Renfro ways even further. He makes love to her, saying,

Say now you'll love em a little bit. Say you'll love them too. You can. Try and you can.
     . . . Wouldn't you like to keep Mama company in the kitchen while I'm plough-ing or fencemending, give her somebody she can talk to? And encourage Ella Fay to blossom out of being timid, and talk Elvie out of her crying and wanting to grow up and be a teacher? You can give Etoyle ladylike examples of behav-ior. . . . Once it's winter, Papa just wants to put up his foot and see pictures in the fire. You could crack his pecans for him, perched there on the hearth. (*LB* 346)

Jack's vision of Gloria is that of a traditional mother, wife, and daughter-in-law who takes care of his family and their needs. We know that, as she seeks to keep her husband's love, Gloria will betray even further the "*promise*" of intelligent, independent action Julia Mortimer saw in her (*LB* 313).

It is Jack (not Gloria Renfro or Miss Julia Mortimer) who is the hero of this tale—with all his foolishness, lawlessness, ignorance, and naïveté. And it is the women—his mother, his grandmother, his aunts, and his wife, Gloria, herself, everyone except Miss Julia Mortimer—who continue to support him in his role as eldest son and family savior (whatever real doubts and disappointments they admit to feeling in pri-vate). As Aunt Birdie announces to the reunion, "And when Jack jumps out in those fields tomorrow, he'll resurrect something out of nothing. Don't you know he will?" (*LB* 313).

Not only do the Renfro women help to tell the story of Jack's hero-ism and bolster family pride in his feats—"You can't keep children of *mine* shut up in school, if they can figure there's something going on somewhere! . . . They're not exactly idiots!" Beulah Renfro brags about Jack (32)—but they punish Miss Julia Mortimer's female independence much more harshly than they have their new, young relation Gloria

Renfro's. Miss Lexie Renfro's story of "nursing" Miss Julia in her final days, battling with her, as Aunt Beck says, to be "content with her lot. . . . Like an ordinary Christian" (*LB* 270), becomes the dark underside of this comic novel. Miss Lexie Renfro, herself a spinster woman and former schoolteacher, another past pupil and admirer of Miss Julia's, as well, recounts this tale of punishment (and female self-punishment) with pride:

If I got to the door and locked it first, she'd try to get out of her own house. . . . Shake—she'd shake that big oak door! . . . I tied her, that was the upshoot. . . . Tied her in bed. . . . Every day, Miss Julia there in her bed called me to bring her her book. "Which book?" I ask her. She said just bring her her book. . . . I couldn't make her tell me which book she meant. So she didn't get any. (*LB* 268-69)

Denied her books and her school bell (to call for help), eventually Miss Julia is denied even the use of a pencil and paper. While Miss Lexie admits to having thrown Miss Julia's earlier letters in the pig pen after reading them and determining they had "something . . . bad to say about human nature" (*LB* 273), finally she refuses Miss Julia any means of communication at all: "I hid her pencil, and she said, 'Now I want to die.' I said, 'Well, why don't you go ahead and die, then?' She'd made me say it! And she said, 'Because I want to die by myself, you everpresent, everlasting old fool!'" (*LB* 274). Defiant to the end, Miss Julia manages to sneak out one last letter to Judge Moody before her life is over—and *Losing Battles* reveals both the great physical cost and the absolute futility of that valiant effort to help Gloria Short Renfro escape marriage into the Beecham Renfro clan and eventual defeat of her intellectual potential. Miss Julia dies, embattled and isolated, before Judge Moody can reach her, a virtual prisoner in her own home, visited by no one and reminded cruelly by Miss Lexie Renfro that Gloria has "forgotten you. . . . like everybody else has. . . . you've been put out to pasture—they're through with you" (*LB* 270). Defeat has proved inevitable for Miss Julia Mortimer. Hers is yet another tale of a woman who has challenged the traditions of southern patriarchal culture only to end up paralyzed, crippled, isolated, rejected, mad, or dead. Such has been the tradition of twentieth century fiction as told by white southern women writers.[5]

I believe that it is only in the works of the last few decades that white women writers of the South have begun to "come of age" and create what Zora Neale Hurston portrayed for African-American southern women in *Their Eyes Were Watching God* in 1937: mature, purposeful female life independent of male authority and authorship. In *Their Eyes Were Watching God*, the reader follows Janie Crawford as she moves through three marriages. In the first two relationships, Janie is dominated by husbands who silence her and treat her as a dependent child in imitation of male/female patterns found in white patriarchal culture. By the end of the second marriage, however, Janie has found her own voice and begun to speak out in opposition to her husband Jody Starks's dominating and insistent "big voice" (*Their Eyes* 75). When Janie marries a third time, at the age of forty, it is as a way of expressing her selfhood, her adult choice, her own autonomy within a larger society.

Janie enters into a more egalitarian relationship with Tea Cake Woods, sharing hard work and easy pleasure at his side, enjoying with him the rich world of black-centered culture Jody Starks had forbidden her to engage in at his store. As Elizabeth Meese explains,

Janie rejects the "race after property and titles" in favor of "uh love game" (p. 171). Recognizing that the exclusion of others is the repression of differences within one's self, she merges her life with the life of the black community, telling big stories, listening to them, working along with the other women, and rejecting Mrs. Turner's politics of color—a pecking order that privileges white features over black. (49)

As Mary Helen Washington has said, in her quest Janie Crawford journeys "deeper and deeper into blackness, the descent into the Everglades with its rich black soil, wild cane, and communal life representing immersion into black traditions" (ix). Janie insists

on a different (black and female) determination of meaning and value, and through her own narrative art as the teller within the tale, Hurston resists the binary opposition of phallocentrism as it inhabits Western metaphysics. . . . [She] propels the past, itself a former present, toward a future that exists only as an anticipated possibility for black women. . . . [Janie] learns to be one of the people; thus, this is a story of her acculturation into black womanhood and her artistic entitlement to language. . . . [Hurston] presents feminist readers with a map of a woman's personal resistance to patriarchy, and feminist writers—in particular Alice Walker —with the intertext for later feminist works. (Meese 53)

In *Their Eyes Were Watching God*, Janie Crawford/Killicks/Starks/Woods is empowered to tell her own story, determine her own life, and value her own experience apart from her several husbands' approval or the consent of her society.

Contemporary African-American southern writers such as Alice Walker in *The Color Purple* (1982) and Sherley Anne Williams in *Dessa Rose* (1986) have followed Hurston in creating black southern heroines who discover their own strength, give voice to their own stories, and create alternative, independent, black communities as havens in a hostile world.[6] Black southern women authors have written out of a different cultural tradition than southern white women authors, a tradition that has identified being black and being female as sources of strength and vision rather than as inevitable signs of weakness and defeat. As Richard King explains, "for [black writers] the Southern family romance was hardly problematic. It could be and was rejected out of hand. Their great theme was the attempt (literally) to escape the white South which had historically oppressed their people" (King 8). The myth of the heroic white father held little power over black women's imaginations. Alice Walker remembers in *In Search of Our Mothers' Gardens* that her inspiration came from women's voices raised high in singing negro spirituals; the flowering abundance of their carefully tended gardens; the artistry of their handmade quilts; and the stirring narratives of their ongoing struggles—all testimonies to black female endurance, resistance, and creativity.

Considering this legacy, it is no wonder that Carolyn Heilbrun finds that "the novelists Toni Morrison and Alice Walker, among others, have more profoundly and dazzlingly discovered new narratives for women, and new ways of understanding old narratives, than any other contemporaries I can name" (60-61). Heilbrun agrees with Toni Morrison's assessment of contemporary American women's fiction that there is

an enormous difference in the writing of black and white women. Aggression is not as new to black women as it is to white women. Black women seem able to combine the nest and the adventure. They don't see conflicts in certain areas as do white women. They are both safe harbor and ship; they are both inn and trail. We, black women, do both. We don't find these places, these roles, mutually exclusive. That's one of the differences. White women often find if they leave their husbands and go out into the world, it's an extraordinary event. If they've settled for the benefits of housewifery that preclude a career, then it's marriage or a career for them, not both, not and. (Morrison, *Black Women Writers* 122)

As Toni Morrison has said, black women and their heroines have had to be both aggressive and nurturing, adventurous and domestic, at the same time.

We see contemporary southern white women struggling in their fiction to create new patterns of womanhood for their heroines which no longer equate femininity with defeat, gentleness and kindness with self-sacrifice and submission. They, too, along with contemporary white southern male writers, find themselves "deal[ing] with a new cultural situation. . . . [one that demands that] the fathers and Faulkner must both be transcended" (King 292). Southern white women writers have awakened to the fact that the power of the mythical, heroic father need no longer constrain and direct them. Yet, as Jean Wyatt argues in *Reconstructing Desire: The Role of the Unconscious in Women's Reading and Writing*, "Unconscious fantasy structures [deriving from the traditional family] pose the most formidable opposition to change, for they seem immutable, channeling desire forever into recreating old patterns of relationship" (210). In their works, white southern women writers continue to struggle against the constraints of traditional familial structures and social roles, striving to "transform desire" and create alternative "patterns of family life that [women readers] can assimilate and use" in their own lives (Wyatt 219). In doing so, they are joining other contemporary American women authors in seeking to imagine "new territories of social possibility" that no longer entail southern white female subordination and degradation, as Dana Heller notes (13). They are struggling to find ways of combining what Heller has called

opposite impulses of separation and connection. Their journeys must affirm the need to reroute heroic destiny through these paradoxes of female psychic development: How is a capacity for both autonomy and relationship, attachment and independence, to be expressed? What forms will explain female development and embrace these seemingly irreconcilable forces? (13)

I believe that southern white women writers now are searching for answers to questions Hurston's Janie Crawford resolved for herself more than five decades ago. They, too, are beginning to create narratives in which their heroines can explore new territories; question race, class, and sex hierarchies; and forge new relationships for more full and fulfilling lives—without feeling overwhelmed by suffering, isolation, and defeat.

The works of the three contemporary southern women writers focused on in this study show how arduous this ongoing process of self-discovery and redefinition has been. In their fiction we find a gradation of responses to the death of the myth of white male authority in the southern family and in southern society. Shirley Ann Grau's novels fixate on the father's death. They reveal the long collusion of southern white women with southern white men in supporting and bolstering the white patriarchy and illustrate that female recognition of the mythic father's death does not result in immediate freedom for his daughters. The legacy lives on in the ongoing confusion, hypocrisy, greed, misery, and corruption of the living. In Grau's works we find an ironic sense of loss, of numbness, paralysis, and pain on the part of white women who seek, at times, to maintain the tradition of their fathers, repeat familiar patterns, or submit to the burden of history in their lives. Anne Tyler's fiction, too, attests to the continuing paralysis resulting from the weakness, absence, or actual death of the heroic father. Yet her comic fiction seeks to promote human understanding in her characters and to heal their grief and pain. Her novels suggest that—with or without the mythic white father—the traditional family structure seems incapable of satisfying the basic human needs of many of its members. Families may continue to provide the basis of community in southern society, but the end of the southern family romance has challenged and freed the family to restructure itself in more flexible, open, tolerant, and elastic ways. Family members must reconstruct and reshape the institution of the family and ultimately reshape a more tolerant, less hierarchical, less materialistic society in Tyler's fictional world. Finally, in Gail Godwin's fiction, the demise of the southern patriarchy is seen as positive—as an end to the southern family romance and as a new beginning for present generations of white men and women. Her heroines are free to explore new possibilities and opportunities for themselves, their families, and their communities—to deconstruct and reconstruct the southern white family in more nurturing, socially responsible, less class, race, sex and profit-oriented ways. In a final chapter I will explore other white southern women writers of contemporary fiction and their responses to a changing southern society, from Lee Smith to Ellen Douglas, Lisa Alther to Bobbie Ann Mason, Ellen Gilchrist to Fannie Flagg, Josephine Humphreys to Rita Mae Brown.

I believe that all of these writers convey a sense of loss—loss of clearly defined sex roles (confining as they may have been) and of the romantic myths and reassuring certainties of long-held traditions. Yet their novels also record a gradual coming to terms with this loss—from the social paralysis and reactionary postures of Grau's characters, to the family confusions and experimentations of Tyler's protagonists, on to the adventures and solutions devised by Godwin's men and women. Their heroines begin to undertake inward journeys which lead away from the family and from the past toward greater maturity and self-knowledge, before coming home to the possibility of new communities and newly restructured families. And, as they move out from under the weight of the past, these writers and their many contemporaries range from the seriousness of Grau's fictional worlds to the comic modes of

Tyler and Godwin. The new loneliness, the new uncertainties, and the loss of tradition, one more time in the white South's history of loss, are no longer tragic burdens. These writers move beyond death and despair to envision new forms and new structures where white southern men and women can begin to heal, to grow, and to interconnect as they undertake together the responsibility of leading full adult lives and changing the world inherited from their fathers.

2

Shirley Ann Grau's Keepers of the House

The women of Shirley Ann Grau's novels (except her last one, *Roadwalkers* [1994], with its "fatherless" black heroines) remain very much in the tradition of white southern women's writing described earlier. They are their fathers' daughters—whether they remain dutiful in fulfilling their obligations or act out in rebellion against male control. They belong to men—men whose houses enclose and restrict their lives. Grau's white women spend their time remodeling, decorating, and taking care of structures which have been built, bought, and owned by men. As Grau puts it in *Evidence of Love* (1977), "A man maintained his own home, his own cave, in his own city. Though he might never set foot inside during the long summer months, he knew his house waited for its master" (18). Her white patriarchs luxuriate in their power, using it with deliberation and skill to protect their interests (their property and their women) and extend their control (both politically and economically). Their sisters, wives, and daughters are the bit-players in the unfolding drama of their lives—background figures who exist on the periphery of the story, along with the black servants—persons who must be taken care of, spoken for, and used to profitable end as much as possible.

But at this point, having established the world of the traditional South, Grau removes the structure's main support beam—and positions her white female characters at the center of the drama. The patriarch dies in *The Keepers of the House* (1969), *The Condor Passes* (1971), and *Evidence of Love* (1977)—while, in her earlier novels, the father's abandonment and betrayal thrust daughters into rebellious action (*The Hard Blue Sky* [1958] and *The House on Coliseum Street* [1961]). At the end of each novel except *Roadwalkers*, where the female protagonists are black, Grau's women are left on their own. They find themselves in control of their own destinies and, in most cases, of large inheritances. They no longer need be told what to do. They are left to make choices by themselves—even to dictate now to others.

With the exception of Lucy in *Evidence of Love*, the result is not promising. At the outset, there is grief, dismay, confusion. The passive lives of the white women in Grau's novels have not prepared them for central roles, for decision-making or hard choices. When they do act, they do so by and large in imitation of their fathers and husbands before them. They scheme, manipulate, grasp for control, and carry out acts of revenge. The patriarch's house still stands, unstable though it might be, and his legacy appears pervasive. The women and the men, the whites and the blacks, left behind by Grau's fathers, find themselves caught in tangled social, economic, and political webs that extend as far as they can see. The past weighs heavily upon the present; in fact, Grau's white women most often seek to maintain the tradition of their fathers, grandfathers, and husbands before them, however burdensome that tradition might be, however honorable, or just the legacy they have been given. In Grau's vision, women, black servants, and less powerful white males do not simply play the role of victims in the southern family and in southern history. They are, as well, its inheritors, its new perpetrators, and its maintainers, the "keepers of the house" of a soiled southern past.

The most important of Grau's works (if the most neglected, as well), *The Keepers of the House*, won the Pulitzer Prize for literature in 1969. While the novel is divided into five sections—two for Abigail, one for William, one for Margaret, and an epilogue—it is Abigail Howland Mason Tolliver who tells the entire story. The narrative, however, is only incidentally her own. *The Keepers of the House* is really a story about the Howlands—and one Howland, Abigail's grandfather and the patriarch of her family, in particular. Through her narrative, Abigail reflects on her current situation and concludes that it is the consequence of all that has gone before:

> I stand on the porch of the house my great-great-great-great-grandfather built. . . .
> I was a child in this house once too, rushing through those halls and up and down those stairs. It was not as nice as it is now—that was before the war, before my grandfather made his money—but it was the same house. For them, for me. I feel the pressure of generations behind me, pushing me along the recurring cycles of birth and death. . . .
> They are dead, all of them. I am caught and tangled around by their doings. It is as if their lives left a weaving of invisible threads in the air of this house, of this town, of this county. And I stumbled and fell into them. (5-6)

At the very moment when Abigail realizes the extent of her new power, she feels helpless and trapped in her family history. The Howland house may now belong to her—and all of her grandfather's enormous estate, besides—but she feels "pressured" and "pushed," she is "stumbling" and "falling," in her new role (5).

Ironically, Abigail felt more comfortable playing the part of a bit-player, the secondary, supportive, traditional female role which was hers throughout the first forty years of her life. Suddenly, now, she is, "shivering with rage and fury. All my life I had been trained to depend on men, now when I needed them they were gone" (275). It makes little difference that she has been no more real to the men in her life, her grandfather or her husband, than blacks have been for most whites in the South, including, at times, herself, "I had done what most white people around here did—knew a Negro and dealt with him for years, and never found out his name" (233). Decades earlier, her grandfather had been amazed to learn that his daughter (Abigail's mother) had had her own concerns, "She thought, she worried. . . . He had never before imagined her as having thoughts or feelings of her own. She had always seemed so content" (41). William Howland did not see women as fully human, as capable of deep thought or reflection; nevertheless, he had learned that white women in the family were to be pampered and patronized—"spoiled." William remembered how his father had indulged his mother's taste for cut glass and china, how he had made sure that her life remained as simple and uncomplicated as possible. Day after day,

she crocheted capes and gowns for all the babies in the county, white and black—and William smiled to himself in the dark—the same pattern over and over, only the ones for black babies did not have the three tiny ribbon bows stitched on top. . . . Poor old lady, he thought, with everything hanging on those three bows of ribbon. . . . And that was your whole place in life. (132)

Despite his momentary pity for the monotony and shallow pretense of his mother's life, William abides by his father's dictum (at least where the white women in his life are concerned): "Should have your women spoiled. . . . Leastways, Howland women is always spoiled" (132).

The flip side of spoiling white women, however, is contempt—something William Howland betrays when he tells his granddaughter Abigail (after maneuvering her back into college following her expulsion for attending a wedding), "You're a child . . . and like your mother you have very little sense" (192). Twenty years later, Abigail's husband, John Tolliver, will echo this same sentiment, chastising Abigail, "Think for once, God damn it. Just don't ooze good will and female charm" (219). When Abigail is afraid their telephone is being tapped by her husband's political opponents, John mocks the triviality of her life and her concerns, saying, "After all . . . what does it matter if they know who we're going to have dinner with—they could get that much out of the servants for a few bucks. Or what you're going to send to the church fair, or if Mr. Shaughnessy sent you a lousy roast" (241). In other words, Abigail could never reveal anything of importance because her life has been lived at such great remove from all matters of real significance in John's life. It has been easy for Abigail to collude with her grandfather and her husband in this patronizing attitude since "after all, there are lots of southern men who treat their ladies that way. It's quite pleasant, really" (190). She has been relieved of the task of acting or thinking on her own the majority of the time. Instead, she seems happy to continue existing in the background when she moves from her grandfather's house to her husband's, merely conforming now to John Tolliver's wishes in becoming "the perfect wife for a [political] candidate. He had chosen and trained me well" (257). She visits hospitals and attends teas to help out John's political career simply because "John always wanted me to go, and I always did what he wanted" (302).

As her husband's political life advances towards the state governorship, Abigail's private life moves from child to child (eventually there are four) and house to house. She asserts herself briefly only when John wants to live in a "substantial" old house to present a better image for his career:

"I want a new house," I said, fearfully, because if I got in an argument with him I always lost. I just didn't want to have him talk me out of this, so I said something I'd never said before. "It's my money. . . ."

"Anyway," I added quickly because I was afraid I'd said too much, "the only old house I ever want to live in is my grandfather's." (208)

Getting her way, Abigail contentedly occupies her days making arrangements for the house:

I built my shiny new house, and my children slept in shiny ruffled bedrooms. The whole town buzzed when I had a contractor from Mobile do the kitchen and the bathrooms. The master bath had a sunken tub and a tiny sun-bathing patio. The kitchen was right out of *House and Garden*: it had everything, every gadget that could be installed. (209)

Abigail "keeps house" for her husband and her children in their new residence in Madison City until William Howland dies and her grandfather's house finally becomes her own. She asks few questions; she remains busy and happy.

Pregnant again, Abigail finds herself

placid and lazy, and John took charge of the remodeling of my grandfather's house. He brought an architect from New Orleans and the two of them worked for months over the plans. There was plenty of money now, and John used it well. I'd never known it was such an imposing house. John had been clever enough to go back to the original style, the massive solid farmhouse—of the sort that preceded the rage for Greek Revival. It was heavy and rather African, but it was beautiful. (225)

After giving birth "at last" to a son, then moving into her grandfather's house (now restored through the efforts of the other man in her life, John Tolliver), and finally acquiring a "proper staff" of servants to finish out-fitting the place (226, 229), Abigail feels serene and fulfilled. She thinks,

It was so elegant now, quiet and dignified and obviously very expensive. It was a magnificent house for entertaining, the house of a man who knows what his future is. I worked hard on the decorating, and John was pleased. "Looks great, old girl," he said lightly. "You've got good taste."

He so seldom complimented me that I felt myself blushing.

"You look prettier when you do that," he joked. "You should always be doing a house. Agrees with you." (228-29)

Abigail's achievement, once more, has been to enhance "the house of a man" (*KH* 228), and, better yet, an important man, helping to ensure his future and elevate his community stature in whatever way possible

The price of such acquiescence and collaboration is, of course, self-contempt. Abigail admits, "I just stared at [John]. I would never have thought of that, but then I never thought of anything" (213). She feels "sick with disappointment" after giving birth to a mere daughter, her namesake Abigail, and "cried bitterly" when a second daughter, Mary Lee, was born. She wanted to "do better. I'd always pictured myself with a great family of sons" (206-07)—but otherwise she feels satisfied.

Although about to be propelled into the ugly red brick governor's mansion (another house to decorate and keep for her husband), Abigail admits, "I sat in the quiet familiarity of my house, the house where I had lived as a child, in a country I had known as a child, and I was happy and content. My children were healthy and my husband successful" (254). Abigail has allied herself with a grandfather and a husband whom she finds she loves but cannot respect (216, 204); with men who may "love" her, as her grandfather loved black Margaret, too, but for whom she has been no more fully human than the black servants (including Margaret, whose place was always in the kitchen fixing food for others, even on the day of her husband's death); and with a political system that has empowered a few white men (among them, William Howland and John Tolliver) while denigrating blacks and ignoring white women's lives in speech after speech, act after act.

Vaguely disquieted by the racist comments of her husband, John, his involvement in the White Citizens Council and the Ku Klux Klan, his media tag as "the brightest hope of the southern segregationists" (210), Abigail still agrees with John's own self-assessment, "I'm no worse than anybody else, and I'm maybe even a bit better," telling Margaret's son, Robert Carmichael, "You got rid of John and got something ten times worse" (253, 266). Abigail has compromised her integrity, forfeited her independence, simplified the problem of her own identity by borrowing that of others, and has not yet been made to feel unhappy with the consequences. She has gone along with her husband's segregationist political stance, as well as her grandfather's secrecy about his "other" family, and has felt no need to take a stand of her own.

Ultimately, however, she finds herself alone, without adult friends or family to help her. Her error, she believes, is having "chosen the wrong man" (257) in marrying John Tolliver—a man she had always known married her for reasons of political expediency—a man, in fact, who made every move in life for that same reason, but whom she had never expected to desert such a loyal and dutiful wife as she has been. Now, however, Abigail has become a political liability. Her family history has been called into question; her wealthy, powerful grandfather is no longer a political asset for John Tolliver. Robert Carmichael has released to the newspapers information about his father William Howland's legal, if secret, marriage to his black housekeeper Margaret Carmichael in 1928. The "Carmichael" children, Robert, Nina, and Crissy, can no longer be seen simply as the comfortable "wood colts" about whom everyone has known but need not worry (242); they are legally William Howland's own children, related, in fact, to Abigail Howland Mason Tolliver herself as the lawful offspring of her grandfather William Howland.

Abigail's familiar, cozy world has been turned upside down:

It's like this, when you live in a place you've always lived in, where your family has always lived. You get to see things not only in space but in time too. . . . I don't just see things as they are today. I see them as they were. I see them all around in time. And this is bad. Because it makes you think you know a place . . . [and] the people in it. (248-49)

But Abigail is having to reassess everything and everyone she has known and to re-evaluate her own role. She thinks, "[T]he old structure of innocence—childish, it was—disappeared. [John] was no longer the husband I loved, he was simply the man I had married. I think now that it was amazing that it had lasted those fifteen long years" (258). She realizes that she has been a foolish romantic (like her mother) in marrying for love and trusting a man who will abandon her when it no longer suits his needs (as her mother was abandoned, as well). She begins to understand her grandfather better, too, and how her own dependency had affected his life:

He'd protected and cared for so many females in his life, that he just looked on us as responsibilities and burdens. Loved, but still burdens. . . . Sometimes he must have felt that he was being smothered in dependents. . . . All those clinging female arms. . . . And then there was Margaret. Who was tall as he was. Who could work like a man in the fields. Who bore him a son. Margaret, who'd asked him for nothing. Margaret, who reminded him of the free-roving Alberta of the old tales. Margaret, who was strong and black. And who had no claim on him. (222-23)

Abigail comes to understand that she has most often been merely a dependent, a burden, someone no one need listen to, someone who has to be told what to do and protected from too much knowledge about reality (especially about property and money). Only gradually has she learned about her grandfather's power and wealth, his real relationship to Margaret and "her" children, the effect of William Howland's life and decisions upon her own. And now, borne down by all this new knowledge, Abigail—the dutiful daughter and wife—must stand on her own.

Yet Abigail's response to all that has happened and all she has learned is merely to realign herself with the most significant male presence in her life, with her grandfather, William Howland (or, rather, with the ever-present ghost of her grandfather). Three months after John Tolliver has left, the townsmen have burned down the Howland barn, and Robert Carmichael has returned to the Howland estate with reporters (putting an end to both John's political aspirations and Abigail's marriage at the same time). Abigail is keeping alive simply through remembrance and hate. She vows,

I am alone, yes, of course I am, but I am not particularly afraid. The house was empty and lonely before—I just did not realize it—it's no worse now. I know that I shall hurt as much as I have been hurt. I shall destroy as much as I have lost. It's a way to live, you know.

It's a way to keep your heart ticking under the sheltering arches of your ribs. And that's enough for now. (4-5)

Although the Howland house may be "empty and lonely," it continues to provide structure to her life. Within its walls, Abigail determines to defend the Howland name, the name of her grandfather and his forefathers before him. She remains the keeper of "the house [her] great-great-great-great-grandfather built" (5), "tangled around by . . . [the] doings" of William Howland and his predecessors (6), a handmaiden to white male history, the inheritor of an estate which has come to her by default (instead of to Robert Carmichael, William Howland's only, but mixed-blood, son), a property she plans to pass on to her third child and only son, John, to handle as he sees fit.

In the meantime, she takes revenge on "outsiders," on John Tolliver, on Nina and Robert Carmichael, and on the entire town of Madison City itself. First, Abigail hires a lawyer to take everything back from John Tolliver that she brought into the marriage—all of the Howland property and assets—divorcing John and shoving the one reminder of his family (his own grandfather's yellow oak desk) out of John's old Madison City office into the street. Next, she tells both Nina and Robert Carmichael that their mother committed suicide (knowing that Margaret Carmichael may have died by accident) and suggests their betrayal and neglect have caused their mother's death (believing that Margaret died, lonely and heartsick for her dead husband, William Howland). Abigail intends that the Carmichael children will suffer as much as she has had to suffer, threatening Robert with telephone calls and the possibility of exposing him to his white wife and family as he has exposed Abigail's black relations and cost her her marriage. In fact, she wishes Robert Carmichael dead.

Finally, the entire community of Madison City must suffer, too, for the misery they have caused Abigail and her family, the destruction they have wrought upon Howland property. She tells the women at Mrs. Holloway's tea: "There's precious little around here that didn't belong to Will Howland, one way or the other. Only you forgot. But watch now, and you'll be seeing it shrink together, you'll be seeing Madison City go back to what it was thirty years ago. Maybe my son will build it back, I won't" (305).

She has already closed the town's hotel and sold her livestock. She will no longer supply the slaughter yards and packing-plant with Howland cattle, or the ice-cream plant with Howland milk, so necessary for the community's economic well-being. When her current contracts run out, she promises to end all sales of Howland timber to the local lumberyard, admitting, as its main supplier, "It'll cost me to do this, but I will. I figure to have enough money to live. . . . This town's going to shrivel and shrink back to its real size. . . . It wasn't Will Howland you burned down, it was your own house" (306). It has been a Howland family tradition to take revenge, then preserve mementos of the past by which to remember assaults on the family and its property. Abigail uses her new power and freedom to carry on this Howland family tradition, to emphasize William Howland's continuing importance to the community that despised and turned on him, refusing to mend fences that have been torn down, literally and figuratively.

It is true that only a few months have passed and Abigail is still reeling from the many blows she has taken. By November, at the narrative's outset, she has begun to progress from her condition in the spring after the Holloway tea party, after shoving John's desk out the door, after her first call to Robert Carmichael. Then, she was "locked" into her "own sob-wracked echoing world," oblivious to the people who came and went around her, "crying until I slipped off the chair. And cried on the floor, huddled fetus-like against the cold unyielding boards" (309). From temporary regression into infancy, into a state of total helplessness, Abigail has gone on to carry out her plans for revenge. She vows, "I want to remember" (4).

Abigail has not tried to think things out for herself. She has merely followed patriarchal family tradition. Like William Howland before her, she continues to repay hurt with hurt and to act to uphold family honor (even against members of her own family, as did her grandfather before her): "I once asked my grandfather why we didn't see some cousins who lived only a little way out of town and who had four sons and the oldest was the star basketball player on the high school team. He shrugged. 'Damn-fool thing, child, but they were right mean to my grandmother.' He didn't try to change it though" (164). Family traditions carry on, even when the family itself is undergoing profound change, as in the time of William Howland and Margaret Carmichael or, as now, splintering apart.

Abigail admits to being confused: "Sometimes I feel that my grandfather was my father. And that Margaret, black Margaret, was my mother. Living in a house like this you got your feelings all mixed up" (142-43). She acknowledges that the housekeeper Margaret's "life got mixed up with ours. Her face was black and ours were white, but we were together anyhow. Her life and his. And ours" (78). Why then, if Margaret has mothered Abigail far more than Abigail's own tubercular, invalid mother, and Abigail has named her youngest daughter after Margaret, is Margaret not one of Abigail's ghosts? Why is she "not part of me" (290)? And why does Abigail continue to defend William Howland for using Margaret to fulfill his sexual needs while continuing to deny her her personhood, her dignity, her visibility, within the family as well as in the community? (Abigail has only once seen a gesture of affection

pass between them in all the years she has lived in the Howland house.)[1]
If William Howland has attempted to do the "right" thing by legally marrying Margaret and validating the births of their mixed-blood children,
he has also done so secretly, thereby perpetuating a system that he
knows is morally wrong and damaging the psyches of the children he
must send away from their mother (and their father—himself), their
home, and the South.

John Tolliver might have spoken for William Howland himself, jus-
tifying such action by saying, "I'm a practical man. . . . I've got to deal
with things as they are. It's hell for them, but my saying so won't help
them or me. . . . It's the credo, and though I don't like it, I don't mind it.
I'm no worse than anybody else, and I'm maybe even a bit better" (253).
While it's true that John Tolliver cannot understand why William Howland felt that he must officially marry Margaret two months before their
first child (William's only son) is born, it is also true that John and
William are alike in their practicality, their acceptance of the status quo,
their acquiescence to the way things are. And if John is correct, that Abigail has wanted him "to be a knight on a white horse fighting [racial]
injustice" (253), will she now—disappointed by the white men in her
life—take on that role for herself? Will her acts of personal and familial
revenge in any way improve the shared lives of whites and blacks in
Madison City? Will her actions restore dignity and personhood to blacks
such as Oliver Brandon who had managed the Howland estate for
twenty-five years without a proper title or adequate compensation (51)?
Will Abigail see to it that Oliver Brandon will have his rightful title, and
a salary commensurate with his many responsibilities, as a reward for his
bravery on the night of the barn burning, his continuing to be the Howland family's faithful black retainer? There is no mention of such a plan.

At the novel's conclusion, we are left to wonder why Abigail has so
little sympathy for the Carmichael [Howland] children who, unlike her,
have not been able to stay in the comfort of the family house, inherit the
Howland estate, bask in family tradition, or continue to live without fear
in the South, if they chose. It is she who now squats in the house that
they can never enter, she who lived there under Margaret and William's
care until her marriage. If they are angry and vengeful, do they not have
far more reason than does she herself? What will she do to restore the
Howland house to all of the Howland family and heal its divisions? And
how will Abigail attempt to restore and decorate the soiled house of
southern history? Hers is a disturbing voice, her story that of a modern,
southern white woman trapped in the patriarchal, familial past, isolated
from the rest of the world, unwilling to open the doors of her house, to
set forth and seek constructive change, to try to bring about a better

future, a more just way of life, for others as well as for herself and her children, or take responsibility for the future through acts of compassion and courage (now that the family patriarch is dead and her dependency on men is at an end).

Equally as troubling is the critical assessment of the novel and its characters, to date. Can we really be meant to see Abigail Howland Mason Tolliver, as Paul Schlueter suggests, as "one of the strongest, most memorable women in recent American fiction"? (64). Is William Howland really meant to be an "exalted" and "heroic patriarch" whose heritage is "worth preserving"? (Schlueter 66). While Abigail does, indeed, show courage and affirm what Eleanor Nobuko Chiogioji defines as "her own identity and . . . her niche in the Howland lineage" (108) by standing up to the townspeople and defending her grandfather's house and property, shouldn't her self-image be based on more than the Howland name? In fact, Pamela Lorraine Parker believes that the novel reveals how Abigail, in fact, "fails in her search for self" (129) through her very overidentification with her grandfather and her Howland heritage—a view which I share. And shouldn't Abigail's long-term goals be more positive and constructive than simply hurting those who have hurt her—for her own sake as well as for others'? Revenge, admittedly, is a way to stay alive—but is it an exemplary way? As Shirley Ann Grau explains, "[I]f there is a moral, it is the self-destructiveness of hatred" (qtd. in Campbell), not only for the townspeople Abigail punishes but for Abigail herself, the family she seeks to defend, and the South she exemplifies. Shouldn't Abigail learn to care for others beyond her own already considerably advantaged children; shouldn't she want to use her power and wealth to lead the community forward?

While Eleanor Chiogioji presents a thoughtful argument that *The Keepers of the House* rebutts the pessimistic view set forth in the novel's epigraph from Ecclesiastes, suggesting the importance of the Howland family heritage, their struggle against adversity (129-32), Shirley Ann Grau seems to offer little else in the novel that might be seen as fending off the future darkness foretold in the biblical passage of the epigraph or discouraging "the mourners [from] go[ing] about the streets" of the land she has described.[2] No one in the town, in state government, or in the Howland-Carmichael family has been shown to have a vision large enough to include two races; a will determined enough to heal ancient divisions; or a desire strong enough on which to build a future (other than one which merely repeats the animosities of the past). Surely much more strength and leadership will be needed to restore comfort and beauty to the South's decaying mansion than we see displayed anywhere in the novel, by Abigail Howland Mason Tolliver, her powerful grandfather William Howland, or by the stately Margaret Carmichael herself.[3]

Only in the last two novels, *Evidence of Love* and *Roadwalkers*, does Shirley Ann Grau offer hope for the future. The white heroines of all her other works follow a pattern similar to that of Abigail Howland. They remain their fathers' daughters even when out from under their fathers' control. Lacking self-esteem and self-direction, they imitate their fathers' actions and perpetuate their fathers' values. They have followed so long, they cannot lead; all their lives, they have allowed others to do their thinking for them. Like the nineteenth century's Edna Pontellier of *The Awakening*, they seem to act spontaneously, without thought, making choices without taking control of their lives.

In Shirley Ann Grau's first two novels, *The Hard Blue Sky* (1958) and *The House on Coliseum Street* (1961), young heroines gain their independence, but only (as in *The Keepers of the House*) by accident, squandering its privileges and possibilities through the same passivity, lack of vision, and negative behavior we have seen revealed in the actions of the newly "freed" Abigail Howland Mason Tolliver. Annie Landry, of *The Hard Blue Sky*, has been the center of her father's life as his only child for sixteen years and his main support after her mother's death a year earlier. Suddenly, she is displaced as keeper of her father's house and apple of her father's eye by his unexpected marriage to Adele (who comes to live with them, accompanied by her young son, Claudie). Annie rebels, refusing to accept Adele or obey her father; aiding an arsonist from Terre Haute before he can be found by her neighbors from Isle aux Chiens; then running away with an outsider from New Orleans (and a convenient father substitute), Inky.

For all the appearance of decision and activity in Annie's life, as Eleanor Nobuko Chiogioji comments, "Annie is passive: rather than initiating action, she waits for things to happen to her" (45). Annie Landry decides to marry Inky "to get away" but remains bewildered as to how she has made this choice:

She'd wondered about [getting married], off and on for years: could she find anybody for a husband? Was there going to be anybody around who'd want her? And she had that too, and not just an island man, nor even one from Petit Prairie or Port Ronquille. But one from the city. One who'd seen a lot, a whole lot. And still wanted to marry her.

That was something you couldn't forget.

But it was strange now, because it wasn't at all exciting. It wasn't sad either. It was just something you had to do because you'd planned it that way a long time ago. (*HBS* 414)

Programmed to marry because it was expected of her, to think of it as her way out of loneliness and isolation, a way to have a man hold her in his arms, comfort her, and take her father's place, Annie prepares herself "woman-fashion" for the disappointment that will inevitably follow "when things did not go well with Inky. . . . She loved him and there wasn't anybody else. Maybe, she found herself saying silently, she loved him *because there wasn't anybody else* [my emphasis]" (426). Inky fills the emptiness in Annie's motherless, fatherless, friendless life; he is what she has been prepared to find and waiting to accept.

Further, as they leave her home on the Isle aux Chiens behind, Annie "relinquishes control of the boat to Inky" (Chiogioji 46), giving her life over to him, ready to keep Inky's house now in place of her father's, to follow where Inky leads. At this moment of great change in her life, Annie takes no control over her own destiny. Instead, she turns the helm over to Inky and stands "waiting, waiting for things to happen to her. Things that could be handled and changed. And things that could just be handled. She felt herself grow great and passive in her waiting" (427). Annie might just as well have remained huddled with the other islanders she has left behind, awaiting her fate before the lashing rains and winds of the oncoming hurricane, rather than setting forth on a new adventure, undertaking a new life, with so little sense of direction, of hope, or of self as she displays at the end of the novel.

Eleanor Nobuko Chiogioji has noted the similarity between Annie Landry and Joan Mitchell, the protagonist of Grau's second novel, *The House on Coliseum Street* (1961). Chiogioji explains, "Both are passive about their own destinies, content to let others determine the course of their lives" (67). And Chiogioji points out that critics who blame Joan's passivity on her abortion, arranged for her by her mother, Aurelie Caillet, misread Joan's character and the action of the novel. Chiogioji explains,

the abortion does not *cause* the seemingly irrational behavior that characterizes Joan's emotional deterioration; the abortion merely aggravates a propensity Joan has toward such behavior. Her apathetic "waiting," her withdrawal into herself, and her divided self all evolve from Joan's passive nature and are, in fact, amplified manifestations of that passivity. . . . Joan has never been a strongly assertive person, especially where her mother is concerned. With no clear cut-goals to give her life direction, Joan lacks a certain vivacity for living. She is already biding her time, "waiting," even before she meets Michael, for with no expectations other than to someday get married (in all probability, to Fred), she indifferently pursues a course of study at the university, once even failing, for a while, to attend classes because she forgot that she had registered for a particular course. (76)

Like Annie Landry, then, Joan has little sense of her own self, knowing only that she is expected someday to marry (in all likelihood, the lackluster Fred whom she does not love) and that she someday will inherit the house on Coliseum Street left to her by her father (and built by her great-great-grandfather in 1840). Meanwhile, she, like Annie Landry, feels abandoned by her father, first through his long-ago divorce from Aurelie and then his death, as well as displaced from a house which is rightfully hers by a mother who has brought forth four other sisters, each by a different father, to create a "house full of bitches" (171). Joan's female self-loathing is revealed in her agreement with her sister Doris's disparaging remark that they are all bitches; she needs a man as much as her mother and Doris to feel important in herself. Like Annie Landry, Joan Mitchell, too, seeks a father substitute to fill the emotional void in her life; carry out her female destiny as a mother-woman (and man-dependent woman), as Aurelie has defined the role for her (Parker 156; Chiogioji 52-53); and, perhaps, as well, prop her up in the face of the strong, overbearing mother she submits to and relies on, but deeply despises (Chiogioji 65).

Increasingly, Joan's weakness in *The House on Coliseum Street* becomes injurious not only to herself but to others as well. She allows the "ghost-child," the "seaweed" shape, within her to be destroyed because her mother has arranged for her to have an abortion (217, 204). She punishes Michael not for getting her pregnant in the first place but for rejecting her through his later attentions to a young student and then to her sister, Doris. Joan twists the truth for Dean Lattimore and his wife, placing all responsibility for her pregnancy on Michael and ignoring her own instigative role in their relationship in order to destroy his academic career. In addition, Joan hurts the ever-faithful and attentive Fred by telling him that she won't miss his telephone calls if he never calls her again, then wonders, "Why did I say that? When I know it isn't true. Why did I? Why did I want to hurt myself?" (185).

While destructive of others and herself, Joan nevertheless persists in viewing herself as helpless, insignificant, and confused. If she has been made independently wealthy through an inheritance from her father, Joan can conceive of no bright future for herself, no constructive course of action, no purpose in moving forward with her life. Instead, she finds herself "waiting. . . . Waiting for what? And she didn't have an answer. Even for herself" (173). In the final scene of the novel, Joan Mitchell, like Abigail Howland Mason Tolliver of *The Keepers of the House*, huddles in a fetal position on the porch of the house on Coliseum Street, at once locked out yet still trapped inside all that this structure represents in her life. Joan is dwarfed and diminished by "everything that had gone on in the house for the past hundred and twenty years. . . . the living that had gone on between the walls " (230). She knows, "I should have found a way to go off somewhere [after the abortion]. But I didn't. . . . I'm back and caught just where I was four months ago" (20). Now she will have to leave in the wake of the scandal she has created by destroying Michael's career, yet there is nothing in the work that points to a positive course of action or a more hopeful future for Joan Mitchell. As Pamela Parker concludes, the introduction of the novel makes clear "that Joan's attempt to define herself and understand her identity is thwarted by the presence of tradition" (67). She has been trapped into seeing herself, her life, her world, in limited ways and in repeating self-destructive, vengeful, negative patterns of action from the past. The sins of her gambling, tax-evading father and her proper, yet ruthless, mother weigh heavily upon her. They have modeled negative patterns of behavior and enclosed her in the (comfortable) house of (unworthy) southern tradition. Joan's "independence" is tied to her dead father, the house on Coliseum Street, a debilitated past. She has no idea how to use her inheritance constructively—or escape her dependence upon it. Joan may leave, but she cannot conceive of doing so freely, much less exuberantly.

In Shirley Ann Grau's next two novels, *The Condor Passes* (1971) and *Evidence of Love* (1977), the past continues to dominate the present, and the white southern patriarch, his successors, even beyond the grave. In *The Condor Passes*, Stanley and Robert remain the patriarch's unwillingly enslaved black and white "sons," Anna and Margaret, their father's dutiful daughters—most of all when they believe they have eluded his grasp. The Old Man (Thomas Henry Oliver) exists at the center of a house (run for him by his daughter Margaret) where "everything . . . had a fixed and ordered pattern. Unchangeable" (11). He is determined that this world will stay intact, even though he has no natural male children to carry on the family line. What he wants, he has always bought: whores, servants, housekeepers, business partners. In *The Condor Passes*, the Old Man buys his immortality as well. He intends to perpetuate his world, unchangeable and unchanged, and he "die[s] beautifully" (6) in the course of the novel, accomplishing this end even as he seems to relinquish his control and dissolve the old order.

His chauffeur and valet, Stanley, who is black, admits that his salary of $300 a week, superior to that of any man in Gulf Springs, white or black, is enough to hold him in place: "How's that for a nigger's salary? For that I'll stay invisible and jump out their way" (3), confessing, "I say I'm going to leave sometimes. Twenty years on any job is long enough. But I don't go" (6). At the Old Man's death, Stanley finally walks away, "Like the Old Man, he was finished here" (421). However, like the Old Man before him, his pockets now are filled with gold. The Old Man has given Stanley two hundred acres of marshland soon to be developed into an interstate and a shopping center, as well as more land for residential development, worth three-quarters of a million dollars (Margaret figures that it could be worth twice this value) (397). Stanley understands the Old Man's motives, "He thinks he's keeping me forever. [Like the condor of Indian legend] I'm his messenger and my feathers are full of gold" (403), but Stanley believes he can elude the Old Man's grasp. As he turns his back on the Old Man's world for the last time, however, he finds that his fingers have metamorphosed into claws, his body into a bird's, "black wings fluttering on each side" (421). Transformed, he is trapped like the caged birds he has tended for Thomas Henry Oliver for years. Stanley carries the Old Man's gold away, tucked underneath his feathers. Weighed down by the Old Man's money, he can no longer soar and fly away.

Denying their relationship—he is not "a white nigger," he insists, "not . . . like the Old Man" (381)—he has actually been bought long ago:

The reason was buried back in his mind, with vague atavistic pictures of burning crosses and hanging black bodies. An anger he would do anything to vent. An anger that increased steadily as he grew more and more successful in the white world. He felt his whole body shake with it sometimes; he would then rehearse to himself his list of accomplishments: I got a new house better than any white man, a kitchen with every gadget any white man's wife could want, and I got a better salary than anybody in this little town; I got stocks in my bank box. . . . All that and I still got a black face. . . . Jesus God.

"Yea," Stanley said. "I'd like to have a lot of money." (404)

His anger over his treatment as a black man at the hands of whites and his desire for revenge have led Stanley into the Old Man's trap. Believing himself in control, the "secret thief" preying on the Oliver family fortune (29), Stanley wakes to find: "I been thinking that I was the big black hawk spying on people's lives. But now it looks like there was a skinny sparrow right up under my nose, watching everything, watching me. Who's fooling who? The Old Man. It's always the Old Man" (35). Unwittingly, Stanley has become the Old Man's dupe, his messenger, Thomas Henry Oliver's successor. The Old Man will live on through Stanley.

And so, too, Thomas Henry Oliver lives on through his chosen son-in-law, Robert. Early on, Robert Caillet finds that the Old Man "could order and arrange things, play God" (135) with his life. Having picked him up, a poor, hungry Cajun boy without a family, the Old Man quickly comes to dominate every part of Robert's life, proving to him, "Nothing money won't do. Fill out a boy, turn a child into a man. . . . Whole thing courtesy of the Old Man. He fed it, he grew it, and to hell with him" (135). Desperate as he becomes to escape Thomas Oliver's grip, Robert finds that the Old Man won't let go. He refuses to let Robert quit working for him (135) and breaks up Robert's first engagement by reporting (erroneously but effectively) that Robert is already married and has two children (126). Soon afterwards, Robert stumbles into marriage to the Old Man's beautiful daughter, Anna, hardly knowing what he is doing or that the Old Man has planned for this to happen. Robert wakes to find: "He was married now. His life was organized and planned. . . . Bask in the approval of your wife's brown eyes. . . . Me, the man of property, the successful businessman, growing distinguished gray hairs, the soft cushions of money all around. . . . And what the hell was bothering him?" (215-16). All his dreams fulfilled, Robert feels himself "shrivel and die" (220).

The Old Man is the stronger force, his money the lure Robert can't resist (Margaret tells her father, "That poor slob's so crazy about money he'd do anything for it. Even Anna. He wouldn't look at her if you weren't paying for it" [268]). Robert submits to the power of "the Old Man. The family's force and drive and shrewdness came from him. Robert knew and he did not really mind. He even suspected that those successes which he called his own had been suggested to him by the Old Man, deftly, cleverly, invisibly, so that he was not aware of the hint" (337). Robert knows that he has been possessed by the Old Man. He has become the Old Man's mechanical toy, admitting, "I see and I think but I don't really feel. I have a life and a business and a good wife to take care of me; people stand up to shake my hand. I am respected. I watch my money grow, I can feel it grow like grass under my care. Even the Old Man nods now and then. I am his son, the one he looked for and found" (340).

However Robert might attempt to disengage himself from the Old Man, he finds himself destined to fail. He has become so entangled in the Old Man's gold-filled web that his desperate acts of rebellion and denial only serve to entangle him further. He may hand over his resignation to try to free himself from the Oliver business empire, reject Anna for teenage girls who give him a temporary sense of his own manhood, get drunk day after day, or refuse to appear at the Old Man's deathbed, but the patriarch holds him fast—forever. Robert is a kept man.

Thomas Henry Oliver has had to buy his heirs (Stanley and Robert) because his wife has provided him with no male children of his own. Desperate for sons, Thomas Oliver brought about his wife's death through her repeated pregnancies: "He had hurt her again, when he should have protected her. . . . The fragile dark-eyed girl had had nothing from him but blood and pain. . . . As if he himself were destroying her" (103). Of the five children Stephanie D'Alfonso Oliver produced for her husband in eleven years of marriage, three sons died. Only the daughters, Margaret and Anna, survived—and they were not enough for their father (as they themselves soon came to realize). Many years later, Anna asks herself:

Why, she thought, do I always get angry at my mother? For not leaving me a memory, for being so vague and gentle and so busy with her job of procreating that she hardly noticed her children once they left her womb. . . . She would ask her father about this obsession to breed; had he wanted a son that much? He had one now, she thought smugly, in Robert. (169-70)

Anna's importance, she determines, will be in being married and keeping house for Robert; yet she determines, at the same time, to make that house "belong to me. Not like my mother. If I died, people could see my reflection in these things. My mother left no reflection. Nothing but some clothes hanging in the closet. And me. And Margaret" (171).

Anna is driven by her own invisibility (and her mother's) in the scheme of things, as is her sister Margaret, who knows that, in her father's eyes, "No penis, no use. He had to have a son, one way or the other" (267). As it stands, she knows that all her father has been left with are "two insignificant girls" (267). At twenty-one, still getting an allowance from her father, Margaret tells Robert, "I want to choose too. . . . To have what men have. To initiate, to choose. Not to wait, not always to wait. For the sleek, preening male. Because I need him. I don't want to need him" (266-67). Margaret would like to be male, to be her father's son, to be his partner and his heir.

When she asks her father if she can go into business with him, however, he refuses. Margaret insists, then, on receiving her own money, demanding,

"I want what's mine, Papa," she said slowly, distinctly. "I'm not going to sit around any more and be grateful for my living. . . .

Half of whatever you had was my mother's when she died. Her estate goes to me and Anna. I want mine, and I'm willing to go to court to get it."

His face was bright red. "What the hell are you saying?"

"I tried asking you politely and you said no. You want what's yours, Papa, and I want what's mine."

He began to chuckle very softly. "Take it and good luck to you," he said. (269-70)

The Old Man, as always, has the last laugh. Despite her new-found independent means, three marriages (and three divorces), several houses to decorate and keep up, Margaret clings to her father's home in New Orleans because

I guess it really is my home, she thought; it's where I go when I can't think of any other place.

. . . Margaret considered this tall old man with the ruddy wrinkled face, the shiny bald head. Because of a couple of convulsive movements with my mother, here I am. Related to him forever. How do you shed a father? Snakes shed their skins, leave them lying on the ground. How do you get rid of your beginnings, your genes?

"I'll find you a proper house, Papa, and I'll run it for you. I'll live with you like a dutiful daughter." (277)

In seeking independence and self-expression, Margaret ends up being the "dutiful daughter," keeping house for her father as Anna has kept house for her father's chosen son Robert.

The two women are, despite their individual attempts at rebellion, the white southern patriarch's dutiful daughters—even, like their mother, producing sons in a futile attempt to extend the patriarch's family line. As Margaret says, "I wouldn't have a girl, not me. I wouldn't make a mistake like that" (284). It would seem, despite Margaret and Anna's efforts, however, that the Oliver family is destined to die out, that Thomas Oliver has been thwarted in his goal of achieving immortality because he has not had a proper son. As Paul Schlueter explains, the Oliver dynasty will cease:

for Anna and Robert's only child has died and Margaret's is a priest. Robert has proven to be an extremely poor choice, not just as a son-in-law but even more as a human being, since his entire existence is spent with extremely young girls. Among the Old Man's last decisions is eliminating Robert from the control and operations of the financial holdings of the Oliver family, with the two daughters thereafter determining all policy. . . . Money may indeed have bought for Oliver everything he wanted, but it could not produce the kind of love needed to assure that his "success" would continue beyond his death, no matter how vivid his memories of youthful poverty. (74-75)

Perhaps not. But Oliver has achieved a kind of immortality that does not require love, a proper heir, a natural son. He lives on through the money he has amassed and doled out—the way of life he has created and perpetuated—carried on now by his dutiful daughters (who have all along kept his houses in perfect running order) and by his rebellious "sons" (who remain bound to him still by their greed and need).

Margaret and Anna pretend they both have escaped their father's dominance and any family resemblance they might share with one another, yet they stand firm, united as their father's daughters, two sides of the same coin, in control, at last, of the family fortune at the end of the novel. Self-contempt has bound them to their father and to each other throughout their lives. Despite their carefully cultivated differences, they are "truly their father's daughters, as callous of others, self-centered, and selfish as Oliver is" (Chiogioji 159). Anna immerses herself in her traditional white southern female role with a single-mindedness of purpose and a lavish display of wealth that are mind-numbing in their proportions:

> She began, with infinite care and precision, to acquire her household goods. At fifteen, she had an entire convent of Guatemalan Carmelite nuns doing her needlework. . . . A Belgian convent stopped everything but prayers to make her lace tablecloths. Slowly, steadily, her closets and chests began to fill. . . .
>
> At sixteen she ordered her china, her own design, executed by Minton. It took two years and arrived barely in time for her wedding.
>
> At sixteen, too, she bought her house. . . . She planned the remodeling with her usual thoroughness—more sketches, more books. (161-62)

Anna is determined to have the most perfect house, the most perfect marriage, the most perfect life money can buy. She tells Robert, "[W]e are going to be the happiest couple that there ever was in the world. . . . Two loves put together, the way God intended them to be. I wouldn't want to live without you" (219-20). What money can buy, God will most certainly ordain.

Anna seeks perfection through God and money, attempting to remove the stain of being female (the one stain in an otherwise picture-perfect existence) from her person forever—becoming more and more afflicted in the process of cleansing herself of her imperfections (even covering her body with angry bites from the red ants she applies to scourge away her sins). Margaret scoffs at her sister's other-worldly image, saying, "Anna, why don't you stop being the perfect housewife and the great mother and the Holy Virgin and all those other things?" (282). Anna's husband, Robert, recoils from her self-proclaimed "purity," feeling himself "shrivel and die" (220) in her presence, seeking humanity and pleasure in the company of other women (including her sensual, earthly sister Margaret). And Anna's son, Anthony, at first believing his mother to be the Virgin Mary, finally attempts to punish her for withdrawing from him into her aura of godliness when he very much needs her real warmth and comfort on earth, here and now, as he finds himself in the throes of a last battle with leukemia. Feeling trapped in his mother's unreal house of perfection, fearing he "won't be able to get out, my mother will have caught me inside that house forever" (313), he escapes both live-burial in the immediate, and real burial soon afterwards, by drowning at sea. Anna has revealed herself to be her father's daughter, denying Anthony love as she has been denied love by her father, maintaining large, expensive, well-polished houses instead of refurbishing the spiritual house within. She may affect a pose of other-worldliness; however, to others she appears very much a woman of the world, one who speaks in a voice that is "level and correctly modulated, neither affected nor coarse, the smooth voice of the perfect lady. Like that sleek shining head of hers, with its gray-dappled hair. Lady of wealth and dignity. The polish that only money gives. As beautiful as money itself, Stanley thought" (411). Anna is the epitome of white southern aristocratic womanhood, carrying on a tradition that, for all her works of charity, affirms hierarchical and materialistic values and a will to carry them on.

Anna's sister, Margaret, embraces these values knowingly and openly. Having attempted to gain power and control directly by confronting her father and demanding partnership with him, she gradually learns to play out her female, subordinate part, keeping his house for him and maneuvering behind the scenes to help maintain the family empire and control over the life it affords her. Margaret cultivates a style that seems the exact opposite of Anna's in its sensuality, spontaneity, and earthiness (Chiogioji 171). Sexually impulsive, Margaret seeks affirmation of herself through erotic power over men, embarking on one relationship after another. She marries three times, then divorces three times, entering into countless relationships (including one with her brother-in-law Robert) both before, during and after her marriages in fruitless attempts to seek self-fulfillment and self-expression. In the same way, she rushes from house to house, decor to decor, in her material search for spiritual well-being, finally redecorating her father's house a dozen times, bragging to her father, "Papa, do you know how foolish this whole house is? . . . Good God, no. This is the best house in New Orleans; it's taken me years to get it to this gorgeous point. . . . There isn't a single thing in it that's not overdone" (366). Margaret revels in personal indulgence, expanding from redecorating houses to collecting works of art, confessing, "Well, I make money and I like to spend it on me. Anna can do the good works" (366). However frantically Margaret searches, however self-indulgently she may spend money, however passionately she ventures through life, she is unable to avoid the truth, that she is "short and square. . . . [with] kinky hair and stupid brown eyes" (189), a woman who finds herself unattractive, a woman unloved by her father, a woman who feels inherently (as a female) unworthy and unlovable. She may be less attractive physically than Anna, and far more crude, outspoken, and promiscuous than her ladylike sister, yet Margaret is united with Anna in being her father's unwanted child—a daughter who may be "astute," in her father's words, but a daughter, all the same. While the Old Man ends up leaving his estate in the control of both Margaret and Anna, they have disappointed him by being born female. Nothing they have ever done has made the slightest difference in affecting their father's indifference to them. At the end of his life, when Stanley asks him, "Shouldn't we call your daughters, sir", the Old Man answers, "I don't want them" (418). They need not hear his words of dismissal at the end of the novel; Margaret and Anna have heard them all along.

Thomas Oliver has ignored his daughters, exploited Robert in his poverty and need, and rendered Stanley and his wife Vera invisible. Yet the Old Man has depended on them all to do his bidding while, at the same time, denying each of them full, real and significant lives of their own. Thomas Oliver has remained in control, manipulating everything and everyone, building his empire. A majority of critics have remarked that, despite all his efforts, Thomas Oliver has failed to perpetuate his dynasty; his attempts at immortality have proved futile. Anthony Bukoski and Pamela Lorraine Parker argue that the black valet Stanley finally escapes the Old Man's grasp (Bukoski 171, 188-89; Parker 122). Mary Rohrberger believes that the Old Man has failed because "there is nothing left of him but memory and that only in the minds of the people who actually knew him. When they are gone he will be extinct—as we all will be" (98). Eleanor Chiogioji believes that *The Condor Passes* "chronicles the gradual extinction of the family that is its subject" (156), revealing "the inherent sterility and corroding destructiveness of the family's values" (183). Indeed, it is that very "sterility" and "corroding destructiveness," however, that triumph in the work. Thomas Oliver's values (if not his family line) will survive and carry on in the world he leaves behind. All of those who remain have been manipulated through their neediness and greed; all have been caught up in a cycle of corruption and selfishness they will continue and spread. Perhaps, as Anna says at her dying father's bedside, if they had been different people, capable of showing love and compassion, "We all would have done things differently" (413). But they are Thomas Oliver's true heirs. Stanley will have the money and, through it, the revenge on whites he has sought. Margaret, with her father's money, will have all the "love" that money can buy and the power she seeks over men (such as her brother-in-law and sometime lover Robert). Anna can continue to spend lavishly, decorating houses, building hospitals, doing "good works" in her need for love and veneration while maintaining control over her world and, as part of this, her helpless husband Robert. Anthony, wasting away with leukemia, has symbolized the disease they all carry out into the world. Only Joshua, Margaret's son, holds himself apart from the family sickness, determining to become a mystic and cure "the lost society" he finds around him (374). If Joshua's act of entering the priesthood "condemns [his] family to a future oblivion" (Chiogioji 184), it will do little to diminish the negative forces Thomas Oliver has methodically cultivated, legitimately and illegitimately increased, and successfully unleashed upon the world. Anna and Margaret, his dutiful daughters, stand at the center of the family drama at the novel's conclusion, once more Grau's "keepers of the house" of an unworthy, patriarchal, southern tradition.

In Shirley Ann Grau's *Evidence of Love* (1977), another dutiful daughter (or, in this case, daughter-in-law), Lucy Roundtree Evans Henley, stands beside the deathbed of her wealthy father-in-law, Edward Milton Henley, observing him with "a watchful, penetrating, patient gaze" (226). She has just given him an overdose of Seconal pills, administering to his wishes when no one else will assist him in dying. At the same time, she assumes a new position of strength and authority over a man who has been used to wielding power and assuming all the control himself:

"I'll put them in your hand," she said, "but you'll have to take them yourself."

Could I do that? And who was she to exact conditions from me?

Alas, her muscles still coordinated properly, her legs still functioned, she was not held prisoner by a corps of white-coated nurses. . . .

And so she could indeed demand conditions from me, who once would have laughed at her.

Now she is my escape. An angel visiting me. (224)

No longer someone to "laugh at," Lucy appears to her father-in-law a ministering "angel," helping him escape the withered frame of his ailing body as she has earlier freed his son Stephen's spirit to set it loose on its final journey: "Returning from a meeting, Lucy Roundtree Evans finds [her husband Stephen] dead inside the house. Until she opens the door, thus freeing his spirit, she can feel it trapped within 'hissing and singing' (141). She herself stands fifty feet away from the house to await the police" (Bukoski 190). Lucy helps both her husband and her father-in-law out of the world, continuing to tend to the needs of others at the last as she has cared for her family's day-to-day, worldly wants all along. At the same time, unlike earlier Grau heroines, she frees herself from her dependence on men, gains power over her own life, and moves beyond male control (as have the black Mary and Nanda Woods in Grau's last novel *Roadwalkers*).

For thirty-four years of marriage to Stephen, Lucy has attended to the "details" of both their lives, raising their two sons, freeing Stephen for the more important duties of his Unitarian church ministry and his classical scholarship. Stephen calls her, "Lucy the perfect, Lucy the thoughtful. Lucy, who kept lists of wedding presents for thirty-four years," the woman who "supervised the actual moving [from Pennsylvania to their Florida retirement home] . . . while I went to Washington for two months' work at the Library of Congress" (106). Lucy has kept her pledge to her father-in-law, "I have been teaching at Greenwood College, but now all my time will be devoted to my husband and my home" (47). Yet, the upshot of her dutifulness is that her father-in-law dislikes her, her ascetic husband Stephen forgets her, her crazed first husband tries to kill her. Edward Milton Henley admits, "To be truthful, had I met her first, I most certainly would have tried to seduce her. And she most certainly would have refused me. As it was, I disliked her immediately and intensely" (48). Her husband Stephen confesses, "Lucy has been a comfort, a support. She has matured into a handsome woman, far more beautiful than when I married her. She is quiet, thoughtful, busy. And yet when she is out of the room, I have trouble remembering that she was ever within it. She seems strangely shadowy to me, without substance" (97). On the night of his death, as he tries to open the door of his study and the house lights seem to fail, Stephen thinks, "And what was her name? My wife's name. I couldn't remember" (136). If Lucy's first husband, archeologist Harold Evans, had loved her, he had also planned to kill her at the same time that he shot himself. Lucy realizes, "The cat's death had averted mine. Harold had intended to kill me, and had killed the cat instead. . . . Harold had loved me enough to want me to be buried with him" (190, 192). Nevertheless, Lucy continued to serve her first husband even after his death, finishing his book from research notes he had left behind, assuring Harold of "a scholar's immortality" (195).

Twice Lucy Roundtree Evans Henley has been a faithful wife and a dutiful housekeeper. Yet she has maintained, all along, despite the traditional role she has played, an independence of spirit from the family patriarch and from family ties that distinguishes her from other Grau heroines. Born in British East Africa of English and Boer parentage, she is an outsider to America, a woman of mixed heritage from a "timeless" culture, one who is bound neither by the American past nor by a life-long dependence on men:

Time had no real meaning in Africa, there were no marks of the past: no grave-yards, no temples, not even a recently abandoned farmhouse. The shambas van-ished quickly and completely. People had lived here for thousands of years without leaving a mark on their earth.

Everything was transient; everything was timeless too. (162)

After her first husband's death, Lucy teaches and publishes children's books in order to "refuse an allowance from Harold's family. And I did not need to return to my parents in Africa. They asked me to come. But I couldn't" (195). Capable of supporting herself, she nonetheless chooses to marry Stephen Henley rather than continue publishing and teaching at Greenwood College. While her father-in-law is contemptuous of her, as he has been of each of his own wives and of women in general, never-theless Edward Milton Henley has "been impressed by Lucy's charac-ter"—so much so that he pays tribute to his daughter-in-law by setting up a trust fund for her, "to be used at her discretion. . . . an outright gift, so that she need never deal with me. I know she will find that a pleasant prospect" (86).

If Lucy's strength of character and personal integrity have won her a trust fund from her father-in-law, they have not changed his views on women in general—or, it seems, on her, in particular. Edward Milton Henley later warns his son Stephen to beware of Lucy's spirit, revealing a deep fear of women underlying his contempt for the opposite sex:

"She has carried you off to her lair," his father wrote, "and she'll devour you there like the Black Widow spider. My dear boy, you are only discovering what I found out before you, and all men before us. Women get you at the last. For a while you think you have them, with their soft bodies and their beckoning dis-tances that lure you on as if there were something waiting for you. But you grow tired and they don't, and in the end they have got you. Look at me now. Nurses, goddamn nurses. I shall be carried to my grave by women. Clotho and Agapos and Atropos—women again; measuring your life."

And Stephen said, "I'm always amazed at how well read that man is." But he did not really deny the substance of his father's thought. (201)

Lucy, like other Grau heroines, does outlive the family patriarch (and her husband, Stephen, besides); at the end of *Evidence of Love*, Lucy also has been made independently wealthy by that patriarch, as have Abigail

Howland, Joan Mitchell, Anna Oliver Caillet, and Margaret Oliver before her.

Yet Lucy's predecessors seem to have been caught in the patriarch's web and consumed there by his values and concerns (rather than the other way around, as Edward Milton Henley contends). This time, in *Evidence of Love*, Lucy frees herself from the influence of the past, feeling no need to carry out acts of revenge, manipulate others, or grasp for control, as had the family patriarch before her. Family concerns do not weigh heavily upon her; she is no longer a "keeper of the house" of family tradition, a "dutiful daughter" to an unworthy father. Because Lucy has side-stepped gracefully what Eleanor Chiogioji refers to as "the emotional tug-of-war that seems to absorb the Henley males" (240)—Stephen rejecting the ways of his father; her own sons, Thomas and Paul, at war with each other, "the inheritors of the values advocated by Henley and Stephen, respectively," as Chiogioji explains (231)—she can go her own way and follow her own values:

Female principle, life force, touchstone of love—Lucy is the measure that reveals the personalities of those with whom she comes in contact. Her own personality is, in turn, revealed by what Stephen calls her "retirement haven, the dream house of her later years" (107), for unlike the house in which she and Stephen make their home for thirty-four years, Lucy's Florida house has an ambience created by her alone. . . . Her openness to life is reflected in the fact that her house is architecturally "open" to nature. The wide windows and large sliding glass doors in every room allow visual contact with the outside world. . . . [it] provides a "natural" environment . . . . [which] brings her full circle to her beginnings, for born and raised in British East Africa, Lucy is no stranger to the kind of ungenial environment that had in large part shaped her character. (Chiogioji 241-43)

At sixty-two, alone in this house, Lucy rejoices to find, "I have reached the security and independence Stephen planned for me. He arranged for me to climb over his dead body into freedom and dignity and peace" (147), and she is grateful for the arrangement her husband and father-in-law have made between them to provide for her old age (despite their lack of true love for her).

But Lucy does not feel obligated by her inheritance, as do other Grau heroines, to uphold the family honor and continue family traditions. Recognizing the lack of love at the heart of her family—"the first effect of my legacy . . . [was] a fight between my sons" (148)—she neither gives up her inheritance as Paul wants her to do nor "buy[s] a new husband," as Thomas jokes. She will not enter the family warfare, joining forces with Paul and his father, Stephen, (whose love Paul seeks) to purify the family legacy nor entering into Thomas and his grandfather Edward Henley's game of vulgarizing the family in quest of life's full sensual and material pleasures. She admits that she cannot keep her sons at peace or her family together: "I couldn't put it back together. That was true. My family was gone. My sons were not brothers anymore; they were men who kept an uneasy truce. My husband was dead" (149). She finds "love between the generations . . . a burdensome chore" (156); the past is over, *"And that is that"* (156).

In the face of her initial fear upon being alone, she asks, "What could happen? What could possibly happen to you? Everything horrid and evil has already happened. What else is there? You could die. And would you mind? Would you really mind? And the answer drifted by so clearly: *Not really*" (202). She delights, instead, to realize her own powers and to take life a day at a time, on her own terms:

Matter of fact, I could feel myself firming and hardening, as if I were developing emotional muscles. I began to feel that I could look more directly at things than ever before. Old clear-eyed beady-eyed Cowboy Me, straightest glance in the West. . . .

I felt that for the first time in my considerably long life I was seeing things truly. I began to see that I was born to be old.

I may even marry again. . . .

But I am not sure I want to marry again.

Because now I have freedom. If I want to go for a drive at three in the morning, there is no one to argue about it. I take the car keys and I go. I drive along the beach and stare across the Gulf, wondering if I see the same horizon that pirates saw four hundred years ago. (203)

Lucy is on her own, independent and free to enjoy life as she wishes—and she likes it that way. When the telephone rings, she often chooses to ignore it. Picking it up, she might hear her son Paul's voice, "angry and hurt. 'Why don't you answer the phone, Mother? We only worry about you because we love you'" (204). But Lucy will not let herself be drawn into the trap of family needs and responsibilities again: "God save me from love. And the proof of love," she prays (204).

The heroines of Grau's last novel, *Roadwalkers*, also embody Lucy Roundtree Evans Henley's strength and independence. They, too, are free; moreover, they find themselves able to keep their houses *in partnership* with their husbands, rather than as mere handmaidens and slaves in the tradition of Grau's earlier "keepers of the house." Through their strong sense of self, these women turn their houses into palaces through which they walk like queens and princesses. Not incidentally, however, these women are black—and in touch, as the white Lucy has been with her past in British East Africa, with a "timeless" African heritage (162) which frees them from southern patriarchal tradition. Baby (Mary Woods) survives as a parentless "roadwalker" in the Depression, becoming a child of the woods, a wild creature in tune with the cycles of nature, a wild enchantress who can never be completely "civilized" by the orphanage nuns who take her in and care for her. Running away from the nuns' proud offer of a job as a housemaid or cook's helper for a wealthy white man, Mary Woods chooses to make her own way in the world rather than be caught in the white patriarch's net once more (as when she was captured by the patriarch's farm manager and sent to the orphanage to be "civilized" and pray for the whites who had rescued her). Mary becomes a seamstress and, in the words of her daughter Nanda, "a black prostitute" (195)—giving birth to her daughter after a brief affair with "an Indian King," a salesman of Worthington electric pumps (195), a man she finds worthy of her love and makes into the father of her little "princess."

Mary's daughter, Nanda Woods, begins her story by saying, "I have been, for most of my life, an inhabitant of my mother's magic king-dom. . . . 'You are,' my mother would say, 'the queen of the world, the jewel of the lotus, the pearl without price, my secret treasure'" (167). Together, mother and daughter become "wizard and apprentice," with Mary teaching Nanda "the greatest enchantment of all: how to walk like a princess in kingdoms of our own making" (181). Nanda learns to do this even through her lonely years spent integrating a convent boarding school for white girls, and later in college, all the while "plunder[ing] the only valuable thing [whites] possessed: knowledge" (193). Graduating Phi Beta Kappa, she then takes over her mother's "second kingdom . . . rooted in reality, based on money and property and the logic of commerce. Its treasures were measured by bank accounts and corporate statements," standing erect and strong in her own right while following her mother, "a woman of flickering eyes, setting traps for dollars. A sorceress of spells and illusions of beauty whose customers followed her devotedly" into both stores: that for white customers and that for black (182). Nanda thinks of herself as using her years at St. Catherine's convent school the way her mother earlier used her employment at Lambert Brothers Department Store, "transform[ing the school's offerings] all into me, leaving nothing behind. This citadel of whiteness has been looted by a single black thief, whom they declared invisible. Their magic has become mine, and I will now carry it away to my mother" (195).

Mary and Nanda work together to create a world in which "black and white were reversing themselves" (234), refusing to accept their degraded status in society and turning their "inferiority" to their advantage. As Nanda concludes at the end of *Roadwalkers*, "I came into my kingdom. My portion, neither more nor less" (292). She "prevails" in the words of the novel's epigraph:

> Stand now with thine enchantments,
> and with the multitude of thy sorceries,
> wherein thou hast labored from thy youth;
> if so be thou shalt be able to profit,
> if so be thou mayest prevail.
>
> Isaiah 47:12

At the novel's conclusion, Mary and Nanda Woods keep their own houses and enjoy inheritances of their own making. Their inner strength (which Grau's white heroines, other than Lucy of *Evidence of Love*, still must learn to acquire) empowers and enriches their lives. They have each other—and husbands who admire and love them. In addition, Mary has her flower gardens and Nanda her creek turtles; their houses, filled as they are with worldly goods (the symbols of their material successes), still remain close to the natural, primitive sources of their sorcery. They have remained free from captivity by white society and, therefore, in touch with their own power: successful *in* southern culture but never *of* it.

In her novels, Shirley Ann Grau dismembers and dissects the southern patriarchal romance. Her white patriarchs are, for the most part, corrupt, greedy, and vengeful, parodies of the heroic fathers of southern mythology. Grau's dying fathers make deals, struggle for control, take risks, and run roughshod over less powerful males. They are, for the most part, supported in this by white females who have given birth (preferably to sons), faded away in pale delicacy, or lived on to remodel houses, decorate kitchens, and defend white male actions. It is a world where black servants still prepare dinner, chauffeur cars, and polish silver as silent (if often seething), attendant, background figures. Yet the white patriarchy is dying. Blacks—Stanley in *The Condor Passes* and Mary and Nanda Woods in *Roadwalkers*—have become the unexpected new inheritors and "keepers of the house" of the southern past, along with the patriarchs' passive, white southern daughters. Mary and Nanda Woods, like Lucy in *Evidence of Love*, now stand on their own and maintain houses free from southern tradition and the corruption of the "family romance" (as the embittered Stanley in *The Condor Passes*, crippled by his years of servitude to his white master, finds it difficult to do). For the most part, Grau's white heroines remain in a state of paralysis and arrested development, carrying on the ways of vengeful or greedy fathers, and maintaining their houses of the past. Shirley Ann Grau exposes the private family ills infecting her white heroines as sources of public corruption and disease in the modern South.

3

Anne Tyler's "Homeless at Home"[1]

With the exception of *Evidence of Love*, Shirley Ann Grau's novels reveal the long collusion of southern white women with southern men in supporting and bolstering the white patriarchy. They reveal that the father's death does not result in immediate freedom for his survivors. The legacy lives on in the ongoing confusion, hypocrisy, greed, misery, and corruption of the living. In Grau's works we find an ironic sense of loss, of numbness and paralysis on the part of remaining family members—women who continue to maintain the tradition of corrupt fathers and to feel its burden in their lives. Anne Tyler's fiction, too, attests to the continuing paralysis resulting from the weakness, absence, or actual death of the white southern father. Yet there are important differences in Tyler's response to the passing of this southern patriarchy.

White southern fathers do continue to cast long and often debilitating shadows over Tyler's thirteen novels. Several of her patriarchs are alive, but they remain detached, remote figures, as are Elizabeth Abbott's disapproving father in *The Clock Winder* (1972); the distanced and distancing fathers of Joan Pike and James Green in *The Tin Can Tree* (1965); and Jesse and Daisy Moran's deflatingly candid father Ira in *Breathing Lessons* (1988). Other fathers are ineffectual, watching helplessly as their children struggle through life: Evie Decker's in *A Slipping-Down Life* (1970), who dies of a heart attack before the end of the novel, and Ian Bedloe's bewildered father Doug who prefers to fix things for the foreigners down the street rather than prove utterly useless at home in *Saint Maybe* (1991). A majority of Tyler's fathers, however, have deserted their offspring before the works even begin: Dr. Hawkes, Ben Joe's father, first by living with his "other-side-of-the-tracks" mistress and then through death in *If Morning Ever Comes* (1964); Billy Emerson in *The Clock Winder*, who dies leaving a decaying mansion and a dwindling estate for his inexperienced wife and children to manage; Mr. Pauling in *Celestial Navigation* (1974), who disappears one day after going out for a breath of fresh air, never to return; Justine Peck's father, who dies of a heart attack rather than accept his daughter's marriage to her first cousin Duncan in *Searching for Caleb* (1976); Mr.

Emory, "a stooped, bald, meek-looking man with a mustache like a soft black mouse" (10), who has a heart attack and dies on the first (and only) day his daughter Charlotte attends college in *Earthly Possessions* (1977); Morgan Gower's father, who stuns and bewilders his family by committing suicide during Morgan's last year of high school in *Morgan's Passing* (1980), or Emily Meredith's father, in the same novel, who dies in an automobile accident when she is just a baby; Beck Tull, who walks out on his wife and three children in *Dinner at the Homesick Restaurant* (1982); Macon Leary's father, who dies, leaving Macon, his brothers, and his sister in the hands of their flighty mother Alicia in *The Accidental Tourist* (1985); Ira Moran's father, who disappears into living quarters above his picture-framing shop on the day Ira finishes high school, leaving his business and two unemployed daughters for the young Ira to take care of in *Breathing Lessons*; Danny Bedloe, who dies in a car crash (possibly by suicide), deserting his wife and three small children in *Saint Maybe* (1991); and Dr. Felson who dies abandoning his forty-year-old married daughter Delia Grinstead to her husband and children in *Ladder of Years* (1995).

Anne Tyler's white southern world is essentially a fatherless one, whether family patriarchs are living or dead, whether the children they abandon are past forty or in the first decades of life, whether they are still living in the same house or far away. From ten to fifty, Tyler's characters often feel confused, bewildered, sad, and frightened as they struggle to cope with everyday lives and plot out destinies in the midst of domestic and cultural chaos. As Joseph Voelker explains in *Art and the Accidental in Anne Tyler* (1989), "the Tyler myth . . . begins with an absconded father" (25). He suggests, further, that Tyler's fathers

are merely weak, never wicked. Tyler's abdicating fathers have nothing in common with King Lear; they always seem to act with an inadvertence that surprises even themselves. While it usually turns out that in some way they were stifled by the closeness of family life, they often are not able to articulate their position until years after their departure. . . . [Tyler] denies the demonic. Fathers are absent, and that absence does mark a world without authority, but the lack is a result of the fathers' incompetence. (Voelker 26, 111)

Shirley Ann Grau's corrupt white patriarchs have given way to Anne Tyler's inept ones. Family structures continue to sag and totter. In Tyler's fiction, however, no one—including the failed white southern father—is to blame.

Anne Tyler's sympathetic vision embraces fathers who have been hurt by life. In *Breathing Lessons*, Ira Moran wakes from his mid-life resentment at having been abandoned by his father to the burdens of both his own life and his father's, as well, to realize that

the true waste was . . . not his having to support [his father and two sisters, as well as his own wife and two children] but his failure to notice how he loved them. He loved even his worn-down, defeated father, even the memory of his poor mother who had always been so pretty and never realized it because anytime she approached a mirror she had her mouth drawn up lopsided with shyness. . . . [But] no doubt he would forget again. (175)

Responsible as Ira has been, refusing to abdicate his own responsibilities as a husband and father, he, too, feels as "worn down" and "defeated" by family life as has his father before him: "He was just as sad as [his wife] Maggie was, and for just the same reasons. He was lonely and tired and lacking in hope and his son had not turned out well and his daughter didn't think much of him, and he still couldn't figure where he had gone wrong" (280). Even Anne Tyler's most dutiful fathers end up feeling defeated and lost, uncertain of how and where they have erred.

Their failures can be measured through the ever-present image of the ideal family which lingers in the background of their lives. As Morgan Gower tells Emily and Leon Meredith (when pretending to be a physician and delivering their baby daughter in *Morgan's Passing*): "My daughters are growing up . . . doing womanly things with their mother, leaving their father out in the cold. Each one when she was born seemed so new; I had such hopes; I was so sure we'd make no mistakes" (19-20). Despite gay photos of family vacations where all the Gowers look happy, Morgan asks, "Where were the tears and quarrels, and the elbowing for excessive amounts of love and space and attention? What about all those colds and tonsillectomies? Where was Molly's stammer? Or Susan's chronic nightmares? Not here" (26). Morgan wants to move from his large, sprawling, family house (which his wife, Bonny, has been given by her father), discard past problems, and change his life:

Morgan never lost the feeling that something here was slipping. If they could just clear it out and start over, he sometimes thought. Or sell it! Sell it and have done with it, buy a plainer, more straightforward place. . . . [Bonny's dead father] never saw the mysterious way the house started slipping downward, or sideways, or whatever it was that it was doing. (29-30)

While it is possible that other factors might be responsible for the house's decline, Morgan blames himself, feeling that it is his fault as a failed father. After all, Bonny's prosperous father had taken care of his family and his house quite competently, and Morgan believes that there still exist other fathers and other families more perfect than his own. In fact,

> Morgan had the feeling that a younger, finer family lived alongside his, gliding through the hallways, calling for tea and hot-water bottles. Evenings, the mother sat by the fire in a white peignoir and read to her children, one on either side of her. A boy, a girl; how tidy. At dinner they discussed great books, and on Sunday they dressed up and went to church. *They* never quarreled! *They* never lost things or forgot things. They rang and waited serenely. They gazed beyond the Gowers with the placid, rapt expressions of theatregoers ignoring some petty disturbance in the row ahead. (100)

Morgan, as patriarch, has failed to create a family that lives up to the old-fashioned, romantic ideal that is very much a part of his everyday, imaginative life—if not his real life in his "slipping" house (29).

Instead, it is Bonny who can be seen moving smoothly through the chaos of their lives, barely aware of Morgan's existence, rejecting his help as she copes with crisis after crisis. Morgan's children, too, seem to exist only to expose his every failure:

> The trouble with fathering children was, they got to know you so well. You couldn't make the faintest little realignment of the facts around them. They kept staring levelly into your eyes, eternally watchful and critical, forever prepared to pass judgment. They could point to so many places where you had gone permanently, irretrievably wrong. (106)

And so Morgan has become a protean figure, adept at shape-shifting, trying on identity after identity, costume after costume, in order to keep his sense of failed manhood at bay and his family at a distance. He does not want to be pinned down—to have all his faults publicly revealed— until, finally, Morgan leaves the family to whom he has proved such a disappointment.

It is this same sense of personal inadequacy and defeat that causes Beck Tull to follow in Morgan Gower's footsteps in deserting his family in Tyler's most famous and most studied novel, *Dinner at the Homesick Restaurant*. Beck Tull, too, has learned to shy away from intimacy (and the self-revelation it brings) after his marriage to Pearl:

> when she got close to me . . . [she] didn't act so pleased any more. Oh, it's closeness that does you in. Never get too close to people, son. . . . [Pearl] saw that I was away from home too much and not enough support to her, didn't get

ahead in my work, put on weight, drank too much, talked wrong, ate wrong, dressed wrong, drove a car wrong. No matter how hard I tried, seemed like everything I did got muddled. Spoiled. (300)

After Beck leaves, Pearl Tull attempts to cover over the gaping hole which has appeared at the very center of her small family, keeping Beck's desertion a secret so that "outsiders would go on believing the Tulls were a happy family. Which they were, in fact. Oh, they'd always been so happy! They'd depended only on each other, because of moving around so much. It had made them very close" (11). Pearl takes a job as cashier at Sweeney Brothers Grocery and Fine Produce, continuing the fiction of the intact, happy family even with her own children, telling them only that their father has gone away on business and "she needed something to keep her busy . . . now that they were growing up and going off on their own more" (12). It is not until the oldest boy, Cody, is leaving for college that Pearl decides to tell the "children" that their father (who has been away four years now) will not be coming back!

Pearl prides herself on her successful coverup, as well as her ability to take over Beck's role in addition to her own. She delights in the thought that

[the children] never asked about him. Didn't that show how little importance a father has? The invisible man. The absent presence. Pearl felt a twinge of angry joy. Apparently she had carried this off—made the transition so smoothly that not a single person guessed. It was the greatest triumph of her life. My one true accomplishment, she thought. (What a pity there was no one to whom she could boast of it.) (20)

And yet the competent, self-sufficient Pearl admits to feeling at a loss and afraid at times, telling her son Cody, "I know you must think I'm difficult. I lose my temper, I carry on like a shrew sometimes, but if you could just realize how . . . helpless I feel! How scary it is to know that everyone I love depends on me! I'm afraid I'll do something wrong" (63). Despite the happy family myth she has created, Pearl admits later in her life,

her family has failed. Neither of her sons is happy, and her daughter can't seem to stay married. There is no one to accept the blame for this but Pearl herself, who raised these children single-handed and did make mistakes, oh, a bushel of mistakes. Still, she sometimes has the feeling that it's simply fate, and not a matter for blame at all. (184-85)

The Tull family has failed to measure up to the white southern family romance in virtually every way Pearl can imagine—with its father gone, its mother imperfect, its children unhappy.

Always, just visible over the horizon, are those other, ideal families with whom Pearl Tull (like Morgan Gower) must compare her own:

Often, like a child peering over the fence at somebody else's party, she gazes wistfully at other families and wonders what their secret is. They seem so close. Is it that they're more religious? Or stricter, or more lenient? Could it be the fact that they participate in sports? Read books together? Have some common hobby? Recently, she overheard a neighbor woman discussing her plans for Independence Day: her family was having a picnic. Every member—child or grownup—was cooking his or her specialty. Those who were too little to cook were in charge of the paper plates.

Pearl felt such a wave of longing that her knees went weak. (185)

The family romance remains powerful, all the more so as Tyler's modern-day families struggle with the reality of desertion, disorder, and divisiveness at home.

Most of the criticism to date on *Dinner at the Homesick Restaurant* attempts to analyze the extent of the damage borne by the three Tull children—Ezra, Jenny, and Cody—at the hands of their angry and domineering mother (desperately trying to hold her family together) and the absentee father who has delivered them into her clutches. Novelist John Updike speaks of the novel as a "genetic comedy . . . [which] deepens into the tragedy of closeness, of familial limitations that work upon us like Greek fates and condemn us to lives of surrender and secret fury" (107). He speaks of the way in which the novel examines "the easy wounds given dependent flesh [that] refuse to heal and instead grow into lifelong purposes" (Updike 108). Joseph Wagner believes that Beck Tull's absence "is the single most powerful factor in the development of the central characters" (74). Wagner traces the patterns in the lives of each of the Tull children to reveal their "father hunger"—to be found in "Cody's aggression, Jenny's detachment, and Ezra's passivity" (75). And Frank Shelton calls *Dinner at the Homesick Restaurant* "a somber and powerful study of family determinism," noting how Beck Tull's desertion "isolates" his children and makes it difficult for them to be intimate with others ("Necessary Balance" 181, 182-83). These critics and others have noted that in Anne Tyler's fictional world, the family seems the ultimate shaper of its members' lives, the absent father a larger-than-life influence on his children's development (or lack thereof).

But Anne Tyler's world view is more complex than these interpretations suggest. Ultimately, she reveals that total family intimacy is neither possible nor necessary for the mature development of her characters. Tyler's subject may be the family, but it is also, as Joseph Voelker declares, "her characters' need to establish identity in opposition to family myth" (13)—an important theme of many contemporary women writers. Mary Ellis Gibson also believes that Anne Tyler's fiction concerns a conflict being played out between family fate and the individual will of her characters (168). If family past can never be eradicated (as even the resilient, ever-changing Morgan Gower in *Morgan's Passing* admits, saying "we [are] all sitting on stacks of past events. . . . [and] sometimes a lower level bleeds into an upper level" [133]), nevertheless Tyler reveals that the family need not have the last word in our lives. Morgan Gower, for example, struggles all his life against his father's suicide, against seeing life as so boring and insignificant that it is not worth continuing, striving perpetually to create a life of adventure and possibility for himself (even if that means deserting his wife and grown daughters to begin anew with Emily Meredith and their new son).

Anne Tyler refuses to allow family determinism to triumph in the lives of her successful protagonists. In fact, as Mary Robertson asserts, "Anne Tyler's narrative strategies disrupt the conventional expectations of the family novels and thus the disruptions themselves also constitute a second-order system of signs that helps to dislodge the ideology of the enclosed family and the notion that the family is the main forum for making history" (186). Of *Dinner at the Homesick Restaurant*, Robertson concludes that "it places the family's children, Jenny, Ezra, and Cody, in various exogenous relationships that prove as formative and valuable to them as do their family ties" (187). In her important essay "Anne Tyler: Medusa Points and Contact Points," Robertson shows how Pearl Tull, by failing to acknowledge Beck's absence from the heart of her family, undermines the very family intimacy she desires. Her children more and more "give up on real candor and expression of feelings in the family arena" (as Tyler's characters are often forced to do in the very bosom of the family), finding that they must seek meaningful lives and greater intimacy in the larger world beyond their front door (Robertson 190). Ezra, Cody, and Jenny Tull develop other relationships outside their "claustrophobic" home as they "turn their eyes away from the monster of family self-absorption . . . to seek their maturity and identity by means of other resources" (Robertson 190, 191). Ezra becomes close to Mrs. Scarlatti (as he has earlier in the novel to his friend Josiah's mother) and takes over Mrs. Scarlatti's restaurant. There, in the refurbished and renamed "Homesick Restaurant," Ezra nurtures complete strangers, regular customers, and on occasion, his own family members through a culturally diverse cuisine that offers the broadest appeal possible (while continuing to care for his ailing mother at home). Cody establishes a separate family unit with his wife, Ruth, and son, Luke, (although old layers "bleed" through, as Morgan Gower has warned, when Luke seems more like his brother and rival Ezra than like Cody himself), traveling with his new family from town to town as he establishes a successful career as a time management consultant. Jenny marries three times, has a daughter, mothers the six children of her third husband, Joe, and takes care of many other children through her flourishing pediatric practice in Baltimore. As Jenny explains to her stepson Slevin's teacher (when Slevin is having problems at school, having been abandoned by his mother as Jenny had been deserted by her father at a young age), "I don't see the need to blame adjustment, broken homes, bad parents, that sort of thing. We make our own luck, right? You have to overcome your setbacks" (196). Anne Tyler reveals that family need not, and should not, control personal destiny; characters can resist their family fates, make individual choices, and alter the pattern of their lives. When Jenny shows Slevin a photograph from her youth, he refuses to believe that the miserable "concentration camp . . . victim" in the photograph could be the cheerful stepmother-survivor he sees before him (203). It is true, the Tull children have not established ideal, perfect, adult lives. They still remember the past, at times ruefully and angrily, and long for the home they never had. Nevertheless, they have developed into adults who have coped and created busy, generally fulfilling, useful lives for themselves in the modern world.

In doing so, they have changed the nature and meaning of family in their lives. By the end of *Dinner at the Homesick Restaurant*, "the boundary between who is real family and who is not" has been "blurred" (Robertson 194). When the wayward father, Beck Tull, returns for Pearl's funeral and the following family dinner at his son Ezra's restaurant, he is amazed at the "great big, jolly, noisy, rambling" family he sees before him (294). Cody lashes out at Beck in self-pity, setting his father straight on the nature of this "intact" family unit that has had to stumble forward without Beck's guiding, paternal presence, telling Beck,

It's not the way it appears. Why, not more than two or three of these kids are even related to you. The rest are Joe's, by a previous wife. As for me, well, I haven't been with these people in years. . . .

You think we're a family. . . . You think we're some jolly, situation-comedy family when we're in particles, torn apart, torn all over the place, and our mother was a witch. (294)

Yet even Cody cannot sustain such a pessimistic view either of his family or of his life, as his final, gentle memory of his mother and the pivotal day of his youth (when he was responsible for her being shot with an arrow, "ending" their family life together) makes clear:

Overhead, seagulls drifted through a sky so clear and blue that it brought back all the outings of his boyhood—the drives, the picnics, the autumn hikes, the wildflower walks in the spring. He remembered the archery trip, and it seemed to him now that he even remembered that arrow sailing in its graceful, fluttering path. He remembered his mother's upright form along the grasses, her hair lit gold, her small hands smoothing her bouquet while the arrow journeyed on. And high above, he seemed to recall, there had been a little brown airplane, almost motionless, droning through the sunshine like a bumblebee. (303)

Placing a hand on his father's elbow, Cody steers Beck Tull back toward the "rambling" family that has gathered to honor Pearl Tull.

The novel affirms the importance of family (in a new, extended form) at the same time that it counsels resistance to the negative forces and mythic power of family in our lives. In addition, it changes the very concept of family itself to render it a more vital, positive, diversifying, and inclusive institution than in the past. Again, Mary Robertson points out that the always-unfinished family dinner in *Dinner at the Homesick Restaurant* becomes a symbol for the open-ended nature of the surviving family in American contemporary life:

Ezra does not follow an orthodox plan for family meals. They occur in a public place, the restaurant, where the members of the family are always in marginal relation to others, such as Mrs. Scarlatti, the kitchen crew, the friend, Josiah (whom Pearl had made unwelcome in her house), and the other customers. That is, Ezra upholds the tradition of the family meal in one way, yet he revises it, loosens its joints, forces it to articulate with outsiders who remain outsiders. . . . the composition of the [Tull] family has become less pure. The direct descendents among the grandchildren, Cody's Luke and Jenny's Becky, are vastly outnumbered by Joe's gaggle of children, who are technically outsiders. . . . The Tull family is finally like the restaurant itself: the shell of the original still stands, but the interior has been demolished and refashioned through the beneficial agency of significant outsiders. (196-97)

Anne Tyler redefines the structure of the family, "loosen[ing] its joints," extending and revitalizing it (Robertson 196), thereby breaking the paternal mold of the past and opening the family to the present and future. As Caren Town has said, "[The Tull] family speaks not with one voice—the voice of the father—but in the raucous chorus of guests at a dinner party, inviting us to join in, grab a chair, have some more" (21). The multiple narrative perspectives Tyler gives us in this and so many other of her works stress differing interpretations and individual responses to family experience—the separate parts that fashion the sum of the family "unit," making it both receptive to and needful of outside influence.

In novel after novel, Tyler affirms inclusive over exclusive worlds —ones that incorporate diversity and resist class and gender hierarchies, the decaying remains of the past. Even the most reclusive of her characters, Jeremy Pauling in *Celestial Navigation*, must turn his family home into a boarding house and teach the occasional art student in order to be able to stay afloat financially and alive emotionally (as the passive homebody Ezra Tull must run his restaurant to stay in contact with the larger Baltimore community and his full potential to nurture in *Dinner at the Homesick Restaurant*). Tyler suggests that isolation in the house of the past is a form of personal and cultural suicide. Morgan Gower (posing as Leon Meredith) and his new wife Emily Meredith relate to the larger world by joining the Holy Word Entertainment Troupe in *Morgan's Passing*, while Justine and Duncan Peck become members of Alonzo Divish's Habit-Forming Entertainments touring carnival in *Searching for Caleb* (1976). Ben Joe Hawkes leaves home, his new bride-to-be beside him, to return to the less incestuous and less familiar, newly challenging—if frightening—world of Columbia law school in New York at the end of Tyler's first novel, *If Morning Ever Comes*. Joan Pike will continue to live away from her parents in the house she shares with three different families in *The Tin Can Tree*; and Elizabeth Abbott is transformed into the competent, useful "Gillespie" Emerson through immersion in the lives of the Emerson clan and its chaotic household in *The Clock Winder*.

By opening themselves to the larger world outside the home and forming connections with outsiders to their families, Tyler's white southern protagonists find that they rejuvenate their lives and escape burial in a suffocating past. Karin Linton in *The Temporal Horizon: A Study of the Theme of Time in Anne Tyler's Major Novels* traces a movement in Tyler's narrative structures away from the past toward the present and the future. As Justine Peck has learned from Madame Olita early on in *Searching for Caleb* (and Tyler's other characters also discover as they travel through life), people can take action to create new futures for themselves as well as reduce the hold of tradition on their lives: " 'No, [she tells Justine] you can always choose to *some* extent. You can change your future a great deal. Also your past. . . . . Not what's happened, no,'

Madame Olita said gently, 'but what hold it has on you' " (129). Tyler's white southern characters resist the hold of the past on their lives not simply by choosing "change," according to Barbara Harrell Carson, but by complicating their lives and their relationships to others. In her analyses of Tyler's *Earthly Possessions, The Accidental Tourist, and Breathing Lessons*, Carson shows how

it is the complex life that Tyler presents as the more rewarding [in each novel]. Simplified lives, on the other hand, veer dangerously close to a kind of living death. For Tyler, selfhood comes not in isolation but in connectedness. . . .

Even though Tyler does not limit this complex life to women, it reflects a traditionally feminine rather than a traditionally masculine system of values. (24)

Connection to others remains crucial for the continued growth of Tyler's characters, their understanding of present-day realities, and their ability to project meaningful futures for themselves. However, there are no "traditional, generally accepted rules" available to guide her protagonists in making their choices concerning the people with whom they should connect (Carson 31). For example, Carson explains:

In Macon's case [in *The Accidental Tourist*], the better choice seems to be to leave his wife; in Charlotte's [in *Earthly Possessions*], it is to return to her husband. Each arrives at a sense of moral responsibility far more complex than that associated with the notion that endurance, self-sacrifice, and adherence to commitments are, of themselves, heroic. Charlotte learns to see her relation-tangled home as a place to build rather than give up, a self. Macon reaches his decision to leave Sarah, whom he loves (in a way). . . . because of the growth Macon experiences [with Muriel Pritchett]. (32)

In her fiction, Anne Tyler rejects conventional notions of right and wrong to reveal what Beck Tull calls "the grayness of things; half-right-and-half-wrongness of things" (301) that accompanies the complicated life, the growth of the self, risking the future. As Anne Tyler herself has said, life is "a complex, inconclusive, intriguingly gray-toned affair" ("Trying to Be Perfect" 48).

In *The Accidental Tourist*, Macon Leary confronts this "grayness," as well, finding that he must leave his wife Sarah (even though he still loves her) in order to include, for his own sake as well as theirs, new people in his life. He finds that he has become a better person, able to give more of himself, with Muriel Pritchett, than with Sarah. From the early days of his courtship with Sarah, throughout their long marriage,

Macon has been "locked inside the standoffish self he'd assumed when he and she first met. He was frozen there. . . . No matter how he tried to change his manner, Sarah continued to deal with him as if he were someone unnaturally cool-headed, someone more even in temperament than she but perhaps not quite as feeling" (53). When Macon's marriage begins to dissolve, after their son Ethan's senseless murder in a fast-food restaurant, Sarah leaves Macon. Macon feels at a loss as to how to win her back since the self she seems to demand from him is the very one that has driven her away: "He felt he'd been backed into a false position. He was forced to present this impassive front if he wanted her to love him. Oh, so much was expected of men!" (52). In their conventional marriage, Macon and Sarah have become locked into stereotypical—if outmoded—gender roles. He is the strong, silent provider; she is the dependent, emotional wife.

On the other hand, Muriel Pritchett provides a refreshing change. She is fiesty, young, disorderly, talkative, lower-middle class—everything that the Princeton graduate Macon is not. A survivor, she has had to support herself and her son Alexander through job after job, telling Macon,

I've *had* to be inventive. It's been scrape and scrounge, nail and knuckle, ever since Norman left me. . . . I've lain awake, oh, many a night, thinking up ways to earn money. . . . I've got about fifty jobs, if you count them all up. . . . Like those lessons at Doggie Do, or another time a course in massage at the Y. . . . Twice now I've paid for an entire Ocean City vacation just by going up and down the beach offering folks these box lunches me and Alexander fixed in our motel room every morning. (189)

Most importantly, however, Macon finds that he changes into a different person when he is with Muriel. In her company, Macon comes to a new understanding of himself and of life:

Then he knew that what mattered was the pattern of her life; that although he did not love her he loved the surprise of her, and also the surprise of himself when he was with her. In the foreign country that was Singleton Street he was an entirely different person. This person had never been suspected of narrowness, never been accused of chilliness; in fact, was mocked for his soft heart. And was anything but orderly. (212)

Macon has been offered an opportunity to break from the past, from convention, from the stereotypical male role he has assumed with Sarah, and create a new life for himself with the androgynous Muriel.

Before Macon comes to live with Muriel on Singleton Street, he returns to the womb of his Grandfather Leary's house to live there (as in his childhood) with his sister, Rose, and their two brothers. Once there, however, he finds that it is not the reassuring presence of the dignified, upright Grandfather Leary that he feels, at all. Instead, it is the ghost of the old man when his "mind . . . began to wander," who armchair-traveled to the fantasy island of "Lassaque," and who created new inventions to make his fortune when he believed himself "poor again, struggling to earn his way in the world" (145, 147). The conventional Grandfather Leary turns even more unconventional, appearing to Macon in a dream, calling on his grandson to renounce his old life for a life of adventure. Grandfather Leary warns him: "You want to sit in this old house and rot, boy? It's time we started digging out! How long are we going to stay fixed here?" (148).

In *The Accidental Tourist*, Macon Leary emerges from his state of ossification, both in his marriage with Sarah and in his continued immersion in his childhood past, to reject tradition and loosen the hold of the past on his life. Macon overcomes his fears, embraces change, and takes new and purposeful action in his life:

He reflected that he had not taken steps very often in his life, come to think of it. Really never. His marriage, his two jobs, his time with Muriel, his return to Sarah—all seemed to have simply befallen him. He couldn't think of a single major act he had managed of his own accord.

Was it too late now to begin?

Was there any way he could learn to do things differently? (351)

Telling Sarah he has decided to go back to Muriel, Macon explains, "It wasn't easy. It's not the easy way out, believe me" (352). Sarah's response, however, is a conventional one:

I suppose you realize what your life is going to be like. . . . You'll be one of those mismatched couples no one invites to parties. No one will know what to make of you. People will wonder whenever they meet you, "My God, what does he see in her? Why choose someone so inappropriate? It's grotesque, how does he put up with her?" And her friends will no doubt be asking the same about you. (352)

But Macon realizes that it is not so easy to know whether couples are "right" for each other or not: "[H]e saw now how such couples evolved. They were not, as he'd always supposed, the result of some ludicrous lack of perception, but had come together for reasons that the rest of the world would never guess" (352). Macon decides to complicate his life, adding Muriel and her son, Alexander, to the relationships he has already established (and will continue, albeit at a distance) with Sarah, his brothers, his sister, Rose, and those who are already dead (his son, Ethan, and Grandfather Leary). Macon chooses to embrace a larger world and a larger self as he ages and matures. At the end of the novel, Macon feels "a kind of inner rush, a racing forward. The real adventure, he thought, is the flow of time; it's as much adventure as anyone could wish" (354). Macon Leary looks forward to the future as he opens himself to life, establishes new relationships with others, and explores unfamiliar aspects of his own character.

For Tyler's characters, home is not always the best place to be. Family often becomes a trap, a hindrance to personal development rather than an asset. Macon Leary finds that he needs to leave his wife and twenty-one year-old marriage because "people could, in fact, be used up—could use each other up, could be of no further help to each other and maybe even do harm to each other. He began to think that who you are when you're with somebody may matter more than whether you love her" (317). In choosing Muriel Pritchett, Macon is choosing fulfillment of his own potential and active, adult decision-making to benefit himself as well as others. Muriel and her son Alexander need Macon—and Macon needs them: "There was so much that needed fixing! [with Muriel on Singleton Street]" (235).

Anne Tyler's characters want to feel needed—to be useful to others. Her novels are filled with wrench-wielding, competent, take-charge women—from Pearl Tull in *Dinner at the Homesick Restaurant*; to Elizabeth Abbott in *The Clock Winder*; to Rita DiCarlo, the Clutter Counselor, in *Saint Maybe*. Many of her male figures, too, are happiest when they are making or fixing something, from the handyman Morgan Gower who works at Cullen Hardware in *Morgan's Passing*; to the resourceful (if restless), and scientifically curious, Duncan Peck in *Searching for Caleb*; to the skilled craftsman Ian Bedloe who provides for his "family" (only Daphne of his orphaned nephew and two nieces may be his brother's own) through his carpentry skills in *Saint Maybe*. When they believe their skills aren't needed or appreciated at home, Tyler's characters often find they must leave. Sometimes, as with the retired Doug Bedloe in *Saint Maybe*, leaving takes the form of paying short, frequent visits to the house of the foreigners down the street to rescue them from electrical and mechanical disasters (since there seemed so little he could do to be of help at home). At other times, as with Morgan Gower's father (also, like Doug Bedloe, a high school English teacher), unused talents can lead to a final leave-taking from the family

—and from life. Morgan's father commits suicide, leaving behind him no clues except a file box filled with "alphabetized instruction sheets for assembling bicycles, cleaning lawnmowers, and installing vacuum-cleaner belts. Repairing, replacing, maintaining" (47) were significant to him in an otherwise humdrum, inconsequential life. He is able to pass on only one piece of advice—"buy the best tools for the job: drop-forged steel, hardwood handles" (46)—to help his son Morgan through life.

Morgan Gower puts this small inheritance from his father to good use at Emily and Leon Meredith's apartment when he finds he is not needed at home:

Like a household elf, he left behind him miraculously mended electrical cords, smooth-gliding windows, dripless faucets, and toilet tanks hung with clever arrangements of coat-hanger wire to keep the water from running. "It must be wonderful," Emily told Bonny, "to have him with you all the time, fixing things," but Bonny just looked blank and said, "Who, Morgan?" (208)

Morgan finally leaves Bonny to be with Emily, a woman with whom he can feel "joyous and expansive. What could he not accomplish? He was a wide, deep, powerful man, and it was time he took some action" (242). With Emily Meredith and their little infant son, Morgan begins a new life (albeit one with his mother and sister still in tow), believing "an assignment had been given him. Someone's life, a small set of lives, had been placed in the palm of his hand. Maybe he would never have any more purpose than this: to accept the assignment gracefully, lovingly, and do the best he could with it" (246). In committing himself to these little lives, Morgan Gower joins Macon Leary, Joan Pike, Ben Hawkes, Elizabeth Abbott, Ian Bedloe, Duncan and Justine Peck, as well as Jenny, Ezra, and Cody Tull, in loosening traditional family ties and reaching out to embrace a new future.

Anne Tyler, as Mary Robertson suggests, creates in her fiction a pattern wherein

a member of the family typically both sheds—somehow becomes unencumbered from his other family relations—and incorporates—forms significant new relationships with outsiders. . . . Tyler designs narratives in which there is constant oscillation between shedding and incorporation without any suggestion of some final resting place, either totally within the family or totally outside it. (186, 199)

To incorporate the new and shed the old, Tyler's characters—in a further complication she offers her readers—occasionally find themselves remaining at home. In *Earthly Possessions*, for instance, Tyler's heroine Charlotte Emory finds that growth, adventure, and new relationships await her—in her own home. Anne G. Jones notes, "[I]n her forced march with Jake chained into a moving island of a car, she finds travel more isolating than home, and Jake less of a stranger to her than her own husband Saul, whose 'leathery, foreign smell . . . [had] called up so much love.' To meet new people, then, she goes back to her family. . . . to travel, she goes home" ("Home" 8). Charlotte Emory has found that her home overflows with family outsiders as well as insiders: her husband, Saul, himself; her own daughter; an adopted son; assorted boarders from Saul's church; Saul's brothers; as well as customers who come to her little home studio to have their photographs taken. There remain plenty of strangers for Charlotte to help in her own house—both "real" family and the many others who call on all her strengths.

Similarly, Delia Grinstead in *Ladder of Years* leaves her Roland Park, Baltimore, home, feeling inadequate and unloved, to acquire a sense of herself as important and useful among strangers. In the small town of Bay Borough, Delia finds herself valued as a surrogate mother, daughter, and wife, a reliable friend, and a responsible employee. Away from home, she finds that "she seemed to have changed into someone else—a woman people looked to automatically for sustenance" (183). When Delia finds that she is actually needed at home, as well—that she has been missed and her complicated family seems to have fallen into disarray without her—she returns: "Was there anything that would, you know. Would persuade you to come back," her husband asks, and she replies, "Oh, Sam. All you had to do was ask" (324). Delia recognizes that her year-and-a-half journey away from family has "worked" (326). Forming new relationships with strangers has created a sense of her own self-worth and enabled her to renew past family relationships in more positive, effective ways.

Thus, Anne Tyler's male and female characters seem remarkably alike in the challenges they face as they attempt to develop mature identities and more satisfying, inclusive lives. Yet there exists a delicate balance in male-female relationships in Tyler's novels.[2] Her fatherless men often seem more vulnerable than her equally fatherless women. For example, Jeremy Pauling in *Celestial Navigation* watches as the motherly Mary Tell befriends their young boarder Olivia, thinking,

in the old days he had assumed that what women knew came to them naturally. He had never suspected that they had to be taught. But listen to Mary, to the firmness of her voice, not issuing concrete instructions so much as showing

Olivia how to *be*. . . . Were there no such tutors for men? Was it only women who linked the generations so protectively? (183)

And Mary Tell, herself, admits to the help she has received from other women, especially from her mother-in-law Gloria Tell:

When I think back on it—on my mother reading to me from that newspaper, smoothing the hair off my forehead—it seems that starting right there I began to live in a world made up of women. My mother and Guy's, the neighbor women who gave me their old baby furniture and their bits of advice—women formed a circle that I sank into. (70)[3]

Mothers, mothers-in-law, and female friends pass on the secrets of womanhood, human interconnection, and day-to-day survival to the young women who follow after them.

Tyler's men and women may both find themselves in a world devoid of fathers, ultimate authorities, final instructions, and over-arching game plans for the future, but her women often seem more able to cope than her men. As Larry McMurtry notes,

Her men slump around like tired tourists—friendly, likable, but not all that engaged. Their characters, like their professions, seem accidental even though they come equipped with genealogies of Balzacian thoroughness. All of them have to be propelled through life by (at the very least) a brace of sharp, purposeful women—it usually takes not only a wife and a girlfriend but an indignant mother and one or more devoted sisters to keep these sluggish fellows moving. They poke around haphazardly, ever mild and perennially puzzled, in the foreign country called life. If they see anything worth seeing, it is usually because a determined woman on the order of Muriel Pritchett thrusts it under their noses and demands that they pay some attention. (136)

Even the least sensitive, and seemingly most resourceful, of Tyler's male figures, Duncan Peck in *Searching for Caleb*, admits to being at a loss on his own:

He could always leave [Justine], of course. He could settle her in Baltimore and then go off again on his own. But he knew that he wouldn't. If he didn't have Justine he wouldn't even know how to see things, what to look at; nothing would exist for him if he didn't tell Justine about it. (300)

Tyler's men often feel weaker than her women, no matter how resourceful, clever, and independent they may seem.

With no fathers to guide them—or fathers who remain disapproving, abstracted, and bewildered, cut off from their families even while at home—Tyler's sons often falter as they try to establish their individual identities and find intimacy with others. The most nurturing and androgynous of Tyler's male characters, Ezra Tull of *Dinner at the Homesick Restaurant*, admits to his mother, "I'm worried I don't know how to get in touch with people. . . . I really, honestly believe I missed some rule that everyone else takes for granted; I must have been absent from school that day. There's this narrow little dividing line I somehow never located [between being too close and too distant from others]" (*DHR* 125). Described by his brother Cody as a "feeder. . . . There was something tender, almost loving, about his attitude toward people who were eating what he'd cooked them" (*DHR* 161), Ezra—like the sensitive Jeremy Pauling in *Celestial Navigation*—lives with his mother until her death, fails to marry the woman he loves, and remains alone at the end of *Dinner at the Homesick Restaurant*.

A few of Tyler's female characters prove more frightened and sad than her men. Charlotte Emory's obese, housebound mother in *Earthly Possessions* becomes a symbol of stagnation, of total female dependence first on her father, then on her husband (both of whom die before her), and finally on her daughter Charlotte and Charlotte's new husband, Saul —a woman completely entombed in her own flesh, the decay of her family past and her family home, the nucleus of her immediate family. In Tyler's *Saint Maybe*, the young, attractive Lucy Bedloe, too, has always depended on men to support herself and her children. Coming from a poor family background, Lucy marries early, is deserted by her husband, is left with two small children to care for, then marries her rescuer Danny Bedloe (when she is possibly already pregnant with another man's—and her third—child). When Danny dies following the birth of "his" new daughter Daphne, Lucy finds herself undereducated, untrained for work, and unable to attract someone to care for her and her three small children. Lucy is overwhelmed by her responsibilities, takes sleeping pills to ward off the painful realities of her life, and dies of an accidental overdose. She is one of only a few Tyler women who fail to transcend the traditional female role, remaining caught in the snares of her past life, succumbing to the predicament of white female dependence and helplessness.

The majority of Anne Tyler's women, however, are so resourceful and energetic that they threaten to (and sometimes do) overwhelm the men in their lives. These women find that they can support themselves and their dependent children, as well as repair the plumbing and insulate their houses—all too well, seemingly, for their own good. Such competent, take-charge women predominate in Tyler's fiction: Mary Tell, Muriel Pritchett, Pearl Tull, Elizabeth Abbott, Justine Peck, Sarah Leary, Rita DiCarlo, Agatha and Daphne Bedloe, Bonny Gower, and Jenny Tull, to name a few. Anne Tyler has created a list of resilient, at times formidable, women—women who can, without knowing it, overpower and frighten husbands, lovers, and sons from their lives.

At the end of the novel *Dinner at the Homesick Restaurant*, Beck Tull tells his eldest son Cody that marriage to Pearl "wore me out. . . . Used up all my good points" (300). He has spent his entire life—he tells Cody—trying to impress Pearl, years after their separation, even as he has moved from job to job, state to state, and woman to woman: "I do believe that all these years, anytime I had any success, I've kind of, like, held it up in my imagination for your mother to admire. Just take a look at *this*, Pearl, I'd be thinking" (302). Whatever he has been able to accomplish, Beck acknowledges that it is Pearl who has been the strong one, the triumphant one, the one who deserves all the credit for her children's well-being and her own remarkable struggle and survival, telling Cody, "Haven't you all turned out fine—leading good lives, the three of you? She did it; Pearl did it. I knew she would manage" (302).

This pattern of the strong female overshadowing the male can be traced throughout Anne Tyler's fiction. In *Morgan's Passing*, Morgan Gower admits,

he had married his wife for her money, to be frank, which was not to say he didn't love her; it was just that he'd been impressed, as well, by the definiteness that money had seemed to give her. It had hovered somewhere behind her left shoulder, cloaking her with an air of toughness and capability. She was so clear about who she was. (29)

Yet, with the indefatigable, capable, oh-so-substantial Bonny at his side, Morgan comes, by comparison, to feel useless, cast-off: "old! . . . ruined! I seemed to have . . . fallen apart" (184). In *The Accidental Tourist*, Macon Leary, too, finds himself attracted to Muriel Pritchett's "spiky, pugnacious fierceness. . . . He had to admire her. Had he ever known such a fighter?" (230, 279). But, at the same time, "he felt awed by her, and diminished" (280). Jake Simms, Charlotte Emory's kidnapper in *Earthly Possessions*, becomes dependent himself on Charlotte's strengths, points them out to her, and suggests the effect they may have had on her seemingly confident, self-righteous husband, Saul: "Maybe . . . you just had him figured wrong to start with. I mean, it could be he really does believe you're good [despite the fact that you don't believe in God], and worries what that means for his side [as a preacher]. Ever thought of that?" (164).[4] Tyler's strong women must take great care not to overpower the men in their lives.

Anne Tyler's favorite novel, *Celestial Navigation*, provides her most in-depth, richly provocative and sympathetic portrait of an imbalanced relationship between a vulnerable male and a strong female, as Frank Shelton has shown in his article "The Necessary Balance" (178-79). Mary Tell seems to thrive on desperate situations; she is a risk-taker and a survivor. She comes to Jeremy Pauling's boarding house, having left home, eloped at sixteen (without ever even having had a date!), with her small daughter at her side. As Mary explains, she has rejected her parents' religion and their way of life as stultifying: "What bothered me was not my parents or even their way of living, but the fact that it seemed to be the only way open to me. I would grow up, of course, and go to college and marry and have children, but those were not changes so much as additions. I would still be traveling their single narrow life. There was no hope of any other" (63-64). Later, Mary leaves her husband Guy Tell for the same reason: "It's as if I have to keep trying different lives out, cheating on the rule that you can only lead just one. I'd had six years of *Hot Rod* magazine and now I was ready to move on to something new. I picture tossing my life like a set of dice, gambling it, wasting it. I have always enjoyed throwing things away (69).[5] Now, having fallen in love with a man who is separated from his wife, Mary Tell awakens to the dismal reality of the situation her gambling ways have created: "If things don't work out with John, I have nowhere to go. This is the first time I have really thought about that. . . . I am entirely dependent on a man I hardly know. I have no money, no home, no family to return to, not even a high school degree to get a job with, and no place to leave Darcy if I *could* find a job. I don't even know if I am eligible for welfare" (73). Unlike Tyler's later creation, Lucy Bedloe of *Saint Maybe*, however, Mary Tell refuses to see herself as helpless.

Mary Tell determines her course of action—a Plan A and a Plan B—both of which she will put into effect by the end of *Celestial Navigation*, not in her relationship to John but, instead, in that to Jeremy Pauling. She concludes,

This is what I resolve: if it works out that John and I are married, I am going to save money of my own no matter what. I don't care if I have to steal it; I will save that money and hide it away somewhere in case I ever have to be on my own again.

Only I won't be on my own, not if it's up to me. I won't leave anyone else ever. It's too hard. (73)

After John returns to his wife, Mary lives happily with Jeremy Pauling (despite Guy Tell's refusal to grant her a divorce) and has six children by him. She seems to grow stronger with each new addition to her family. Although she realizes the artistic, reclusive Jeremy is "not dependable," Mary admits to "lov[ing] him more than I ever loved anyone" (142). Their observant boarder Miss Vinton reports that, over the years, Mary "grew quieter, older, stronger. There was something more loving in the way she treated [Jeremy]. . . . she had stopped expecting him to be like other people" (143). Yet, sorrowfully, Miss Vinton comments, "I never dreamed she would grow to be too understanding" (144).

Mary's strength only exacerbates Jeremy's weakness. Always frightened by the world, terrified even to leave his own house, the agoraphobic artist Jeremy at first responds to his new boarder, the beautiful Mary Tell, by trying to help her in her desperate situation and stretching himself to meet her needs. In the beginning, he feels useful; however, as the years go on and the house fills with their children, the possessions they have accrued together, as well as a continuous stream of boarders, Jeremy (like the heartier Morgan Gower before him) feels overwhelmed —and, ironically, in his own house, extraneous. Jeremy begins to grow even more remote and shut-off from those he loves, retreating to his studio and thinking:

Did anyone guess how his children baffled him? He didn't understand them. He had trouble talking to them. All he could do was watch. . . . Mary watched too, but for different reasons. She was checking for danger and germs and mischief; she was their armed guard. What Jeremy was doing was committing them to memory, preparing for some moment far in the future when he could sit down alone and finally figure them out. (157)

Incapable of understanding or helping his children, Jeremy is made to feel especially small by the very woman he loves: "he felt that she was pointing something out to him: her role as supplier, feeder, caretaker. 'See how I give? And how I keep on giving—these are my reserves. I will always have more, you don't even have to ask'" (160). In awe of Mary's power, Jeremy wonders,

Were women always stronger than men? Mary was stronger, even when she slept. . . . She didn't even believe in God. (Jeremy said he didn't either—how could he, knowing how carelessly objects are tossed off and forgotten by their creators?—but he was haunted by a fear of hell and Mary was not.) Mary was more vulnerable than any man, the deepest pieces of herself were in those children and every day they scattered in sixty different directions and faced a thousand untold perils; yet she sailed through the night without so much as a prayer. There was no way he could ever hope to match her. (167-68)

When Mary receives news of her divorce from Guy Tell, and grants Jeremy his long-awaited desire to marry her, Jeremy—afraid of being swallowed up, of disappearing entirely from his own home—retreats to his studio (where he is working on the sculpture of a man fleeing for his life) and "forgets" to come out until his wedding day has passed.

In *Celestial Navigation*, Anne Tyler's portrait of a couple in love with each other but unable to live with each other is a hauntingly poignant one. Mary Tell admits to having tried "holding myself in check trying to keep the reins in [with Jeremy]. I didn't want to dominate," being aware of Jeremy's wish "that I would shrink a little. He never guessed that I already had shrunk, that this was as small as I could get" (202). Finally, however, she acknowledges failure, conceding that their relationship has become hurtful for both of them, that "it seemed all I could do was give him things and do him favors, and make him see how much he needed me. The more he depended on me the easier I felt. In fact I depended on his dependency" (214). The more Mary's love grows for Jeremy, the more she weakens and threatens him. To protect himself, Jeremy has—as Mary recognizes—"gathered some kind of stubborn hidden strength" (217) to exert itself against her.

Shut out of his life, Mary leaves Jeremy, taking her "household-hints money, my money-back-offer money, my coupon money" (*CN* 196) with her to use to rent a cabin at the Quamikut Boatyard. She feels "so sad. Hadn't I once sworn never to leave anyone ever again? Especially not Jeremy. Oh, never Jeremy" (192). Yet Mary knows that their relationship cannot continue: "He changed. I changed. . . . changes that each of us caused in the other, but they were exactly the ones that have separated us and that will keep us separate. If he calls me back he will be admitting a weakness. If I return unasked I will be bearing down upon him and plowing him under. If I weren't crying I would laugh" (217).

When Jeremy does muster up the courage to come and see Mary, hoping to bring her home with him, he finds her stronger than ever—she and the children seemingly forming "an unbroken circle" together, one he cannot enter (197). When he tells Mary that his "work is going *very* well. . . . better than it ever has before," Mary retaliates by saying, "I'm managing on my own now. I'm not depending on a soul. I'm making it on my own"; and Jeremy thinks, "Well, of course she was. Mary had *always* managed on her own. . . . She would do beautifully anywhere. There was no defeating her. He felt tired at the thought of her" (265-66). Trying to prove his usefulness to her, still hoping to bring her home, all the while thinking, "Yes, but what about me?" [266]), Jeremy works to winterize the cottage (causing Mary to believe that he wants her to stay there) and offers to take the children out on the boat to air the sails and dry them for her. Terrified for the children's safety, Mary pleads, "Jeremy, I—please don't take the children" (272), revealing clearly how incompetent she finds Jeremy. Thus, she ends their relationship forever.

And yet Mary has never wanted to stay on her own, be self-sufficient, and live alone with the children. She has promised herself that if Jeremy came for her, "if he said a single word to keep me with him, I would gladly stay forever" (196). Yet Mary cannot reveal her vulnerability when Jeremy does come to visit, anymore than Pearl Tull in *Dinner at the Homesick Restaurant* can tell Beck that she needs him in spite of her apparent self-sufficiency, her competence in "making each house perfect—airtight and rustproof and waterproof . . . [her ability to] seal up the house, as if for a hurricane" (16). Muriel Pritchett in *The Accidental Tourist* is more fortunate because she is willing to admit the weaknesses underlying her ever-resilient strength: "In bed she said, 'You wouldn't ever leave me, would you? Would you ever think of leaving me? You won't be like the others, will you? Will you promise not to leave me?'" (290). Courageously, Muriel follows Macon to Paris after he has left her and returned to Sarah, admitting her desire to be with him. It is true that, when he first sees her, Macon "actually looked around for some means of escape" (326), and Muriel (when explaining her presence in Paris) also has stressed Macon's vulnerability rather than her own weakness:

"You need to have me around," she said.
"Need you!"
"You were falling to pieces before you had me." (328)

Nevertheless, Muriel allows Macon to see how important he is to her. Muriel cares for Macon, wants to be with him, and reveals how her weaknesses and strengths are bound together into an androgynous—yet still incomplete—whole.

The couples who are most successful in Tyler's fiction manage to find a sense of balance, accommodate their differences, and establish an egalitarian relationship that avoids diminishing either party. Like Elizabeth Abbott of *The Clock Winder*, they can remain androgynous individuals without endangering their marriages. They can bring into relationships and into families (as Elizabeth advises Peter Emerson) the very things that are lacking and needed (as Elizabeth has in her marriage to Matthew Emerson):

"They think I've made a mistake," [Peter Emerson] told [Elizabeth concerning the Emersons' reaction to his marriage to P.J.]. . . .

"Maybe they're right," he said. "You shouldn't hope for anything from someone that much different from your family."

"You should if your family doesn't *have* it," [Elizabeth said]. (311)

Difference can be an asset in a marriage—as an outsider such as P.J., or Elizabeth Abbott herself, can be a revitalizing, strengthening addition for a stagnating family unit such as the Emersons.

Harmony can come from difference, in Tyler's worldview. Through Tyler's fiction, Mary Robertson explains, "greater fullness" can be found even in:

the overstuffed households of Emily and Morgan [in *Morgan's Passing*] and Charlotte and Saul [in *Earthly Possessions*]. Both women realize there is no exit from the disorder of claims upon them by people who are technically outsiders to their own families, but it does not feel like hell to them because they have learned to respect true difference as nourishing. (199, 200)

In the marriage of first cousins Justine and Duncan Peck in *Searching for Caleb*, as well, the two sides of the Peck family—the orderly and the disorderly, the rational and the imaginative, the staid and the wild—are united in harmony with each other and with the outside world. Like Maggie and Ira Moran in *Breathing Lessons* and Delia and Sam Grinstead in *Ladder of Years*, Tyler's enduring couples are resilient, learning to find a balance between them, accommodate personal differences and family fractures, endure everyday hardships, look forward to the future, and remain open to a larger world, even as their "choices [grow] narrower and [they need more than ever] . . . to show real skill and judgment" (*Breathing Lessons* 327) as they enter the final stages of their journeys together. As long as they have something to offer each other and can stay together without using each other up or harming each other (by rendering each other helpless, useless, or despairing), their relationships can continue to be sustaining and nourishing ones—accommodating, and, in fact, enriched by, difference.

Nevertheless, for Tyler's heroines, a longing persists—what Anne G. Jones calls "the lure of that imaginably perfect state of being—the bliss of merging, the self in unimpeded relation to someone else . . . [that] lies at the core of homesickness in many Tyler novels" ("Home" 6). Joan Pike in *The Tin Can Tree* acknowledges that "everything she saw made her homesick, but not for any home she'd ever had" (143). In *Dinner at the Homesick Restaurant*, the Tull children continue to long for the ideal home, the family they were denied. Home is never quite what it is supposed to be. According to Tyler's fellow southern novelist Doris Betts, the title *Dinner at the Homesick Restaurant* "expresses Tyler's useful paradox: sick FOR home, sick OF home" ("Fiction" 35). It is a paradox that Jenny Tull expresses when she learns that her brother Ezra plans to change the elegant Scarlatti restaurant into the home he never had; Jenny warns that many of his customers will reject the "homelike," "family" atmosphere of "The Homesick Restaurant" as reminiscent of the very houses they are longing to escape. Jenny explains, "maybe people go to restaurants to get *away* from home" (75). Anne Tyler reminds us that perfect dinners, restaurants, homes, families, and marriages do not exist outside fairy tales. What her characters long for, they can never fully experience. They remain, as Emily Dickinson wrote of her mother, "homeless at home" (771), restless and searching, unable to be at rest in the midst of family yet homesick in the world beyond.

Yet this does not mean that Tyler's heroines must settle for the status quo, for what they have, for the familiar—and merely "endure" (*Searching for Caleb* 229-30). It is Duncan Peck who warns his wife, Justine, that "enduring" is not a vital or viable philosophy of life. When their daughter, Meg Peck, leaves home in *Searching for Caleb* to marry a quiet minister, saying, "I don't want new experiences, I want a normal happy life," she finds herself, instead, "liv[ing] among *crazy* people!" (229). The ideal life has been shown to be an illusion, once more, and real life, as always in Tyler's fiction, more unpredictable, messy, and confused than Meg had hoped it would be. Justine and Duncan visit Meg, listen to her complaints, and try to give their advice:

"You should leave," Duncan told her.

"Oh, Duncan," said Justine. She turned to Meg. "Meggie darling, maybe you could just—or look at it this way. Imagine you were handed a stack of instructions. Things that you should undertake. Blind errands, peculiar invitations . . . things you're supposed to go through, and come out different on the other side. Living with a faith healer—I never got to live with a faith healer."

"That's what you're going to tell your daughter?" Duncan said. "Just accept whatever comes along? Endure? Adapt?"

"Well—"

"And how would people end up if they all did that?" (229)

Real life can—and should—be an adventure, Tyler illustrates, even though the ideal life always remains elusive, with no easy answers and no straight paths to follow; there are only difficult choices needing to be made and futures waiting to be shaped. We don't know at the end of *Searching for Caleb* what Meg's choice will be, but her parents have presented her with Tyler's two redeeming options: *stay*—if, as her mother Justine tells her, she can see her married life as an adventure, an opportunity to have new experiences and get to know different kinds of people; or *go*—as her father Duncan advises her to do, to search for a more fulfilling life.

In *Morgan's Passing*, as well, Emily Meredith faces a dilemma similar to Meg Peck's. In her marriage to Leon, she has come to feel burdened, confused, and unhappy, "like someone in a story, some drudge. I feel like the miller's daughter, left to spin gold out of straw" (183). Yet, when Emily chooses to marry Morgan, she is able to experience life as an adventure and the world as full of possibility and challenge (despite the fact that Leon has taken their daughter to live with him and she soon finds herself camped in a crowded trailer with Morgan's sister, mother, and their new infant son to care for—still doing puppet shows, although now with Morgan, not Leon, as her co-puppeteer). Earlier in the novel Mrs. Tibbett had questioned Emily's puppet-show version of "Beauty and the Beast," saying, "You had [the princess] living happily ever after with the Beast. But *that's* not how it is; he changes; she says she loves him and he changes to a prince." Emily replies quickly: "It's just that we use a more authentic version" (83). It is this more authentic version that Tyler insists on giving her readers at the end of *Morgan's Passing* when Emily establishes her new, but very real, life with the novel's complex antihero Morgan Gower. Happiness and adventure may be possible, but there are no fairy-tale endings in life, Tyler insists—or in the chaotic, messy, present-day realities of her novels' conclusions.

In fact, in Tyler's fiction, the ideal is actually shown to be dangerous, a trap and a lie that can ensnare the unwary and cut people off from life. As Mary Robertson shows, "family purity leads to entropy," the weight of family history, "in the guise of recording events in time, more often artificially kills time, the beat of time, through concepts, such as the family, that deny history's real randomness and disorder" (203). Justine Peck in *Searching for Caleb* must fight the ossifying Peck family myth, its oppression and decay in her life, in order to stay receptive to the new, to remain vital and open to change. She warns her daughter Meg (a throwback to the Daniel Peck branch of the family rather than its adventurous Caleb side), "Teaching you to adapt is the best education we could give you!" (21). Those who resist change, as do the Pecks of Roland Park, Baltimore, reveal their "alienated attitude . . . a secret, stingy resentment that the world and its many people are different from oneself" (Robertson 200). As Duncan Peck tells Justine, the Peck family is "digging the moat a little deeper. They're pointing out all the neighbors' flaws and their slipping dentures and mispronunciations, they're drawing in tighter to keep the enemy out" (88). To be a Peck is, as Duncan tells Justine, to look down on others as "common. [But, he insists on knowing,] What's so uncommon about us?" (88). Maintaining the "perfect" family not only is an impossible task but one that can lead to self-delusion and stagnation, not to mention snobbishness, devisiveness, and alienation from others. According to Mary Robertson, Anne Tyler reveals that

one can best be oneself if one is connected in some significant way with those in the public who are different from oneself. Charlotte's house [in *Earthly Possessions*] has a room with an outside door which serves as a photography studio that is open to the public. Ezra's "homesick" restaurant [in *Dinner at the Homesick Restaurant*] similarly connotes both the public and the private life. The Merediths' apartment [in *Morgan's Passing*], into which Morgan eventually moves with Emily, is located above a public crafts shop with a common hallway.

Anne Tyler suggests that urban environments are more enriching than suburban ones; in *Earthly Possessions*, "Charlotte's neighborhood changes from strictly residential to partly commercial when Amoco buys the property next door for a filling station. Ezra's is a city restaurant in Baltimore, and Morgan's people reside in Baltimore too" (Robertson 200). Anne Tyler creates characters who learn to embrace the unfamilial and the unfamiliar. The most fulfilled of these come to experience and enjoy the urban, the diverse, the imperfect, and the real—to find their own individual significance in relation to a changing, crowded world.

Barbara Harrell Carson believes that Anne Tyler deconstructs not only the myth of the white American family romance but the dominant myth of white American literature (as typified by Thoreau's *Walden Pond*), as well—the myth of "the heroic isolato" (24). Instead, Carson sees Tyler as offering "a traditionally feminine rather than a traditionally masculine system of values"; she "locates self-fulfillment in complex relatedness rather than in isolation. . . . Instead of the nobility of simplification, Tyler celebrates the painfully joyous enrichment that comes from establishing and cherishing the networks that string us together" (24, 33). An openness to change, to difference, and to others distinguishes Tyler's most fulfilled characters, as well, from the more traditional white heroines of Shirley Ann Grau (including even the most liberated of these, Lucy Roundtree Evans Henley) and points to the greater maturity of their adult lives. Tyler's fictional world still emphasizes the private, but it opens the doors of the narrow white world so that outsiders can come inside and the public commotion and clutter beyond can, at least, be heard and viewed.

In addition, as we have seen, Anne Tyler's fictional world is not the world of the past (as in Shirley Anne Grau's fiction), but the world of the present and future. Her novels are filled with a "sense of transiency that permeates [contemporary] life in the United States," as Julie Papadimas notes (45). The house of the past threatens, in the words of Duncan Peck of *Searching for Caleb*, to "seal [you in] . . . [to cause you] to grow old and stale and finally die" (33). As Frank Shelton explains,

the large, old, reputable houses in Tyler's fiction usually suggest retreat from life and a smothering of the individual; however those houses can be revivified as they are in *The Clock Winder* and *Earthly Possessions*. On the other hand, a more impermanent kind of life in a less respectable residence like the trailers in *Searching for Caleb* and *Morgan's Passing* or Muriel's house in *The Accidental Tourist* can bring with it a receptivity to the vicissitudes of existence. ("Anne Tyler's Houses" 45)

Tyler reveals that "her characters must at least be open to other perspectives and other modes of living. . . . Her characters who are most successful in their own lives are those whose domestic arrangements combine. . . . the opposing human needs for permanence and mobility" ("Anne Tyler's Houses" 46). Some of Tyler's characters learn to travel at home (like Charlotte Emory in *Earthly Possessions*); some learn to travel around home (Justine Peck circles Baltimore as a fortuneteller for a carnival in *Searching for Caleb*, and Delia Grinstead finds Bay Borough offers her a better perspective of her life in Baltimore in *Ladder of Years*); the majority learn to relish the unanticipated journey and flow of time that constitute life itself, wherever it takes place, whether at home or abroad. Even the decorous, staid Daniel Peck, living out his final days with his transient granddaughter Justine (while searching for his wayward brother Caleb), "began to relax. . . . began to enjoy the search itself. . . . learned to concentrate solely on the act of traveling" (*Searching for Caleb* 158). His daughter Lucy watches him and wonders "if he didn't almost *enjoy* this life—these dismal houses, weird friends, separations from the family, this moving about and fortune telling. If he weren't almost proud of the queer situations he found himself in" (202). When Lucy and his other Roland Park children come to visit for his ninety-third birthday, Daniel seems to brag about his newfound ability to cope, remarking needlessly, "After all, we're living in reduced circumstances" (202).

Social movement in Tyler's contemporary white America tends to be downward—yet this is not seen as either negative or depressing but as an opportunity for growth and renewal—as it has been in the life of Daniel Peck. The experience of "a slipping-down life" as synonymous with adult growth and choice in contemporary white American life extends far beyond the world of heroine Evie Decker in Tyler's second novel. Delia Grinstead, Morgan Gower, Emily Meredith, Macon Leary, Charlotte Emory, Justine and Duncan Peck, Pearl Tull, Mary Tell, and Jeremy Pauling all find the "reputable" houses of the white past hard to maintain in the present. Filling stations move in next door (as in *Earthly Possessions*), neighborhoods change (as in *Saint Maybe*), and families (in novel after novel) fall apart. For such a world, Anne Tyler's message is not "endure," but the more complex "adapt" (as Justine Peck has advised her daughter Meg to do in *Searching for Caleb*). Anne Tyler's white protagonists must learn to adjust to decline and change in their lives, experience hardships that enable them to grow, and move freely in both time and place, learning to cast off whatever threatens to diminish, deaden, or distance them from life, and relish new—even "slipping-down"—experience.

The institution of the family is Tyler's training ground for adaptations of every kind—not the traditional white southern family we have found in Shirley Ann Grau's novels but, as Julie Papadimas has said, one "redefine[d] . . . in purely [contemporary] American terms. In spite of belonging to nuclear families. . . . [Tyler's] characters suffer from the greatest degree of isolation when they reach out to their families for understanding. To achieve a sense of belonging, many form surrogate families" (45). Still desirous of family union, still hopeful of finding nourishment and fulfillment within the institution of the family, Tyler's "homeless at home," as we have seen, must often flee mothers, fathers, sisters, and spouses (those, that is, remaining in the family nest) in order to find community and dignity with people outside their immediate family. More often than not, Tyler's white nuclear families not only don't work, they require escape and avoidance for the maturation and well-being of the individual. Family judgments can be unfair and cruel—threatening paralysis and retardation in the development of the self:

"Justine," Sam Mayhew said, "you have been a disappointing daughter in every way, all your life."

Then Justine rocked back as if she had been hit, but Duncan already stood behind her braced to steady her. (*Searching for Caleb* 103)

Justine can prove herself useful and necessary, a valuable person in the new family unit she has created with Duncan in the wider world she explores with him. Yet Justine and Duncan will also fail to provide what their own daughter Meg desires in her adult life:

[Justine and Duncan] were not very parent-like. [Meg] loved them both, but she had developed a permanent inner cringe from wondering how they would embarrass her next. They were so—*extreme.* So irresponsible! They led such angular, slap-dash lives, always going off on some tangent, calling over their shoulders for her to come too. And for as long as Meg could remember she had been stumbling after, picking up the trail of cast-off belongings and abandoned projects. (163-64)

Meg elopes, as did her mother before her, to go off to connect with people outside her immediate family, those with whom she hopes to build a more satisfying life of her own. Tyler's characters form new families, abandon or reconstitute old ones, in order to provide for their deepest needs and begin to fulfill their adult potential.

For this journey, there is no guide. Maps must be designed individually, from deep inside, entirely from scratch. Tyler's men (both strong and frail) and her women (both independent and lonely) attempt to form and maintain alliances that will offer the greatest good or the least harm to themselves and others—rejecting the materialistic quests for success and upward mobility that obsessed the generations before them, as well as past romantic ideals of family loyalty and honor, male independence and female subservience. Tyler's white southern heroines are no longer merely keepers of their fathers' houses or helpless dependents on men. Together, Tyler's male and female characters struggle to survive and remain vital in a complex, urbanized South where faint, anachronistic traces of a more aristocratic, mythically "genteel," white past still cast shadows over everyday lives. Tyler's modern-day Baltimore, however, is very much a part of mainstream American society—a culture decidedly in decline as a world economic power. The fictional world she presents us—filled as it is with random murders, bizarre kidnappings, unexpected car accidents, run-down rowhouses, and despairing suicides—seems all too familiar and commonplace throughout American society. It is a culture very much in need of the creativity, adaptability, and communion (through difference) that her contemporary white southern heroines and heroes have to offer. If this present-day world is a challenging one, requiring resourceful, resilient selves for a complex, even dangerous life, it nevertheless remains far better that the alternative: isolation, decay, and death in the crumbling house of the past.

4

Gail Godwin's Family Reconfigurations

In the fiction of Anne Tyler, as we have seen, fathers are indifferent, ineffectual, or—for the most part—absent. Daughters typically break their remaining family ties to go off and establish new lives—and new families—for themselves. They become puppeteers, nurse's aides, grocery store clerks, physicians, fortune tellers, or nursery school teachers, in addition to being wives and mothers. Only a few remain unattached to husbands, coping on their own, at the conclusion of their stories—Mary Tell, Evie Decker, Sarah Leary, or Daphne Bedloe, for instance. Fewer still prosper in life (most "slip-down" from more secure economic pasts)—and none find themselves in the position of the majority of Grau's heroines: in control of large inheritances from their fathers. Yet the very precarious nature of their financial situations seems to energize and challenge Tyler's heroines, calling upon their androgynous inner resources, requiring them to use old skills and develop new ones, necessitating that they open their doors, look out, and interact with a larger world. Their survival depends on their ability to adapt, meet difficulties, and accommodate differences. As Joseph Voelker concludes, increasingly in the course of Tyler's fiction, her characters learn to be flexible and open to life's possibilities, becoming less distant from and less fearful of the "random and dangerous . . . accidental world" (177) in which they find themselves.

Gail Godwin's daughter-heroines also develop and grow over the course of her writing career. At the outset, they seem as restricted and crippled as most of Shirley Ann Grau's heroines—women who repeat the patterns and mistakes of the past, who have no larger vision of themselves or the world, who are too passive and too fearful of life to take risks. Increasingly, however, they escape from enclosed, claustrophobic family relationships to search for self-knowledge and experience a larger world. Only when they have succeeded in developing their own strengths and talents do they risk returning home to renew old ties. In Godwin's most recent works, her heroines have matured. They no longer despair of change for themselves or their societies. Having undertaken Jung's "task of personality" themselves (Godwin, "Southern Belle" 51), they begin the task of community, working to bring together friends and family, black and white, rich and poor, old and young, South and North, West and Midwest. Joining with Tyler's characters, then moving beyond them, Gail Godwin's latest heroines come to value inclusion and connection over exclusion and isolation in their lives. They seek ways to combine their private and their public selves, open and extend family structures, take political action, and fulfill their social responsibilities (not in the mode of traditional white southern women who have done so by passing on hierarchical traditions and restrictive codes of manners but by trying to create more inclusive, egalitarian communities for the future). In their struggle against southern codes and family strictures that retain a powerful hold even in the late twentieth century, Godwin's daughters of the South grow from a state of dependency and arrested development: they begin to embark on mature, adult lives of their own.

As with those of Shirley Ann Grau and Anne Tyler, the heroines of Gail Godwin are essentially fatherless. As Jane Hill writes,

Certainly, *Violet Clay* and, to a lesser extent, *Glass People*, *The Odd Woman*, *A Mother and Two Daughters*, and *The Finishing School* resonate with the feeling of loss associated with the absence of a father figure, and, with the exception of Leonard Strickland in *A Mother and Two Daughters* [and the father of Godwin's later *Father Melancholy's Daughter*], the father figure bears considerable resemblance to Mose Godwin [Gail Godwin's own playboy, alcoholic father who divorced her mother in Gail's infancy and then committed suicide in 1958, when Godwin was twenty-one and had only recently resumed contact with him]. (3)

The military father in *The Perfectionists* (1970) remains remote and distant from his daughter, and Godwin's more gentle, guiding fathers— Leonard Strickland of *A Mother and Two Daughters* (1982) and Walter Gower, Rector of St. Cuthbert's church in *Father Melancholy's Daughter* (1991)—both die, leaving their daughters to chart life courses on their own. In five of Godwin's nine novels, stepfathers intrude on the heroines' lives, invading the sanctity of the "true" family, displacing real (if deceased) fathers, distancing real mothers, and disrupting traditional domestic patterns. Real families fail, but the mythic family of the white southern family romance retains its power (largely due to the example and teachings of mothers and grandmothers who pass along its dicta). Carolyn Rhodes writes of Godwin's artistic struggle to expose "the dangers of the old ideal of 'Southern Womanhood,' with its constricting effects on the docile daughters of the misguided mother who tried to model and impose the tradition of shallow ladyhood" (55), as did

Godwin's own mother and grandmother in her youth.[1] Godwin's heroines must escape being trapped in the ideal of white southern womanhood, the ideal of the southern lady who has never "strained toward . . .
'the task of personality,'" who has never "confronted her true reflection
beyond the quicksilver image of what her heritage has prepared her to
be" (Godwin, "Southern Belle" 51). In Godwin's novels, Carolyn
Rhodes says, "women reared to reenact the traditional values must learn
. . . to see their fallacies, explore them openly among critical friends and
find new ways to be themselves, continually self-creating [their own per-
sonhood]" (65).

The earliest of Godwin's protagonists, however, fail to meet the
central challenge for the southern woman, evading "the task of personality" for easy submission to the dictates of tradition. In *The Perfectionists*
(1970) and *Glass People* (1972), Godwin's heroines remain trapped in
formulas from the past—in ideal images of the self and family that deny
them vitality, maturity, identities of their own—real lives in the ongoing,
ever-changing present. Dane Tarrant Empson, the protagonist of *The
Perfectionists*, has been given a unique opportunity (as was Godwin herself in her own life story which inspired the action of the novel)[2] to begin
a new life, create a new self. As Penelope MacMahon (her husband
John's patient) declares—while vacationing with John and Dane Empson
and John's three-year-old illegitimate son in Marjorca during the course
of the novel—"Gosh, what strange luck you had. I wish *I* could go to a
new country to work [Great Britain] and within a year find a brilliant
man who wanted to marry me and a ready-made little son who had my
eyes and didn't even have to have his diapers changed anymore" (3).
While Penelope's synopsis of Dane's story sounds very much like a vari-
ation of an old female plot—woman meets man; woman marries man;
woman stays with man in Britain rather than return to her own country
to live; woman becomes mother and wife (even if the child she mothers
comes to her "ready-made")—Dane ironically finds that her life is not
traditional enough.

John Empson is "not *conventional*" (3). He challenges her to grow
with him, admitting to being as protean as Tyler's Morgan Gower of
Morgan's Passing,

I've been a math scholar, philosopher, computer programmer, doctor who deliv-
ers babies—that was fun, very *joyful*—and, of course, I was almost a Jesuit. I've
been all those things and I'm none of them now. Next year I may be something
else again. I'm evolving all the time. I'm not your "finished" man, I'm afraid.
To be finished is to be circumscribed, to have stopped growing. Then one might
as well be dead. (41)

But Dane wants John to be more "finished," to be "more respectable" (41) and more in control. She likes it when John momentarily seems to have "taken over the task of steering their lives" (132). However, John resists the role of hero and patriarch, telling Dane, "[Y]ou're my wife. If I can't expose myself to you, then to whom? I know you would like it if I stayed in my doctor-protector role all of the time. When the uninte-grated, blundering little boy peeps out, it threatens you. But unless he comes out, he will *remain* unintegrated and blundering" (24-25). Dane is repulsed by John's candor, his weakness, his constant analysis and reflection, continuing to desire a more traditional, stoic, in-command "protector," as John suggests.

Dane finds herself overwhelmed by the challenge John poses. He assaults her unquestioned verities and demands mutual experimentation and reflection. Dane longs for the more simple life of the Spanish women she sees leaving mass on Majorca,

the young and virginal, with their white missals and fresh skins; the married and pregnant; and the old and widowed, draped in funeral black. She envied them their definitive stages of womanhood. It was all done for them. They had only to flow along with nature's seasons, being courted, bedded, bechilded, and bereaved. There were not all those interstices of ambition and neurosis for them to fall into. (17)

Dane, whose father was a military man instilling in her a sense of order, hierarchy, and decorum, desires a traditional husband and a traditional marriage like that of the "beautiful young French couple with their two small children" whom Dane watches with a "secret obsession" (38) throughout her vacation. She is eager to give herself over to history, to repeat traditional familial patterns, to have it "all done" (17) for her. She resists the new kind of marriage she shares with John, thinking, "She did not wish to complete, or to understand or to participate anymore. After ten months of this mentally and spiritually exhausting marriage, she wanted to be just a body—and left alone. She felt tight in the head, like something was growing—a flower someone planted in a pot too small" (22). Her mind cannot contain the growth that threatens to uproot her totally; again, she wants to become pure, an unthinking "body," going through the motions of female adulthood and replicating ancient patterns of nature and history.

Dane longs for a more traditional, less complex womanhood, and a perfect marriage that will fulfill her romantic desires. She finds inspira-tion in the model of the Victorian marriage with its "dignity and form," its ". . . privacy, . . . put[ting the] best foot forward" (72), yet Dane has succumbed to John Empson's proposal of an avant-garde marriage because of the idea of relationship he presents, the ideal form that he, too, has promised. It is "Marriage as a Work of Art" (25) that John has held forth to Dane. But Dane wants her postmodern art form *now*, complete and whole, a "finished product" (167) like those passed down through history, something a postmodern structure can never be. Instead, she finds that her husband's

flesh-and-blood failings which he dumped regularly in her lap like so much bruised fruit made it more and more difficult for her to keep the image clean. He could not balance her on his shoulders in the sea, or stride silently as a native across a sandy beach. His daily dealings with life were so much smaller that the panoramic sweep of his mind; his actions were never quite worthy of the clean, heroic beauty of his best ideas. (49)

Dane wants John to have "heroic beauty" in both mind and body; she wants shoulders she can ride on, a vision to supersede her own. When John offers Dane the opportunity "to create [with him] a shared universe greater than either of us could make (or explore) alone" (60), Dane surrenders herself to *his* universe rather than joining with him as he wants her to do in working towards a shared creation. In giving herself to John, Dane "wished . . . now . . . to complete her self-abnegation to the will of this determined man. . . . She had often wondered how martyrs felt, the moment before they were devoured by fire; or nuns, when their hair is being cut off, just before taking the veil. It must be something like this" (67-68). Dane wants to submit to John, not join with him in creating a self, a life, and a marriage of their own.

Thus, inevitably, Dane feels contained and constricted, giving herself over to her husband and his "ideal" of marriage, awaiting passively his creation of an artistic whole that will envelope her, while continuing to endure the "mess" and "disorder" of the real man, the present moment, and the everyday world around her (71). At the end of the novel, she takes out her anger and frustration on John's son, Robin— identifying with and punishing the boy's refusal to be molded by others, at the same time. Dane remains a confused child herself, on the one hand desiring to surrender her being to John in a traditional relationship (an ideal form) and, on the other, needing to find and assert her own personhood against him to escape being absorbed entirely into his vision. Her conflict remains unresolved. As Anne Mickleson points out, "The novel ends with Dane unable to say 'yes' or 'no' to her husband: 'Either answer made her lose' [204]. . . . Our last picture of Dane is of her mouthing the word 'bastard' as she watches her husband scramble over some rocks in the distance" (69). John must be her savior or her enemy; she refuses to accept him as her partner in shaping a new kind of life and a new kind of marriage that might allow for the selfhood and creativity of both partners.

Francesca Bolt in *Glass People* (1972) feels a similar ambivalence, a mixture of love and hate, attraction and repulsion, for her district attorney husband, "the terrible Cameron Bolt"—as the newspapers refer to him (4). Francesca, like Dane Empson, has desired to give herself to a man who will subsume her—who will do all her living and thinking for her. She explains, "It's as though I want some final force to enter me and take over my body, set me on some genuine destiny that can't be changed, that I can't turn back from" (13). In Cameron Bolt she has found just such a man, one who believes he has the right to design containers for others, to hold other people in finite forms of his own construction through the institutions of government and of marriage where he can wield control. At first, Cameron "had sat down with [Francesca] and made her a chart. If she followed it, she could accomplish everything a wife should do and have time left over. But she never could follow it" (5). Quickly, Cameron takes over Francesca's role as well as his own, doing the living and planning for both of them: "Cameron did not mind cooking or setting the table, or even washing up, as long as she sat across from him looking perfect" (11). Important for her appearance and not for herself—her husband "preferred [her] silences. He wished there were more of them. Then her ineffable beauty shone out and she was his mysterious, beautiful woman again" (45)—Francesca becomes more and more an object instead of a person. In desperation, Francesca writes home from California to her mother Kate, "I have lost all my energy. There is no life in me and the days drift by, one exactly like another. The seasons are all the same, you can never know for sure what month it is, no leaves fall or change, this place is like a garden under glass" (9). Later, when Francesca visits Kate, she confesses, "Marriage has been strange for me. It's very strange. It's a little like being frozen, or hypnotized. Sometimes, I feel as though I am slowly becoming paralyzed. I can sit around for hours and do nothing, see nothing. I feel like I am slowly turning to stone" (63). Kate's advice to her daughter comes from her own experience as a woman who has reflected the character of each of her three husbands, "Perhaps the alternative is to let yourself turn into someone else" (63). Rather than resisting by turning into stone or glass, Kate suggests that Francesca should follow her mother's example and take on the shape of her husband, instead.

While Francesca resists Cameron, going home to her mother, having a short affair with a man she meets on her return to California,

and becoming pregnant by him, she comes back to Cameron, still confused about who she is and what she wants. Like Dane Empson of *The
Perfectionists,* Francesca talks to other women and watches the way they
lead their lives, trying to find out from them clues concerning her own
needs and her own existence. What Francesca finds on her brief journey
away from her husband is not reassuring—an elusive woman whose
sickness in the hotel room next door replicates her own illness in marriage; a woman like her husband who has blueprints for the future, takes
charge of Francesca's life, and is willing to use her as a figure in the
background of her own broad canvas (as Cameron has done); another
who tells her how untrained and unprepared she is to exist on her own in
the outside world; and a mother who continues to advise her to take her
shape from her husband.

Francesca has already chosen to do the latter by marrying Cameron
in the first place—a man who "believe[s] in shapes. I believe everything
good has a shape. . . . Relationships are containers. Marriages are containers. . . . In a marriage, a traditional marriage let us say, the husband is
the public container" (98-99). Although she has tried to escape from the
container of her husband and her marriage, feeling herself "useless, both
to myself and him. There is nothing I can do for him that he can't do
better for himself" (157), Francesca ultimately yields to Cameron's will.
He insists,

Some shapes can't be altered once they are made. The sacrament of marriage is
such a shape. There are promises we make which bind us within their terrible
spiritual force-field. You and I might live physically apart for the rest of our
lives. And we will, if that's what you want. But we are eternally together in that
spiritual field of force we created with our own vows. (183)

It is much easier to let Cameron assert his will, choose her clothes for
her (the Byzantine mosaic "Madonna" dress from the St. Axel collection), and take care of her and her prospective child than elude his grasp
and find her own way in the world. He promises, "I shall be a happy,
devoted father [even to a child not his own]. I'm no stranger to the old
traditions, the old miracles, and I assure you I know how to conduct
myself in the awesome presence of this one" (201). Cameron will
require nothing from Francesca (she knows that he will not sleep with
her anymore) except that she remain an object of beauty, a glass figurine,
perfect in every way: "He had insisted that she begin rubbing oil of
almond on her belly at night, even though she was hardly showing. . . .
He didn't want a single stretch mark, he said" (203). In the novel's last
line, Francesca is described as "put[ting] away a hefty lunch, confident

in the secret, rather sly knowledge that Cameron would never allow her to get fat" (208). Francesca remains a figurine for Cameron to care for—an object for him to dust off, polish, and put out on display. There is little else left beyond her surface image.

Although Dane Empson and Francesca Bolt fail even to begin Jung's "task of personality," the protagonists of Godwin's next two novels, *The Odd Woman* (1974) and *Violet Clay* (1978), make that task the central purpose in their lives. Like Godwin's earliest heroines, Dane and Francesca, Jane Clifford of *The Odd Woman* finds herself seduced by ideal, traditional shapes—the ready-made stories of the nineteenth-century literature she teaches and the ready-made stories of women's lives all around her. Unlike Dane Empson and Francesca Bolt, however, Jane Clifford successfully resists these familiar structures, learning to risk being "odd," being "unique," in order to live her own life. The novel's epigraph from Jung identifies the challenge that awaits Jane in the course of her personal development: "In knowing ourselves to be unique in our personal combination—that is, ultimately limited—we possess also the capacity for becoming conscious of the infinite. But only then!" To create her own unique character, and, therefore, discover her position in relation to an infinite universe, Jane finds that she must resist the traditional formulas and constructions others would impose on her.

First, Jane Clifford must resist the role she is given by her family. As she returns home for her grandmother Edith's funeral, Jane sees her relations waiting for her at the airport:

There they stood in a row. . . . They had stood so for years of her landings, these people, waiting for her to come back to them, expecting her to come back, never doubting she had any choice but to fall back from the sky into their nets of family and region and social standing and—most compelling weave of all—their image of her, Jane, their Jane. (83)

Jane resists the pull of family and strives, in the face of the identity each of them would impose on her, to become her own person. Returning to the southern city of her youth for her grandmother's funeral, Jane vows:

I am not going to be pulled back this time. I will be compassionate to them, but I will not betray myself to make things easier for them. I will not show my emotions. I will not show favoritism to Ronnie over Jack [her stepbrothers], and I'll give Jack some of my time if he wants to talk. I will not have the slightest disagreement with Ray [her stepfather] no matter how he provokes me. I will be a person they all respect, and perhaps even like, but I will not give them a single weakness they can fasten on and thus retain me as theirs, their same old Jane.

And I will try, really try, to resurrect the bygone flavor of those talks with Kitty [her mother]. Even if they were fictions, I will revive them into reality with my detached, yet expanding sympathies. It will please her. (85)

Jane knows that to succumb to her family's image of her would mean losing her self. She desires to show her family love and care without becoming weak and giving in to their desires, needs, and visions for her. Jane struggles to discover who she is apart from the identity the family would impose upon her.

The women of Jane's family particularly tempt her to become like themselves with their sculpted, polished looks and lives. Seeing her mother Kitty, Jane thinks, "That woman, that blond woman—anyone can see she is what they call a 'lady,' and thinks of herself as a lady, with her straight-held shoulders and expensive suit with the little silk scarf tucked in the neck; and the black kid gloves covering all of the wrists" (83). The other influential family woman in Jane's life has been her grandmother, Edith Dewar Barnstorff (who dies at the outset of the novel), a woman whom Jane describes to her colleague Sonia Marks as "the perfect Southern lady. She was elegant, snobbish, beautiful to the very end. Her skin—and I'm not exaggerating—when I saw her this past Christmas was smoother than mine. She took exquisite care of herself" (56). Objects of beauty like Francesca Bolt of *Glass People,* Jane's grandmother and mother also embody the southern code of ladylike behavior. Edith had taught Jane, "You had your choice: a disastrous ending with a Villain; a satisfactory ending with a Good Man. The message was simple, according to Edith" (23). Jane's mother (although still very much a southern lady) and her stepsister Emily (who marries young) had both rebelled against Edith's strictures: "Jane's mother, Kitty, not taken in by the ominous program, had eloped twice. Both times with 'questionable' men of her own choice, if nobody else's. And Jane's young half-sister Emily had spotted the man she wanted when she was twelve, and married him with the approval of family and Church, at age fifteen" (23). Both women, nevertheless, follow Edith Barnstorff's script by marrying men who give final shape and meaning to their lives, following the traditional dictates of white southern society. Jane, however, remains unattached at thirty-two, filling a temporary position in literature at a midwestern college, her life still up in the air, incomplete, nontraditional, unsculpted, and unfinished in comparison with theirs.

Feeling a need for "more control of [her] life" (3), Jane "ransacked novels for answers to life, she wheedled confidences out of friends, investigated and ruminated over the women she had sprung from, searched for models in persons who had made good use of their lives,

admirable women who, even if not dramatic, might guide her through
their examples. So much remained unclear" (24). Searching for clues to
help her in her own life, Jane has remained what her friend Gerda Mulvaney calls a "romantic," someone who believes "there's a unit a man
and a woman can make. . . . A communion that insists on two other-
nesses" (41). Jane resists being alone, desiring still to follow in the footsteps of her grandmother, mother, and stepsister by "arranging her existence to accommodate a man" (25) and follow a traditional female plot.
Thus, Jane has taken a lover, a fine arts professor named Gabriel
Weeks—a man who is older than herself, already married for twenty-five
years, someone she has met at a Modern Language Association confer-
ence in New York and has seen only fourteen times in the last two years.
Yet Jane finds in the course of the novel that her relationship with
Gabriel cannot "complete" her life; instead, it fragments it further, leading her away from knowledge of herself. She finds that she is no longer
willing to live in the margins of Gabriel's life—nor marginalize her own
identity to his. Thus, Jane ends up alone at the novel's end—her story
still "unfinished." Nevertheless, she finds that her "ego" remains intact
and ready "to assess the strategic losses and negotiate back lost points"
(279) as she prepares to continue the process of creating her own life
story—one that she is discovering may not require union with a man to
attain its ultimate structure and meaning (in defiance of "the old, old
story" of women's lives (58) and her grandmother Edith's code of the
southern family romance).

Jane Clifford, nevertheless, would like the narrative of her life "to
make sense to the careful reader. . . . [who] would say, 'Yes, this existence felt its acts as irrevocably necessary'" (44-45). She would like the
structure of her life to have a compelling shape and beauty of its own,
and she remains acutely aware of the dramas of other women's lives
around her. As Rachel Brownstein concludes,

The Odd Woman is about women who imagine their lives as fictions, and about
fictions women live by; its heroine sees her life as a plot. Jane Clifford's Great-
aunt Cleva, who ran away with a villain (or was it a hero?) of a melodrama, was
as moved by literary example as Jane the professor is; and the influences on
Jane, for whom Cleva's life is story, are also a mix of real and imaginary
people. Desperately seeking idyllic romantic love on which to base a life as perfectly shaped and finished as literary character or literary form, haunted by the
contrasting examples of women in her family—her coaxing compliant mother,
her delicate lady grandmother, and long-dead Cleva—Jane Clifford is beset by
representations of women, that is, by the idea of other women as representations
of what a woman's life might be. (Brownstein 180-81)

The women in Jane's family, as well as other women in Jane's life, seem to be acting out the plots of ready-made stories: Great-aunt Cleva fulfilling the melodrama of the fallen woman; Edith and Kitty, the drama of the southern lady sacrificing her life for husband and family; her friend Sonia Marks, the life of the contemporary heroine, a superwoman who combines the lives of scholar, teacher, wife, mother, and friend into a perfect whole. Gerda Mulvaney, Jane's oldest friend (and look-alike), has chosen to take on not one plot but a series of roles for herself: "Gerda flung herself wholeheartedly into each successive ripple of the *Zeitgeist* until she had squeezed her own wave out of it. She rode the forefront of movements and dressed vividly in their costumes. She took up people and lovers and causes with a zealous, greedy intensity, seeing her personal salvation in each one" (35). Now Gerda publishes a feminist newspaper *Feme Sole* for solitary women, causing Jane to "wonder what its example might contribute to her own, less colorful life. She was not sure she wanted to sacrifice one god to another, or one sex to another. She wanted, if possible, both sexes and all the gods working for her" (40). Jane wonders if it is possible for a woman to work out her personal destiny apart from men without coming to hate men—or they her—as the inevitable consequence Gerda and her staff suggest comes with female independence and self-development.

In looking at the lives of other women Jane knows, as well as those of women writers such as George Eliot and the fictional heroines of the stories she teaches in her university classes, Jane finds the very idea of "self" suspect, "a myth which had died with the nineteenth century" (*OW* 21), understanding "that the self is a creation of time and circumstance, tailored to occasion and audience," as Gayle Greene notes (95). In her own life, Jane has found that there is not simply a "self" but "many selves that make solitary living such a crowded occupation" (*OW* 54). Jane learns to resist the temptation to simplify her life by adopting a ready-made self, a perfectly shaped story, a plot constructed to appeal to a certain place, time, and audience. She rejects the old costumes and the ready-made parts they would confer upon her life:

The word "mistress" itself was a story. As was "career woman," or "spinster," or "professor of English," or "intellectual," or "Romantic." I am all of these, thought Jane, but all of them are only parts of me. Her lover had called her indestructible. She had a glimmer of what he meant. You remained indestructible by eluding for dear life the hundreds and thousands of already written, already completed stories. . . . You reminded yourself . . . that you had to write yourself as you went along, that your story could not and should not possibly be completed until *you* were: i.e., dead. (44)

Jane learns to live with and value her complex and unfinished state, the very "oddities" that make her unique, and resist conventional costumes, simplifying forms, and signifying structures. As Gayle Greene explains,

She learns . . . to relinquish illusion, accept herself, and depend on her own efforts. . . . Though Godwin makes gestures toward open-endedness . . . probabilities are strongly suggested: Jane is left alone with herself, depending on her own efforts, attaining the self-awareness and self-reliance that make it impossible for her to pick up and follow Gabriel to England [if he gets his Guggenheim to go to London, where his wife is unwilling to live and Jane had planned to join him] or anywhere else. (98)

At the end of *The Odd Woman*, Jane is left to make her own story as she listens to "the barely audible tinkle of a soul at the piano, trying to organize the loneliness and the weather and the long night into something of abiding shape and beauty" (419). She continues to feel a longing to "organize," "shape," and "beautify" her life, needing to fight her desire to impose finished structures, the completed lives of other women, and tailor-made costumes from other eras, on her own life story. At the end of the novel, Jane accepts that "the task of personality"—always incomplete, frustrating, and difficult—has become the ever-evolving structure of her life.

Violet Clay (in the novel by the same name) begins her narrative from a point of greater security than Jane Clifford has attained at the end of *The Odd Woman*. In her retrospective account, Violet looks back on the time when she (like Jane Clifford) was in her early thirties. Since that time, she has become comfortable with her life, stating simply, "I am a painter. I like to listen to music while I work" (3). Nevertheless, the story she tells is of the painful process by which she grew into self-acceptance and self-discovery, struggling against the identity both family fate and the gothic image of woman as victim might have imposed upon her in the course of her life.

Violet has learned that she must not only leave behind her family and the South of her origins but must also struggle against the internalized image of herself that she has developed as a woman, a white southerner, and a member of the Clay family. Her friend Milo—who writes gothic novels under the pen name of Arabella Stone (novels for which Violet has designed covers)—confides in her his discovery of the relationship of family to self-loathing, terror, and fear:

"I think the very essence of what we have come to call 'gothic,' all those winding passageways and trap doors and dark stairways, may have a great deal to do with the family. With things we haven't been able to deal with. So we put them underground or in the attic, whichever you choose. We forget they're there except when they manifest themselves in some form of brooding terror, or a growing uneasiness of something lurking, waiting to do us in."

"What? The parents, or the things we haven't dealt with?"

"I'm . . . not sure it makes a great deal of difference. I've thought a lot about this. It's been on my mind, you see." (233)

Milo here equates the family with what his heroines (and the heroines Violet paints) flee to escape, as well as the force that lures them into final entrapment within the mysterious, gloomy old houses of the past. Violet, too, understands that the fictional heroine of the gothic novel "was running away from the house that would eventually contain her. Why then was it necessary to 'the plot' for her to go through the motions of running away? Because someone had to 'catch' her, and coax her to come back with him into his house" (284) to carry on the nightmare/fantasy of family entrapment.

Violet herself has already undergone such an experience years ago in her early marriage to Lewis Lanier, lawyer son of her grandmother's best friend "Big Violet":

He had been told about me, the orphan of War and a Romantic Suicide. He had had, he said, a frequent dream of "saving" me long before we met. . . . There was something sexy about having been captured, having been forced by the machinations of those two old Eumenides [her grandmother and Big Violet] to lie down in the sweet juices of traditional womanhood and abandon the hubris of an edgy, lonely struggle. I didn't touch a paintbrush those first months of captivity. (31-32)

When Violet finds she cannot endure her captive state any longer and divorces her husband, she is haunted by another gothic nightmare—with which she finally comes face to face in the person of Minerva Means, a "childlike old woman in her glad rags and matching hair ribbons, living out her days in a sepia wash of family history" (196). Violet, like Minerva, is a woman alone, a woman whose parents have long ago died (her father in the war and her mother through suicide), a woman playing out her family role as orphan, victim, and failed artist, understanding that she and Minerva Means share a bond,

I was as alone in the world as Minerva. Only there would be no ancestral fortress for me to hide out in daintily, drawing my consolations from its hoards and shadows, dressing and undressing myself in front of comforting old mirrors that still bore my child's imprint on their old silver surfaces. If I didn't create my own fortress soon, my ravagers were going to be more pitiless than any anticipated thief or prison escapee. (207)

The specter of herself as a pitiful spinster, a child-woman untouched by time or reality, herself metamorphosed into Minerva Means, becomes another gothic horror that haunts the thirty-two-year-old—but still not developing—Violet.

Unlike Minerva Means, Violet has no ancestral fortress in which to hide, but she has inherited her uncle's Adirondacks cabin in Plommet Falls—a place where she can determine her destiny, becoming either a captive of the past or the creator of her own future. There where her Uncle Ambrose Clay committed suicide over his inability to become a successful writer, Violet can determine whether she, too, will play out the family drama of the failed artist and succumb to family destiny. As Carolyn Rhodes explains, "[Violet's] deepest fears are fears of failing if she should dare to aspire to higher art. Violet also compares her life to her Uncle Ambrose's, whose role as Failed Southern Gentleman is relevant because he served as surrogate parent, modeling self-deceit and ultimate hollowness" (61). After Ambrose's death, Violet thinks,

If Ambrose could bow out in a sportsmanlike way, I, too, could be sporting. I might not choose to blow my brains out, but I could at least not whine if it was in the cards for me to become one of the world's losers. There was still time to get a dignified loser's act together, if it came to that. Didn't I come from a part of the country that had made its biggest loss into a sort of debonair victory? (266)

Both the history of the South and Violet's own family history have shaped her destiny as that of the "loser." Her mother had committed suicide after the death of her husband in World War II, and her paternal grandmother had given up her piano career because of "secret fears that I might not succeed" (28-29), instead marrying a dashing young southern man who would leave her "a widow of twenty-six with two small boys to bring up and my fingers too stiff to do any of my bravura pieces anymore" (28). Violet's grandmother sells off pieces of the family estate to support herself and her young granddaughter, attempting to keep up appearances on the East Battery of Charleston, South Carolina (but drinking secretly, giving in to despair over the failure of her life). Early on, Violet finds that she, too, lives a life dominated by shame and despair, having "joined the hallowed clan of The Orphan. I became accustomed merely to holding out my hand and receiving from others the currency of sympathy. But, at age thirty-two, I was discovering I couldn't buy so much with these earnings" (4).

Violet's heritage, thus, is one of weakness and loss. Even as an independent artist who has lived for nine years in New York after the failure of her marriage, Violet knows that she is squandering her talent as "an illustrator, not an artist. I was still spending my skills on other people's visions" (5). Violet is afraid that, as her former lover Jake has said, ". . . you're scared silly as those gothic heroines you paint of taking any real voyages. You're afraid if you got really good at something people wouldn't pity you anymore, and you'd rather have the pity" (4). It is only when Violet has lost both her job as an illustrator and the last member of her family when her uncle commits suicide, both on the same day, that she goes to the Adirondacks alone to confront her failed self, her failed artistry, and her failed life.

There Violet meets Samantha DeVere (Sam), a woman who has refused to play the role of life's victim and failure—a woman who helps Violet to achieve a "breakthrough" (283) in her art and life. Sam is no shrinking Violet (so to speak), no fleeing gothic heroine, but a "powerful female" (285) who presents Violet with "another sort of picture and lots of questions" (284). Victimized in every way possible—by an abusive stepfather from whom she has had to run away; by three college boys who have raped her in her flight from her stepfather; and by the birth of an illegitimate daughter, Cheyenne (conceived through the rape), whom she is left to raise and support on her own when she is little more than a child herself—Sam asks for no pity and allows herself no weakness. She has become a self-taught, skilled carpenter who studies in her spare time for her high school equivalency exam, aspiring to go on to college to become an architect when her daughter is older. Sam has raised Cheyenne to be strong, as well, counseling her not to hide her illegitimacy but to turn it into an asset—a unique, mysterious feature that can enhance her life. Violet, too, draws strength from Sam, finding that she "put me into proportion"—that "never, since I heard Sam's story, have I been able to take my 'Poor Little Me' moods seriously for very long" (315).

Friendship with Sam changed Violet's outlook on life, leading her to a new understanding of her own good fortune,

In my life since Plommet Falls, there have been times when things did not go as I wished. I have been without enough money to provide myself with the sort of life I wanted. I have had to take jobs that took away valuable painting time and painting energies. I have been frequently alone, or without the kind of company I would prefer to my own. It was not until very recently that I got the kind of studio I wanted and had sold enough work to be able to stay home and paint in it. . . . "Well, at least," I say humorously, "I'm not in the middle of South Dakota with nothing but the clothes on my back and a trio of rapists' seeds battling it out for ascendancy in my womb." And things begin to look quite bearable again. (314-15)

Violet gives up her orphaned victim status, no longer dwelling on loss—a white southern pastime—but on the advantages life has bestowed upon her. She is not alone in her quest. As Jean Wyatt states, "It is, finally, relationship that enables Violet to paint something that *does* communicate. . . . Paradoxically, Violet gains a new autonomy by relinquishing her defense of boundaries: identifying with Sam gives her a clear vision of the autonomy she wants for herself" (116).

Sam has given Violet a new self-image and a new subject for her art, as well—a white woman who is muscular yet beautiful, strong yet feminine, a "suspended woman. . . . suspended in . . . well, her own possibilities, what she might do" (323), rather than in her historic powerlessness. Her painting of Sam, entitled *Suspended Woman,* not only begins her career as a serious artist but signals Violet's own self-development. Through Sam, Violet learns to accept herself as a woman with a future, the world as a place of promise and possibility, women alone in states of transition as energetic and powerful beings. Violet remains no longer "crouched in the shadows of [her] own potential" (109), trapped "in the Book of Old Plots" (45) alongside the gothic heroines she has painted. She no longer uses her artistic talent to perpetuate the image of female weakness and victimization. As Elizabeth Fox-Genovese has shown, at the outset of the novel Violet has supported herself through

the culture of female fantasy and aspiration by means of the mass production of Gothic novels. . . . The ambiguous theme of the Gothic—the home as source of evil and as refuge, the man as savior and as rapist—provides a counterpoint to [Violet's liberation] from that dangerous patriarchal domestic legacy. (212-13)

Early in her life, Violet Clay has not only allowed herself to become trapped in her culture's self-defeating images of womanhood, she has helped to perpetrate those same images through her art. In liberating herself from this cultural heritage, she finds herself now aiding other women by creating new images from which they can draw strength—as Godwin uses her own art of fiction to expose the power negative images exert in entrapping women and to explore new female identities for her heroines.

Violet is even able to help the resourceful Sam see herself more clearly and positively through their relationship:

And by the time I left Plommet Falls, possessed of the painting that was her gift to me, the painting that was destined to bring me my first share of the long-wanted acknowledgment, I like to believe I gave her something in return. As she spread out the pieces of her adult life and looked at them for the first time in the company of a friend and saw what kind of picture they added up to, a confident pride grew in her. In spite of having been given some shoddy materials to work with, she had been gutsy enough to build all this? "I really think," I told her, "that the test of a person is, in the end, how well she's used what she was given to use. And, girl, you've used it." "Do you really think so?" she asked. I thought so, I told her. (310)

Godwin shows how women can affirm each other's lives—rather than continuing to assist in holding each other down and keeping each other trapped in houses of the past. By the end of the novel, Violet Clay is in a position to help other women find and use their own inner resources and talents, as she has come to do. As Joanne Frye notes, "Violet Clay is the first of Godwin's protagonists to tell her own story; she is both agent and recipient of the narrative process as she uses narrative patterns to gauge patterns in her own behavior, trying always to arrive at a self-definition continuous with the past and appropriate for the future and to work out patterns for her own sense of autonomous selfhood" (113). At the novel's conclusion, Frye asserts, "Violet Clay has learned not so much the art of painting as the art of narrating the self and acting toward an ever-changing destiny" (130).

Godwin's last five novels all deal, as well, with female evolution. At the same time, Godwin moves steadily beyond this theme to consider the roles of women in society at large as they begin to create new kinds of families and more inclusive communities than those they have rejected. As Jane Hill suggests, "The idea of woman suspended between worlds or options, as represented by Violet's first important work of art, is a major turning point in Godwin's fiction. . . . Godwin's subsequent work . . . will be about characters, primarily women, who learn to live in suspension and to draw power from that state" (54-55). *The Finishing School* (1984) and *Father Melancholy's Daughter* (1991) continue to concentrate their focus on a single female heroine who (like Jane Clifford and Violet Clay) learns to value herself and affirm others, at the same time.

In *The Finishing School*, Godwin explores the paradox of how an older woman who has sacrificed herself for others, living her own life vicariously, can yet exert a positive, liberating influence on a young girl. The woman in question is Ursula DeVane (although the protagonist Justin Stokes's own mother will become an ironically powerful role model for Justin's cousin Becky Mott, as well). Ursula has given up her own career aspirations to be an actress in order to nurture the musical talents of her brother Julian and take care of him after the deaths of their parents. The pattern of Ursula's life has been self-destructive and negative—a life that Justin Stokes comes to renounce by the end of their brief summer friendship in her fourteenth year—the summer she and her family moved to Clove, New York, "the North" she says, "that I had been brought up to hate because its interference and brutalities had destroyed our gracious past" (6). Justin has lost her father (killed in an alcohol-related, single-car accident); her southern-lady grandmother; her surrogate father, grandfather, and namesake, Dr. Frank Justin; and her beloved ancestral home in Fredericksburg, Virginia. The stage has been set for Justin to see "herself as the victim of Tragedy" (5), a forlorn child of the defeated South, as Justin's mother has starred all her life in another southern role of white female helplessness as "The Daughter" (39). As Louise Stokes tells her daughter, Justin, a life of being supported by her father, pampered by her mother, and indulged by her boyish husband has been

the story of the little girl who got her own way for thirty-two years. Recently I have been thinking . . . that it would have been better if I hadn't had my own way quite so much. And I've been thinking about you, too. I know there are lots of things you don't like about our new life, but . . . I think you may grow up to be a better . . . certainly a more useful person than I am because of the very things you suffer now. You'll have to develop strengths I never bothered to. (39)

While Justin's cousin Becky Mott, now a "counselor and psychologist to precocious criminals," can look back on Louise Stokes as "the most wonderful woman I had ever met" (279), she knows that Justin took Ursula DeVane as her adolescent role model instead: "But you I could never understand. With a beautiful, kind mother like that, you preferred to spend time with that ugly, crazy woman over on Old Clove Road" (280). Although it has taken Justin until the age of forty, twenty-six years later, to acknowledge her debt to Ursula, she admits, "For what it's worth, you left your mark on me. Despite everything that happened, I have absorbed you. As long as I live, you live in me. Sometimes I hear myself speak in your voice. And, as you did, I watch its effects on others" (2-3).

What Justin Stokes has done, she realizes, is to take the best that Ursula DeVane had to offer and turn it, DeVane style (as in the DeVane family motto, "Luck is our ruler—and our weapon!" [128]), to her advantage: "I became what she wanted to be. . . . In that sense, I am her creature" (47). Justin has fulfilled Ursula's acting aspirations while rejecting the overall pattern of Ursula's—and her own mother's—life, intuiting even as a young girl that Ursula and her mother, "each in her own style, was cultivating the role of the glamorous martyr" (193). While Ursula positively influenced Justin's choice of an acting career, she might, Justin realizes, have encouraged her into more disastrous theatre, that of making soap opera productions out of her own life:

Would I, if I hadn't made it as an actress, have become a dangerous person, dangerous not only to myself but to others? What would I be doing if I hadn't become an actress? Making up tales of my past to impress whoever would listen? Looking for ways to dramatize my environment—and whoever happened to be living in it—to keep myself from going dead? (171)

After Julian DeVane commits suicide—having asked Justin to replace him so that his sister will have "s-someone else to transfer her ambitions to. . . . Sissie n-needs that" (288)—Justin labels Ursula "a witch . . . able to make me perform in her story, robbing me of the chance to be the heroine of my own story" (307). Only at age forty does Justin understand that Ursula, in fact, enhanced her life, rather than damaged it:

So, here I am, in the middle of my own life, almost the same age she was then. And it has taken me this long to understand that I lose nothing by acknowledging her influence on me. . . .

   Now, my thoughts go forward to meet hers. I know something of life's betrayals and stupidities myself; I know the ashy taste of not living up to some part of your dream. I even know the necessity for making constant adjustments to your life story, so you can go on living in it. She and I would have much to talk about now.

   But I also know something else that I didn't know then. As long as you can go on creating new roles for yourself, you are not vanquished. I believe there is quite a good chance that Ursula DeVane, if she is alive today, does not consider herself vanquished. (322)

Ursula has taught Justin crucial survival skills in her "finishing school" hut in the woods, as Justin later comes to understand.

   Ursula has affirmed Justin at a crucial point in her life, turning her away from seeing herself as a victim—"No, there are things much more tragic than the deaths of pleasant, unexceptional people and having to start all over in a new place," Ursula tells Justin (5)—showing her that a new life in a new region means "she can start her life over and be anything she chooses to be" (90). She opens Justin to the possibilities her life and her name hold forth: "an androgynous name. It gives you more *room,* somehow" (16). Ursula teaches Justin the danger of identifying with groups in order to avoid "having to discover who [she is]" (16) and questions the "goodness" of Justin's grandmother's life of conformity to the ideal of the white southern lady, forfeiting self-knowledge and a "private life" of her own (126). Ursula advises Justin to keep growing and changing,

But what we *ought* to fear is the kind of death that happens in life. . . . at some point, you congeal. . . . You're not fluid anymore. You solidify at a certain point and from then on your life is doomed to be a repetition of what you have done before. *That's* the enemy. There are two kinds of people walking around on this earth. One kind, you can tell just by looking at them at what point they congealed into their final selves. It might be a very *nice* self, but you know you can expect no more surprises from it. Whereas, the other kind keeps moving, changing. (254-55)

Ursula helps Justin appreciate the "fluidity" of the self and fortifies her resistance to being "rushed into womanhood with all its distracting appurtenances" in favor of the "lonely, mysterious side [of herself] I was just beginning to know, a side neither masculine nor feminine but quivering with intimations of mental and spiritual things" (122). Justin will marry and divorce twice; she will play many roles in her acting career; she will reflect on her past and make new discoveries about herself and others in the process. What she will not allow herself to do is to become static and stale—playing out one part for the rest of her life, a state Ursula DeVane has taught her to fear and avoid.

Ursula DeVane, however, had allowed herself (up to the point where Justin parted company with her) to become enclosed in her ancestral home, trapped in the role of female nurturer and family martyr. Her pupil Justin resists family entrapment, remaining "family-less," as does her cousin Becky Mott, as well; Becky's father, Eric Mott, complains about this to Justin when she visits him at his IBM office in upstate New York (170). Instead, Becky has chosen to deal with the children of other people's families, trying to help them heal their broken lives. Some of the children Becky works with have committed murder, including the killing of parents in their anger and pain (170). Justin herself has learned about family destructiveness through her adolescent contact with the DeVane family history: a mother driven mad by an angry daughter and a damaging marriage to an older man, a controlling husband; a vengeful daughter who has betrayed her mother, then martyred herself first to her ailing father and then to her talented brother; and a weak, overly dependent, ultimately despondent son who finally takes his own life.

Families such as the DeVanes can damage their own members' lives as well as lead to larger cultural patterns of destruction revealed in the case histories of Becky Mott's young patients. Godwin shows the destructiveness of family, as well, through the seemingly harmless, well-intentioned Eric Mott. Estranged from his wife, Mona, at the outset of *The Finishing School*, Mott remains protective of her, his daughter, Becky, as well as Justin, her brother, Jem, and their mother, Louise, during their stay in Clove, New York. All the time he watches over them, he is also engaged as well in secret, potentially cataclysmic, national defense work for IBM. Years later, Justin discovers: "What Mott had been doing, that summer when he mowed our lawn every Saturday, and checked Aunt Mona's car under the hood, and played dutiful uncle to his fatherless niece and nephew, was maintaining the vacuum tubes of an enormous secret computer being readied for the military" (164). Mott's job has been an extension of his role as family patriarch and protector of the home, one where he no longer lives:

God, how *needed* Mott must have felt as he instructed the Air Force how to check and recheck that maze of crucial vacuum tubes! He must have seen himself as an angel of surveillance: watching over those tubes that would maintain the computer's ability to survey the free summer skies of North America and sound an instant alert at the first darkening threat of the Russian menace. Maintenance and watchfulness. Protect what you have. Watch out for your nearest and dearest. Mott's religion had served him well at work and had spilled over, that summer, into off-work hours. (164-65)

Mott's protective stance at home, when he goes out after dark to search for Justin, will expose Ursula DeVane's love affair with Abel Cristiana, provoke Julian DeVane's suicide, and create trauma for the adolescent Justin, as well. Luckily, the "ninety-nine percent reliable" (165) SAGE IBM system Mott maintains at work has no parallel misfires in its "protective" function for society—and yet Godwin has revealed the deadly potential for mass destruction just below the surface calm of patriarchal family life.

Instead of closing off from others and adopting a dangerous, fearful, ultimately selfish posture, Justin becomes an adult who remains open to growth through her life and her work. Her "family" extends beyond its Justin-Stokes origins in Fredericksburg, Virginia, and even its Stokes-Mott branch in Clove, New York. Through her mother's second marriage to Craven Ravenal, Justin becomes friends with Craven's ex-wife, Charlotte, and her daughters, who, according to Charlotte, have become "as proud of you as if you were their blood sister. And look at how my grand-daughter Suzie drove up from Randolph-Macon to see you in that play. . . . You are Suzie's *idol*. You'll make it easier for her to get out, if she ever needs to" (321). Justin has become as much a role model for young Suzie as Ursula DeVane was for her—someone who can open up possibilities and liberate younger women through the example she has set in her work and life. Unlike Ursula DeVane, however, Justin is not trapped in her ancestral past nor enclosed in the nuclear family hothouse; she has meaningful work to engage her, as well as a large network of public and private relationships to draw on. Ursula DeVane remains a member of Justin's extended family—an inspiration for the fluidity she counseled rather than the entrapment she allowed.

Margaret Gower, the protagonist of *Father Melancholy's Daughter*, will also grow away from nuclear family enclosure to embrace a larger community and a larger world, one that eventually includes the betraying "witch" of her girlhood (as Justin Stokes's includes Ursula DeVane). At the age of six, Margaret experiences the breakup of her tight, little family (when she is years younger than the almost-fourteen Justin Stokes). Margaret's mother, Ruth, deserts her father to go to England with a former teacher and friend, Madelyn Farley, where (like Justin Stokes's father) Ruth is killed in a fatal car crash. Afterwards, Margaret clings to all that remains of her family—her father, Walter Gower, rector of St. Cuthbert's Church in Romulus, Virginia. Yet, Margaret admits that, early on, she had wanted to have her father dependent on herself alone so that she could be the one, in place of her mother, to soothe him through his bouts of depression: "It would be all my responsibility. And though the task would be daunting, I would conduct myself as a hero. . . . Much as I required [her] company, there was somehow no room for my mother in this particular fantasy" (43). After her mother's death, Margaret is able to fulfill her dream of devoting her life completely to the care of her father.

She does so with such fixation that her best friend, Harriet Mac-Gruder, warns Margaret, "You talk about *his* problems, what *he's* reading. You never start off with how *you* are. . . . it's not healthy. . . . watch out that it doesn't become a form of escape" (130). Harriet challenges Margaret to attend to her own life, saying, "But why not just get on with your *own* overall destiny?" (129). Instead, Margaret remains content to devote herself to her father's life (and "escape," as Harriet has said, the problem of her own character development). Margaret trusts her fate to others, "If I take care of my day-to-day responsibilities in good faith, then my future will take care of itself. I'll get a good ending, like the heroines in the books I like. Not necessarily a *happy* ending but one that I can accept as belonging to me" (152). But the future does not take care of itself. Margaret Gower is held responsible for her own destiny.

When Father Gower suddenly dies of a heart attack, Margaret comes to understand that, in awaiting passively the heroine's "good ending" by putting her father's life before her own, she has forfeited the role of heroine in her own story. Before his death, Reverend Gower has advised Margaret and their young friend, the Reverend Adrian Bonner,

[the Resurrection] means coming up through what you were born into, then understanding objectively the people your parents were and how they influenced you. Then finding out who you yourself are, in terms of how you carry forward what they put in you, and how your circumstances have shaped you. And then . . . and *then* . . . now here's the hard part! . . . You have to go on to find out *what* you are in the human drama, or body of God. The what *beyond* the who, so to speak. (276)

Margaret Gower finds, too, that she must resurrect and redeem herself. She has "sinned," as her father defines it, by avoiding the hard task of self-development, "falling short from [her] totality" (198). She has denied her own potential, allowing herself to be circumscribed by her father's needs and concerns.

In his final act before his death, Reverend Gower performs a healing ceremony, reconsecrating a Venetian statue of Christ—one that has watched over Saint Cuthbert's since Margaret's youth, only to tumble to destruction by miscreants. The statue can never be made perfect again, Reverend Gower admits, "[but] we can bless its broken pieces and respectfully lay it to rest" (308). Margaret Gower follows her father's lead as she begins to heal herself, blessing and laying the pieces of her broken family's past to rest in the final section of the novel. She begins to take responsibility for herself, no longer "want[ing] to be anyone's daughter anymore. . . . I want to be a grown woman with a grown woman's responsibilities" (348). In sifting through the rubble of the past—her love for her father; his mysterious bouts of melancholy; her parents' failed relationship; her mother's desertion of her father and betrayal of Margaret; as well as Madelyn Farley's culpability in luring her mother away from her family—Margaret starts to ask, "Where was my story? When was it going to begin? What would I have to go through to get to the beginning of it, or far enough into it to realize it *was* mine?" (351). It is her old enemy, the witch in her childhood closet, her mother's old friend, Madelyn Farley—with her talk about her new "provocative theater piece" *Holy Desire* on late-night television and her discussion of religion as a "binding together" of pieces "into something new" (353, 354)—who helps Margaret Gower find her new life. Despite her dead father's disapproval of female priests in the Episcopal church and the many obstacles she faces in choosing this controversial way of life, Margaret determines to study for the ministry—and star in a drama of her own.

Margaret is determined to create a whole self from all her scraps and pieces, much as her mother had fashioned her marvelous "Easter Egg" as a last gift for her daughter—a mosaic created from many materials by several different artists (herself, Madelyn Farley, and Madelyn's artistic father). As she prepares to face the challenges of her new life, Margaret reaches out to a large community of diverse individuals. In addition to her own soul-searching diary entries, her letters in the novel's epilogue form a variegated collage of those to her childhood friends; her fathers' former parishioners in Romulus, Virginia; former colleagues of her father; her college landlady; a former professor; and the staff of theological seminaries to which she is applying. She writes with affection to Ben MacGruder (whose love she has rejected) and to Father Adrian Bonner (who has rejected her love, but whose friendship she values and maintains). She lives temporarily with Madelyn Farley, helping to nurse her back to health after a recent operation, and cares, as well, for Madelyn's aged and querulous father. Margaret writes Ben MacGruder that she is not "'sacrificing my life' to the first parent figures I could grab at," in old-Margaret-Gower-fashion, as he has accused her of doing (398). She explains,

Three or four or even six months is not my life. At least I hope it isn't. And if it is, what should I be doing with it instead? Having arguments with you in Romulus or Charlottesville? At least these people need my services. I am good at taking care of older people. I've had some experience, you know. And I am learning valuable things from these two people. Disreputable as you may think they are, I am learning from them how important it is to be doing something you like doing every day until the end of your life, whether it is painting a landscape between coughing fits, or sketching sets for a new theater piece while your ribs mend over brand-new heart valves. (398)

Margaret continues to care for others—but not at the sacrifice of her own life. Now she takes care to nourish and fulfill herself, admitting, "I seem to be learning so many new things I am dizzy some days," feeling "increasingly amazed at the mysteries" of life around her (399). She has learned to combine ministry to others with ministry to her own inner self. She is determined now to live out her life doing what gives her joy and leads to her own spiritual growth. No longer caught in the past of her broken nuclear family, no longer Father Melancholy's dutiful daughter (and surrogate wife), no longer trapped in a drama that denies her own significance, Margaret Gower anticipates the future and delights in her own possibilities.[3]

Margaret Gower of *Father Melancholy's Daughter* learns to give *of* herself without giving *up* herself, a delicate balance that Godwin's heroines in her most mature and sophisticated works, *A Mother and Two Daughters* (1982) and *A Southern Family* (1987), struggle to find, as well. Through the complex structures of these two novels, with their multiple protagonists and multiple points of view, Gail Godwin poses challenging questions for her characters and the contemporary culture that forms their milieu. On the one hand, she voices the same concern that Cate Strickland of *A Mother and Two Daughters* identifies as the central issue of Hawthorne's *The Scarlet Letter*, "Can the individual spirit survive the society in which it has to live?" (179). Godwin seeks to show how strong individuals not only can survive the cruelties of their age (as do Hawthorne's Hester Prynne and the struggling protagonists of the contemporary novels Cate reads) but can affect their age to become what Hester Prynne was for her contemporaries, "the most positive force [her] community had!" (188). Godwin may mock contemporary writers through Cate's critique of their structural and thematic similarities, but they are (as she is) "at least . . . trying to stretch the limits of communal imagination and envision new ways to live. At the moment, they seem to be stuck in wilderness [female authors] or prison [male authors]—both excellent places for reflection and stoking up one's energies for what comes next: what have we done wrong, and how can we do better next time?" (443). Godwin seeks to go beyond such cultural "reassessment" (443) to create visions of new and better communities in her later works.

A Mother and Two Daughters focuses on the relationship of individual women to each other and to their society. Godwin asks, how can daughters reject family entrapment yet still maintain a positive relationship with family members; how can they show care for others without sacrificing themselves, at the same time; how can they develop their inner spirit and yet use their talents without being compromised by the chaos and danger of the world outside; and how can they be a part of the process of cultural change without adding to the modern forces of disorder and entropy everywhere about them? While the novel challenges traditions of white southern family and community by extending boundaries and renouncing social hierarchies, it also, as Katherine Payant notes, "suggests that female unity and community, how we treat our families and friends, can be a paradigm for how we treat each other in the larger fabric of the amorphous thing called 'society'" (62). Self-development and social development go hand in hand.

As the first chapter of *A Mother and Two Daughters* announces through its title, "The Old Guard," the white elders of Mountain City, North Carolina (the setting of *A Southern Family*, as well) are dying out. In particular, one of the most gentle and kind of this older generation, Leonard Strickland, no longer sits at the head of his table trying to maintain order and dignity in the emotionally turbulent lives of his wife, Nell, and daughters, Cate and Lydia. As Jane Hill has suggested, the novel begins by raising questions about its three heroines in the aftermath of Leonard Strickland's death:

Can they move forward? Can they "rescue" themselves? Can they draw on resources they have not previously been obliged to tap? Can they discover salvations in the midst of complications that arise, in part because of the patriarch's death and in part because of the inherent complexities of being female in a time when the old guard and its guardians are disappearing? Can Nell, Cate, and Lydia make new starts? (64-65)

Godwin's answer, Jane Hill finds, is affirmative as "all three women . . . work toward transformations of self" that lead to transformation of the family and society, as well: "The novel's epilogue replaces the shattered image of the nuclear family mourning the loss of its patriarch with a fluid and vibrant extended family, presided over by Cate, in many ways the least likely nurturer among them" (66).

Cate Strickland Galitsky is the daughter who has moved farthest away from home and been the least bound by the constraints of traditional womanhood, having divorced twice and, in the course of the novel, rejected a proposal of marriage from her multimillion-dollar industrialist lover, Roger Jernigan, and aborted their child. Cate, like Jane Clifford of *The Odd Woman*, is an itinerant English professor with a Ph.D. but little job security—a woman with a mind and life of her own that often put her at odds with her more conventional mother, Nell, her sister, Lydia, and Mountain City's "Old Guard" matriarch, her Aunt Theodora Blount. Cate's father has loved her but has worried about her independent lifestyle, her unstable professional life, and her defiant political stances (one of which, during the Vietnam War, brought about her arrest, cost her a job, and lost her Aunt Theodora's affection, at the same time). Ironically, Leonard Strickland punishes Cate for the very independence he admires in her, leaving her money in a trust fund that will assure her of $6000 income a year rather than paying her a lump sum (as with his traditional daughter, Lydia, who has never supported herself but, instead, moved from financial dependence on her father to dependence on her husband, Max). In *A Mother and Two Daughters*, Godwin reveals that Cate's female independence, though a disquieting force that works to bring about family disharmony and societal discord, can—through its insistence on honesty, fairness, love of self, and concern for others—lead to "a vision of community, within the family, the town, and, ultimately, the nation" (Josephine Hendin 3) that will foster a more caring society. In the epigraph of the novel's epilogue, taken from Ralph Waldo Emerson's "Success," self-development and individual strength are allied to community betterment: "We are not strong by our power to penetrate, but by our relatedness. The world is enlarged for us, not by new objects, but by finding more affinities and potencies in those we have" (523). In *A Mother and Two Daughters*, Cate works to "find more affinities" with those who are different from herself, including her mother and sister, increasing her sense of her own individuality as well as her influence upon her community in the process.

The inevitable end of white female assertion and independence need not be the fate experienced by Mountain City's "wildwoman," Taggart McCord, who, having "left her husband, joined the WAVES . . . , played piano in a nightclub, jumped out of airplanes, worked with poisonous snakes in a circus," ends up committing suicide (15). Theodora Blount has warned that "there's a limit to the traces anybody can kick over. I don't care how privileged or intelligent she is" (15-16). Yet the novel shows that women, black and white, need not dissipate their energies hopelessly, without self-understanding or societal purpose. Female independence need not lead to alienation from others or add to societal breakdown. In fact, the novel underlines Cate Strickland's assertion to her mother Nell that "what we need is a few more city *mothers*" (363), strong women who are willing to take purposeful action and play leadership roles in their society. American culture, Cate feels, desperately needs new and more thoughtful leadership:

I really do think we've blown it, Mother. Rich, promising, adventuresome, imaginative America has blown it. We started off with more than anybody else as a nation—more land, more dreams, more freedom—and just look what we've made of our abundance: we poison and blow one another up with our science and technology; we've bought pretty packaged lies for so long that if the truth walked into this restaurant right now we wouldn't recognize it; we've gotten lazy and smug and greedy and inept; no wonder our planes fall out of the sky and kill hundreds of people. . . . And the makers of nuclear reactors and sporty little cars don't give a damn how many people they poison or turn into human torches, as long as they can collect their sneaky profits. (362)

America's problems require adult leadership, Cate asserts, not "assholes like [Mountain City's] Latrobe Bell who sit up there in Washington and play at 'running the country' like it was some kind of *Monopoly* game, or something. Only nobody's told them that if they make a mistake, Mother's not going to comfort them with milk and brownies and tell them to get a good night's rest and they can start all fresh again tomorrow on a clean board" (362-63). However, if childish white men have been playing power games in Washington, childish white women have been unprepared to grow up and unwilling to take on leadership roles themselves.

As Godwin shows with her three heroines in *A Mother and Two Daughters*, white women, too, must work to achieve full adulthood and lead responsible lives in their communities. Female socialization, particularly in the American South, has undermined women's adult lives by requiring their subjugation to the family. Cate concludes that "nobody who is, first and foremost, a 'family member' has a hope in hell of becoming a whole person" (441). Returning home for her father's funeral, then reuniting with her mother and sister in the family cottage on the Outer Banks the following summer, Cate is reminded of why as a teenager "she had gone around in a more or less constant state of alienation from family" (440). She wonders,

Why in God's name did people form families? What made them imprison themselves in the separate pressure cookers referred to as "nuclear families"? Of course, children didn't form them; children came to consciousness and found themselves already bubbling away in the pot. But then what made these children grow up and start another pressure cooker all their own? What an unholy process! First the smug exclusion of all others, of the "outside world"; then the grim multiplication of oneself and one's partner behind closed doors; then the nauseating, unclean moiling about of all the family members in their "nuclear" caldron, bumping against one another, everyone knowing all too well everyone else's worst faults—all of them *stewing* themselves in one another's juices. (440)

Cate has resisted family claustrophobia and the lure of male protection, not to mention the powerful Dracula pull of sexual attraction that causes her "will to resist" to "ebb" away, leading her to an unhealthy desire "to be transformed. . . . A quick, clean bite by some outside force and it would all be done for you, you could stop trying" (65). Cate treasures her "will to resist" marriage, family, and tradition, maintaining her individual responsibility for "transforming" herself and the larger society of which she is a part. At the same time, she finds her ability to bring others together and establish community at the end of the novel depends on a newfound acceptance of differences within her own family and her willingness to mend broken relationships from the past. As she grows more secure about her own life choices, Cate becomes less threatened by and critical of family and friends—becoming more respectful of the varied contributions of others to community well-being.

During their Outer Banks vacation, Cate has belittled her sister Lydia's "little accomplishments" (460): Lydia's divorce from Max, her childhood sweetheart and the father of her two sons; her new relationship with a young Jewish podiatrist, Stanley Edelman; her friendship with two elite blacks, Renee Peverell-Watson and Calvin Edwards; her late-won college education; and her own woman's program on daytime television. Cate has accused Lydia of still existing in a "dollhouse," causing Lydia to lash back in pain: "Well, I may not set the world on fire . . . but at least I've never murdered anybody [alluding to Cate's recent abortion]. If that's 'creating yourself afresh,' I prefer my doll kingdom" (460). At the end of the novel, when Cate organizes a family reunion to celebrate Lydia's eldest son's marriage to Renee's daughter, joining white and black families together, she recognizes the need to heal the breach existing in her own family between herself and Lydia—the sister with whom she must "coexist . . . for decades more" (552). At the reunion, when Lydia compares herself to the now-militant Renee (who has added a law degree to her Ph.D. in sociology in order to combat the racism that has hurt both herself and Calvin Edwards in their adult lives), she admits to Cate,

"[Renee] makes me feel almost trivial sometimes. What good am I doing, really, showing people how they can be healthy and furnish their houses with taste on a budget and be powerful if they organize as consumers and parents? Compared with Renee, I'm so—" She went red in the face. Both sisters realized that Lydia had caught herself in the middle of accusing herself of the thing Cate, on that night five years ago, had accused her of.

"Don't underestimate what you do," said Cate. "People need to feel they can manage their lives. Where would we be if everybody despaired even of putting their own house in order?" (555)

Cate makes amends to her sister, paying her respects to all Lydia has done to change her life, become independent, and make her own contribution to society. Cate assures Lydia that she does help her female viewers manage their lives, budgets, and children more successfully, aiding them in developing their inner resources and affecting a larger world through their collective power as parents and consumers. Lydia may still be more traditional than Cate, but she, too, is driven by what her stepfather, Marcus Chapin, calls "a formidable sense of responsibility"—and Lydia, as a television personality, has acquired enough societal power to "call up the Governor and be put through at once for an interview, or raise a quarter of a million in donations for a youth center in one hour or cause a thousand women to return a certain brand of chutney to their supermarkets because the makers had cheated on the mangoes . . ." (561, 527). By taking responsibility for her own self-development, Lydia finds herself able to contribute to the betterment of her community.

Cate's mother, Nell, also has chosen to live out the rest of her life in a more conventional way than her daughter Cate—one that still enables her to further community well-being, as well. While she has reconciled herself to Leonard's death, finding simple pleasure and peace in the new solitude that comes to her at the age of sixty-three, Nell chooses to give up her quiet life to help others in her final years. Katherine Payant explains Nell's decision to nurse her friend Merle Chapin through a losing battle with cancer in this way:

Should Nell abandon the free life for one of traditional female nurturance, self-denying service, in a sense continuing to mother? Telling herself, "You can be self-contained in the coffin" [520], she nurses her friend, which leads her to further self-discoveries, including the desire to return to her pre-marriage career of nursing. (61-62)

Nell's husband, Leonard Strickland, tried to protect his wife and daughters from the vagaries of the world and "believed in the family as the bulwark of a moral and stable world" (54). Out from under Leonard's protection and the cloister of the nuclear family, Nell begins to extend her care to others beyond narrow family confines—nurturing others out of her newfound strength and skill rather than out of family subjugation and obligation. When Nell marries Marcus Chapin (who has emphysema) after nursing Marcus's wife, Merle, until her death, Nell feels she is enriching her life and fulfilling her own destiny, not betraying Leonard or her daughters:

she had asked Marcus if he also felt at times [a] sense of a double existence: one part of him in the present with her, and one part in the past with Merle. Of course he did, he had replied. And then they had lain in bed, holding each other, and remembering things about Merle and Leonard. It was almost as if the four of them were there, together. And then . . . well, that was another mysterious thing: how, at her age, at Marcus's age . . . how they could enjoy a side of life she had thought was over forever. A warmth spread over her whole body. (563-64)

Nell gives to others from her maturity and abundance, teaching classes in emergency techniques at the new Mountain City Rescue Center and taking the alcoholic Sicca Dowling into her home after Sicca's husband's death, "help[ing] her dry out" in a sunny basement "apartment overlooking the back garden" (536).

Further, Nell shows Cate that nurturing others and being nurtured by them need connote neither subservience nor weakness. When Cate is out of work, Nell offers to help her:

"But why not use your time looking for another teaching job, and let me tide you over until—"

"Mother, I am not going to be another Taggart McCord, sponging off Mother every time she—"

"You are *not* Taggart McCord!" Nell's vehemence shocked them both.

"You're alive; Taggart McCord's dead! When you're alive, you do what you *can* do. That's the duty, that's the privilege of the living." (474)

Nell *can* help Cate out and Cate *can* use her time in Mountain City to good purpose to find work that will allow her to support herself and help others (first through a New York grant foundation and then through free-lance teaching of special-interest courses she has designed and promoted). Cate learns from her mother, Nell, that accepting aid need not diminish her, that aid can be given with respect for individual adult choices.

The end of *A Mother and Two Daughters* marks a new beginning for its heroines. As John Breslin states,

The novel begins and ends with a party. But where the first commemorates an old order dying and concludes with a fatal accident, the latter celebrates a wedding and a new order being born. . . . the story is a comedy in the classic sense, moving from dispersion to reunion. . . . the women's lives are unmistakably late twentieth-century American: mid-life identity crises, academic vagabondage, interracial permutations. Nell Strickland and her two daughters, Cate and Lydia, perform their family dance of estrangement and reconciliation to the music of a society so rapidly in transition that even massive physical landmarks have simply disappeared, like the hill in the middle of Mountain City, or been transformed beyond recognition, like the orchard of Nell's private school now part of a shopping mall. Fragile human constructs like marriage or civility or contractual obligations fare less well still. (305)

Yet, despite the breakdown of the old order, a new order is taking its place. Civility and obligation are undergoing redefinition. Jonathan

Yardley explains that "the extended family that in the end gathers to celebrate itself . . . [is] nothing less than the family of humanity, in all its flawed and perfect glory" (3). Cate's nephew Leo has married Renee Peverell-Watson's British-trained daughter Camilla—bringing American, British, and African cultures together at one time. The new family integrates lower-class Appalachia with upper-class North Carolina in highlighting Wickie Lee's acceptance by the aristocratic Theodora Blount and in staging Cate's family reunion in the simple home and grounds that she inherited from her "hillbilly" relative Uncle Osgood. Godwin also shows how the extended family can bridge divorce in Lydia's sorrow over her ex-husband Max's death and her love for his young daughter, Lizzie, the child of Max's second marriage. Not only does Lydia help Max's second wife by accepting parental responsibility for Lizzie but so also do Lydia's mother, Nell; her two grown sons, Leo and Dickie; and Lydia's Jewish lover, Stanley. In this new age, racial and social tolerance must be integrated into the extended family—one where the aristocratic Theodora and her long-time, black maid, Azalea, share old age together separated only by a bedroom wall, and Cate's rejected, midwestern, wealthy entrepreneur lover, Jernigan, feels welcome to join in the embrace of her eclectic family.

Josephine Hendin describes the novel's spiritual ascendance in this way:

As Lydia moves toward independence, as Cate strives toward a greater acceptance of others, and as their mother reconstructs her life, Miss Godwin achieves a richness of affirmations. In this generous novel, illness and age are enablers. And if time has taken the illusions and promises of youth from these women, it has also pressed them toward recognizing the serious courtesy due one another's pain. In one of the best-realized episodes of the novel Cate, whose face is temporarily paralyzed by Bell's palsy, reaches accord with a former high school friend whose leg was shattered in the Vietnam War. Anti-war activist and veteran—both battered by their choices—comfort each other with exquisite simplicity. (14)

In the process of working on their own self-development, Cate, Lydia, and Nell become more tolerant of each other, more accepting of difference in the world around them, and more capable of creating a caring community.

In *A Southern Family*, Godwin continues to explore the jealousies and hatreds, the dark interior of "the family caldron" (371), to reach a similar point: individual survival and community well-being depend on individual development; respect for each other's pain; and tolerance for

differing perspectives. The story is told from the varied points of view of
Lily Quick; Clare Campion (Lily's daughter); Ralph Quick (Clare's
upwardly-mobile stepfather); Rafe Quick (Clare's stepbrother); Felix
(Clare's Viennese-Jewish lover); Julia Richardson (Clare's lifelong
friend); Sister Patrick (a Quick family friend who left Ireland for Bel-
gium and became a nun in America); and Snow Mullins (Theo Quick's
Appalachian ex-wife). All have shared a relationship with Theo Quick—
who at the outset of the novel kills a woman, then himself, in a mysterious act of murder-suicide which bewilders and haunts his family and
friends.[4] Each survivor has a different interpretation of Theo's character
and his violent death—a perspective that grows out of the differing
gender, class, national and ethnic backgrounds of each individual, as
well as out of each one's particular relationship with Theo Quick himself. What emerges in the novel is the destructive family pattern of this
white southern family and the importance, as in other Godwin works, of
breaking away from family entrapment (as Theo failed to do) to seek fulfillment of one's personal and social potential.

Lily Quick—whom Snow Mullins calls the "Queen Mother" of the
Quick family—has established, in true white "southern lady" fashion, a
destructive pattern of denial and evasion, "meant to protect individual
family members from their failures and limitations, from pain and
shame. Yet the protective stories and secrets have a sinister on-going
function. They block the acceptance of reality and prevent the growth of
individual family members," as Kim Lacy Rogers states (63). Rogers
argues that Lily Quick's lies about her "independence" as a young widowed fiction writer and newspaper reporter (Ralph Quick recalls that
Lily's mother had to balance her checkbook for her and that Lily Campion begged him to marry her and take care of her and her young daughter Clare during this period of "independence" [469]) kept Lily from
"fac[ing] her own limitations as a woman and a mother . . . [and] helped
create impossible expectations for her own children. . . . [resulting in]
Clare's constant sense of impending failure, Rafe's chronic drinking, and
Theo's depression, his passive-aggressive behavior, his suicide" (63).
The Quick family lives in its own closed-off world, an "oxygen-deprived
pressure chamber of family life" (42), with the bickering Lily and Ralph
at the center. In their remote house on the hill, the Quicks, according to
family friend Julia Richardson, "[have] shut themselves up inside, closed
all the windows, turned on the heat or the air-conditioning . . . and continued to provoke and intrigue and smolder, oblivious to the peace and
beauty of their immediate surroundings" (21). They have created an
environment that is physically, emotionally, and mentally unhealthy for
all of them.

Whenever Clare, Lily's eldest child (now a successful novelist), returns to Mountain City, she finds herself regressing to a state of childish helplessness and inadequacy. Entering the Quick family "pressure chamber" (42), she

> had the dismal sensation of never having left home. It was as if, after all, the core of her had never escaped, never traveled or lived in Europe, or met Felix, or written and published books; this part of her remained forever stuck in the nightmare of adolescence, where she would always be thirteen or fourteen, trapped inside the decisions Lily had made, and subject to the whims and tyrannies of Ralph. For some reason, yet—or never—to be discovered, the part of her old life she could not seem to outgrow, from which no amount of love or distance or success had been able to free her, was located somewhere within the rise and fall of those two voices [Ralph's and Lily's] and the world they engendered and perpetuated between them: a place at once provoking and sorrowful and treacherous and vengeful and duplicitous and miasmic—yet perversely compelling. (109)

A part of Clare remains trapped in her adolescent past, angered and threatened by Lily's marriage to Ralph Quick. If the "dynamic, unconventional" (15) Lily Campion could regress to dependence and frail femininity so completely after her marriage to Ralph Quick, if she could remain permanently locked in a hostile relationship with a man she hated but also needed (447), what could prevent her daughter, Clare, from succumbing to her own weaknesses? Clare confesses to her Viennese lover, Felix, that even though she has kept her father's name of Campion, she, too, is a Quick: "[I knew] that [my family would] screw things up just as they always do. As *we* always do. Because I'm one of them, God help me" (443).

Yet Clare does not remain locked in the Quick family past, as she fears, and even Lily is able to make some progress in her life by the end of the novel. Family can, of course, be the destroyer Clare fears it to be—"Well, if guns don't kill you," she has said after Theo's funeral, "families will" (162). The Quick family, in fact, has defeated Clare's stepbrother, Theo, as all agree, whatever other differences there may be in their interpretations of his tragic end. His ex-wife, Snow, theorizes, "Theo was never allowed to live his own life or be his own self. In a sense, it was his own family that killed him, and he let them do it" (238). While families can destroy their own members, individuals can (and must), *A Southern Family* reveals, refuse to comply—must, in Cate Strickland Galitsky's words from *A Mother and Two Daughters*, preserve the "will to resist" whatever threatens to negate the self (65). Theo complied in his own destruction, as Snow understood, allowing himself to become "the battleground" between Lily and Ralph and the Quick "family sacrifice" (309, 238) that Clare steadfastly refuses to become.

Some, such as Clare's lover, Felix, have been "lucky" in their families. Felix had had "a happy childhood" (305) but then "had lost his family at ten" in World War II (295). Felix wonders, when he looks at "the troubling family unit of Quicks . . . how each of them might have been different if, as had happened to himself, fate had untied the knot of family earlier in life" (296). Cut off early from family ties, Felix has felt free to follow his own interests, using his artistic talents as opportunity allowed him, becoming an executive producer with a New York theater of his own. He has not lingered over the tragedy of his family past—as he finds southerners doing, "heavy with history. . . . still carrying a grievance [which] . . . makes them feel separate and proud," dwelling in their own sad past (299)—but has moved forward through life without self-pity:

Not infrequently, Felix found himself in the odd position of feeling embarrassed by his good fortune, by his confident and relatively easy passage through life so far. He and Clare often discussed this: how, despite the fact that both his parents had been killed in a London air raid before they could join him in America, he had managed to retain his exuberance and his optimistic temper. (305-06)

The pattern of Felix's life suggests one route to mature development and meaningful social interaction: freedom from family ties and optimistic forward movement.

Julia Richardson, Clare's lifelong friend, has chosen another direction—one that might have resulted in personal diminishment had she not already undertaken Jung's " task of personality" as a young adult.. The pattern of Julia's life suggests that family ties need not destroy individuals if there is enough respect, tolerance, and privacy within the family to allow for individual expression and self-development. Julia chooses to give up her independent life as an historian in New York (following an earlier four-year marriage and divorce) to help her father after her mother becomes mentally ill. Julia resists her mother's harshness toward her throughout her illness, as she resisted her mother's negative influence as a girl, and enjoys a harmonious life with her father after her mother's death. She continues to teach history at the local community college, feeling "whatever she had lost, or missed, in her life, she knew she could count on her work always to interest her" (40). Further, she admits that she has come to value solitude as her "most natural state" (47), and in the company of a father who also needs privacy, Julia is afforded the distance necessary to sustain their close family relationship. Most importantly, through her self-sacrifice in caring for her parents, Julia is able to transcend her harmful mother. As Kim Lacy Rogers explains,

But even before the collapse of her mind, Mrs. Richardson was an awful woman—status-obsessed, foolishly addicted to her own good looks, hostile when Julia divorced the wealthy heir of a plantation family. By returning to care for her mother, Julia repudiated her mother's life and became her mother's opposite: responsible, nurturing to her friends, firmly grounded—as a historian—in reality. (62)

Julia combats the negative forces at work in her own family by returning home, giving *of* herself (but not giving *up* herself), finding personal and professional fulfillment in her return to Mountain City. Her return to the role of daughter remains a facet of Julia's character development, one that allows her to merge her personal autonomy with care for others. Upon the death of her father, she will need to explore other, broader, possibilities.

Similarly, Felix's daughter, Lizzie, chooses a traditional way of life, marriage, and conversion to Orthodox Judaism. Clare feels that Lizzie is probably deluded by youthful naivete in believing that she can "liv[e] a life where I no longer have to think of myself as the most important person in the world" (490). Yet, as Clare tells Lizzie's bewildered father, Felix, Lizzie probably has chosen this life as a way of finding out more about herself rather than simply denying herself, as she believes she is doing. When Felix complains, "She's been brought up an American girl, with the whole world open to her. Why should she want to shut herself up in a box of tiresome, outdated old rules? Especially since she didn't even *like* Israel. I don't understand. . . . I don't want my Lizzie to lose her Lizzie-ness," Clare replies, "Maybe what she's doing is searching through Jewishness to see if she can find any lost parts of herself. . . . Maybe she's looking for *more* Lizzie-ness" (412, 414). Having known personal freedom in her youth, Lizzie now chooses a traditional life. She is, Clare hopes, in the process of exploring different facets of herself that will both make her more an individual and join her to others in positive ways.

In Godwin's works, according to Jane Hill, it becomes the obligation of all those who are seeking to lead responsible, caring lives to free themselves from the negative influences of their families and culture—to work to find their best selves (9). It is not enough to go along with one's circumstances, as Clare Campion recognizes in critiquing her own writing in *A Southern Family*: "I mean, God, Julia, what if my effects, such as they are, have been achieved simply by learning to satisfy the tastes of the culture that shaped me, rather than trying to sniff out its rotten spots or going beyond it in my imagination? If that's all I've done, what use does that make me to the present or the future?" (51).

Clare realizes the power of outside influences upon every individual, including herself, wondering, "What of me is singularly *mine,* and would be so regardless of whom I was born to and how or where I grew up? What of anybody's was purely her own or his own, if you took away family and religion and upbringing and social class?" (424). As a writer, Clare has used her imagination to extend her own experience by learning about other people's lives "from inside" which "freed her to go on to other human mysteries" (433). She has written about Julia Richardson's southern family in one novel and, over the last three summers on vacation in the Fauquiers' "No Saints" island cottage, studied the aristocratic ways of a people

not interested in impressing others anymore . . . [she has come to understand] why they took a dégagé and fatalistic attitude towards the inevitable decay all around them, an attitude extending from refrigerator wires corroded by sea air to their own deaths. . . . They had transcended the personal, in a way. Everything worth pushing and shoving for had already been won by predecessors. . . . Now one polished the silver for special occasions, or cherished the president's chair, and while waiting for individual extinction, did one's loyal best for one's own family, or served others who were fighting to hang on, or who did not seem to realize that the best days of civilization were over. (432)

But Clare, as a writer who explores human potential, is committed to the future, working to improve herself and her society, not chained (like the Fauquier family) to the past.

Just as Snow Mullins must learn to resist the worst in her Appalachian background, with its racism, its "apathy, blindness to beauty, a refusal to be responsible even for your immediate surroundings" (346), if she is to grow and develop, Clare—by maintaining her relationship with Snow and visiting Snow and Theo's son, Jason, (her nephew) in the village of Granny Squirrel—challenges her own self-satisfaction "as loving chronicler of the complacent middle class, to take an astringent little descent into the land of the have-nots and come to some compassionate understanding of why not everyone can make it" (366). In Granny Squirrel, Clare enters another kind of reality less pleasant than any she has written about or experienced herself. She seeks to grow both as a person and an author from that experience. She also learns from

Theo's criticism of her writing on the eve of his death: "You let [your characters] suffer a little, just enough to improve their characters, but you always rescue them [Theo tells Clare] . . . and reward them with love or money or the perfect job—or sometimes all three" (49). Clare admits her attraction to romantic subjects and endings, confessing to Julia,

Theo taught me something, whether he had read my books or not. He was speaking out of his knowledge of *me* that afternoon. . . . I won't let things be themselves. I arrange things around me the way I want them . . . the way I need them to be . . . and shut the rest out. I shut Theo out all of his life because he didn't fit into the life I intended to have for myself. (371)

Acknowledging her own responsibility for Theo's unhappiness, Clare throws away the novel on which she has been working, and begins, as Kim Lacy Rogers argues,

a long, honest letter to Theo—presumably the seed for *this* novel. . . . In short, she tries to understand her brother's life on its own terms, refusing the familiar dark tangle of the family narrative. In this effort Clare finally frees herself from the deceptions and evasions of her mother's life, her happy endings, her fatalistic and false charm. She moves, in fact, beyond her mother's story of her life and into her own. Clare renounces what is essentially a daughter's story—one that maintains memory and history by remembering and retelling others' stories. In making the break with her role as daughter, Clare moves beyond a replication and repetition of her mother's life and into something more authentically independent: a story that is free of the fantasies imposed by her mother's failure of will. (65)

Clare overcomes her negative family background to embrace a larger, if more real and imperfect, world and create a more compassionate and realistic self.

Even Lily Quick begins to change and grow in the aftermath of Theo's death. In her volunteer work with the elderly, she has become "increasingly involved in preserving the dignity of the ones who weren't as lucky as Mother [who died quickly]. I can't stand it when they're treated like idiot children or . . . or garbage waiting to be taken out, or something. I get so angry. Every one of them is a unique personality. . . . no two personalities—*no two*—are ever alike" (525). Yet Lily has had trouble accepting the reality and respecting the individuality of members of her own family, either denying them love when they refuse to please her or making them over into images of what she would like them to be.

However, Theo's public and violent death has made her habits of evasion and denial more difficult to sustain. His tragic murder-suicide, making headlines as it does, can neither be ignored nor transformed. Further, through his marriage to Snow, Theo has forced Lily into contact with the poverty, ignorance, and deprivation she has tried to rise above. Now Theo's son, Jason, insists that his grandmother acknowledge the integrity of those she has disdained, demanding that she not refer to Snow as "a laid-back hillbilly" (530) but show his mother the respect she deserves. Later, when Lily tells Sister Patrick about Jason's confused life, divided between the Mullinses in Granny Squirrel and the Quicks in Mountain City, Sister Patrick counsels her, saying, "[It] doesn't sound all bad. . . . [Jason] has so many people to love him, to teach him different things" (531). Lily finally admits that the complexity of Jason's life could become an advantage for him, Headstart classes and all, revealing her personal growth when she acknowledges,

You're right. . . . That's the way I'm going to have to try and see it. Mrs. Mullins will teach him to dig potatoes and make biscuits, and all his rough little cousins will teach him to be tough and protect himself, and if I can just teach him to expect the most of himself and help shape his ideals, I will die a happy woman. It's what I care about most, seeing that child grow up strong and intelligent, without being damaged irrevocably by his early bad luck. It's what I am living for now. When Clare called yesterday from Switzerland, to wish me happy birthday, I could tell she was a little disappointed that I didn't get more excited about our relatives in Switzerland. Ten years ago, I might have been. But "roots" don't matter to me much anymore. Ancestors-in-common are just more antique clutter and old debris. I care about what's here for me to do *now*. (531-32)

Lily focuses on her work in the present, the part she can play in helping her grandson Jason develop, and the task she shares with the other members of Jason's extended family in building his future. Lily's family and her community have been enlarged, necessarily, through the course of the novel to include those of different races (her masseuse, Thalia, and Theo's friend LeRoy); religions (Felix); social classes (Snow and the rest of the Mullinses); and nationalities (Sister Patrick and Felix). As in *A Mother and Two Daughters,* so, too, in *A Southern Family*, Godwin's female characters learn to relate to a larger world, tolerate human difference, and envision a more promising future. As Jane Hill has concluded, "Nowhere in her earlier work does Godwin attain such wholehearted respect for a spectrum of essential selves as she manages in *A Southern Family*" (102).

Throughout her novels, Godwin exposes the problems of failing to grow up, escape family entrapment, and cast off the burdens of the past. Her most successful protagonists work to develop a self strong enough to withstand the negative, regressive forces in their lives. Only when they have undertaken the difficult task of developing their own characters can they begin to re-engage with their southern families and communities in positive ways. Finding a successful integration of work, self, and society in their own lives, they begin, then, to help others become more socially responsible and tolerant. Their personal development extends from concern for the self to concern for others; from escape from the nuclear family to a reaffirmation of "family" reconstituted as a more socially inclusive unit; from fear of the larger world to embracing its challenges and shaping a more humane future. Along with Clare Campion of *A Southern Family*, Godwin seeks a vision based not on "false hope" (319) for the future, or narcissistic love for the past, but one that builds on the "constructive sorrow" of deeply felt and processed human experience—life engaged in as widely and as fully as possible (Godwin, "Journals" 195).

It is this full—but not necessarily happy—life that Gail Godwin presents in her novel *The Good Husband* (1994). In this work, each of her four main characters—Magda Danvers and her husband, Francis Lake, as well as their friends Alice and Hugo Henry—carries out the difficult "task of personality"—leading not to happy endings but to the wholeness of self which is their spiritual obligation to themselves and to the world. As Magda Danvers explains to Father Floris,

What we feel *compelled to do*, whether it's making art or giving your life to God—I personally don't think there's any difference between the two—evolves out of the inner fabric of our lives, however disguised the patterns may be to us. The work, the vocation, is an attempt on the part of the would-be artist, or the would-be religious, to fulfill *in an inner way, in a symbolic way* what the outer world is failing to provide him with in the service of wholeness. (24)

In fulfilling their spiritual obligations, husbands and wives may lose each other—as they do in this novel; nevertheless, Godwin reveals that they can still find personal fulfillment and the service they must provide the world, each in his or her own distinctive way.

Francis Lake and Magda Danvers have been "mates who aren't matched" but have found that "this can be a very happy arrangement" (24). Theirs has been a nearly perfect marriage—with Francis fulfilled in his house-husband role caring for Magda, and Magda flourishing in her public role as sought-after and much-admired intellectual. Yet Francis, who has existed until Magda's death "in the radiance of the[ir] partnership" (196), finds himself alone at the novel's end, while Magda, too, has had to face her "Final Exam" on her own, coming to terms with the life she has lived and the death that awaits her, acknowledging, "I have been successful, theatrically successful, if I may say so, in infecting receptive young minds with a desire for wholeness. . . . [yet] I haven't provided the wholeness myself. . . . I was basically an arouser, not a fulfiller" (168). A month after her death, Francis confirms his wife's self-assessment, writing to his mentor, Father Birkenshaw,

One might say she worked to the very end, because it was important to her to understand the meaning of everything, even her own death. I know she has influenced many lives for the better. She certainly influenced mine. She was much beloved by many others as well as by me, and I'm still wondering how I'm going to get on without her. But I'm so grateful to have shared a life with her for what would have been twenty-five years this coming November. (330-31)

But "get on without her" Francis must—and *can*—as he learns when he returns to do odd jobs at his former religious seminary, undergoing the spiritual tutelage of the elderly Father Birkenshaw. Writing to Alice Henry, Francis explains,

Now, through having been accepted as part of the community here, and from my talks with Father Birkenshaw, I've sorted out what I can leave behind and what I want to take away with me. There are many things I might do next, I have some pretty concrete ideas, but I'd like to have the benefit of your advice. Several days before he died, Father B. said a wonderful thing to me. . . . "You know, Francis, just as the monks kept learning alive in the Dark Ages, it's going to be people like you who keep human kindness and charity alive in ours." (465)

Francis learns to value himself and find his own vocation in a world that sorely needs his service of kindness and charity only after his service to his beloved Magda has ended.

The other couple in *The Good Husband*, Alice and Hugo Henry, are perfectly "matched" (unlike Magda and Francis) but not well "mated" (24). They are each other's intellectual equals—Alice as a capable and successful literary editor and Hugo as a well-known, talented novelist (her client). Upon the loss of their newborn child, however, they find that they no longer have a future together. Hugo begins to commit himself to a new novel through which he "knew [he] could address important longings and woes of his own" (328), admitting to himself, "the truth is, anybody can live without anybody" but books "last" (329). He writes a friend, explaining, "As a close friend of my son's [from an earlier marriage], a very educated and generous philanthropist—actually, he's my son's companion—recently said to me: We can't be free until we can tell our story, and only by telling it convincingly can we each do our bit to help the world grow up" (422). Hugo remains engaged in telling his story as truthfully as he possibly can, facing up to his own demons and, thereby, trying to help "the world grow up," as well. He retains his friendship with Alice beyond their divorce, writing her on the anniversary of their child's death, "He would have been two today. It didn't come to pass, the flowering of his life, or that life we might have had, but other good things will. I truly believe that, Alice, and I also believe there is no one who deserves those good things more than you" (459). Freed from marriage to Alice, Hugo can begin to show care for her again.

Alice, who has had to face far too many endings already in her life—the deaths by car crash of her mother, father, and brother, as well as the death of her infant son and the end of her marriage to Hugo Henry—nevertheless learns, with the help of her dying friend Magda, to accept that endings can be "open" as well as "closed," positive as well as negative. As Hugo has said, in creating open endings in fiction (as Gail Godwin has come to do, as well), the novelist must show that

some implicit wisdom deeper than consciousness has guided [characters'] fates all along. . . . If [the author] has been a good creator, you can say, yes, that's okay, they're going their separate ways, but it's the way it has to be for these particular people. . . . In this case, the attraction of each of them going their separate ways, *but having somewhere else to go that is right for them*, is more powerful to the reader than the old satisfaction of seeing them safely at home in each other's arms. (416)

Alice finds that she does have somewhere else she must go and things she must do on her own, after her separation from Hugo. Alone in Magda and Francis's house, doing her freelance editing, Alice writes Francis that she has been "given a second chance to finish my youth in a house where people close to me have lived and moved about their rooms and made their histories together in those rooms. Living in the house you two made together and shared has given me back my sense of *home*, something I hadn't had enough of when I lost mine" (463). She and Francis Lake have not married, as Alice had hoped, but Francis remains her friend and confidant, needing her advice and wanting her to stay on in his house ("I've also come to think of you as being part of the house, and if you are agreeable, I am sure we can work something out" [466]), realizing that, together, they have become a "family," of sorts. As Alice writes to Francis of the adolescent Elberta (an unhappy girl adopted by an Aurelia College benefactor before Magda Danvers's death), "you and I are a bit of Elberta's 'home' in the same way you and Magda are part of mine" (463). Family bonds have been extended beyond traditional boundaries once more in Godwin's *The Good Husband*, as they were also in *A Southern Family* and *A Mother and Two Daughters*. Alice Henry and Francis Lake remain in contact with Magda Danvers's spiritual legacy after her death; Alice and Hugo Henry remain friends despite their recent divorce; Francis Lake and Alice Henry continue to "parent" the difficult Elberta without being married to each other or living together with their spiritual "daughter"; and natural parents learn to love their children and rid themselves of prejudice, as Hugo Henry must do with his son Cal's lover Lawrence—learning to accept not only that his son is gay but also that he is in love with a black man. Alice, Hugo, and Francis have important work to do in the world before their own endings, as does Magda Danvers until the morning of her death: Hugo using his writing talents to tell the truth and foster "maturity" in himself and the world; Alice using her editing skills to help writers such as Hugo live up to their potential for truth; and, together, joining Francis Lake in "keeping kindness and charity alive" (465) through their own personal relationships with one another and in the world at large. They are taking responsibility for their own lives and for creating a more positive future for their societies, as have the protagonists of Godwin's *A Southern Family* and *A Mother and Two Daughters,* before them.

5

Other Contemporary Authors
and Their Fictional Worlds

The novels of Shirley Ann Grau, Anne Tyler, and Gail Godwin represent a small part of a virtual outpouring of works by contemporary southern women authors. It would be impossible to deal simply with the novels of the last three decades alone (even the best of these) in one study. Yet the patterns we have been tracing in the recent works of the three authors under consideration can be found in the novels of a majority of their contemporaries, as well. In a changing South and a changing America—a society where the father's voice of authority has dissipated —contemporary white southern women writers and their protagonists admit to their confusion. Yet they seldom express nostalgia for the simpler, more clearly formulated structures of the past. Instead, white southern women writers continue to reveal personal and social misery at the heart of the patriarchal tradition; the need for women to resist entrapment in houses of the past, for their own good, as well as that of their families and communities; and the importance of female self-realization for the reformation of contemporary society.

Paralleling Grau: Haunted by the Past

A number of contemporary white southern women writers share Shirley Ann Grau's obsession with the patriarchal past—the negative consequences of male dominance and the resulting passivity and child-like dependence of women on men. They reveal that few have profited— even a majority of men—from society's patriarchal arrangements. Competition and jealousy over the ownership of women and property have separated white men from each other, as well as from women and blacks, resulting in murder in Louise Shivers's *Here To Get My Baby Out of Jail* (1983) and Ellen Douglas's *The Rock Cried Out* (1979). In *Here To Get My Baby Out of Jail*, lower-class Jack Ruffin envies Aaron Walston his small, post-Depression farm and his attractive wife, Roxanna, eventually murdering Aaron to run away with Roxy. Dependent first on her father and then, at sixteen, on Aaron; isolated from the company of others on their outlying farm and from a husband who never "really thought about [anything other than]. . . the tobacco crop" (12); burdened by the care of a baby and a house, yet desirous of more, Roxy says, "I'd thought at the time we got married that men got out and did things, made things happen, but life on the farm was just one long hard day after another" (91). Roxy feels confused by "that ragged discontent that came over me. I'd think: You've got a good husband, a pretty house on a good farm. What else could you want?" (49). She succumbs easily to Jack's attentions toward her.

Eager for the love and companionship Jack offers when he comes to help at the farm, then stunned by the murderous outcome of what she had seen as tenderness, intimacy, and joyous passion, Roxy wonders, "How had I let this thing happen between Jack and Aaron? How had Daddy let it happen? How had Aaron let it happen? But most of all, how had I let it happen? . . . How could I have been so weak and drifting to let it come to this?" (106). Only now does Roxy sense within "a self growing. I'd never had a self before" (110), realizing at the trial, as she looks at her father, "I saw I was still expecting way too much from this big-boned man. No matter how many tangerines he brought at Christmastime and pieces of sugar cane he'd walk up with in his hand, I couldn't keep on hiding from the bad things in the world by forever riding around with him in my mind" (139). After Jack is sentenced to death, and Roxy has been denounced in the community for her unfaithfulness, Roxy determines, finally, to salvage a life for herself and her child by assuming control of her life, no longer remaining dependent on a father, husband, or lover, but standing firm and "steer[ing] . . . into something good and strong. I aim to find something" (139). With Jack in jail, she realizes that she too has existed far too long "in a little dusty jail inside my own self ever since I'd been born. With Jack I'd only gotten deeper into a black-barred jail [of female weakness and subservience to men]" (144).

It is to the memory of her grandmother Georgeanna and the direction of her stepmother Ruth that Roxy turns now for female help in shaping a new, more constructive life for herself and her daughter. Although her father has wanted her to go away for awhile to live with a distant relative, Roxy decides to stay on with her family upon her stepmother Ruth's recommendation. Ruth has argued to Roxy's father,

[Roxy is] always doing something some man thought she ought to do. How can she go off to Virginia or anywhere else? She needs to learn how to do some things first. Some civilized things. . . . She can stay right here with us for a while and ride it out just the same as we will. She and Baby can learn along with Callie [Roxy's young stepsister], right here in this house. Then, when she's able and gets good and ready, she can go wherever she chooses. (146)

If Roxy can be successful in her self-development, she will be able to help her daughter, Baby, become less dependent on men, as well as more creative, caring, and thoughtful in making early life choices than Roxy herself has been.

In Ellen Douglas's *The Rock Cried Out*, the jealousy of a young boy over a beautiful girl's attentions, his need to prove his manhood to himself and to her, results, ironically, in the 1964 death of the very girl he desires. The boy, Dallas Boykin, follows his father, Mac, unreflectingly, absorbing from him southern, racist, paternalistic values, rejecting the contrasting ways of his dying mother (who reports the activities of the local Ku Klux Klan in which her husband has been involved to the FBI and the Justice Department before her death, believing it up to women to expose and destroy the Klaverns and end white male violence and hatred of blacks). When Mac Boykin takes the young Dallas and his brother Lindsay Lee to Ku Klux Klan meetings, "it made kids like us feel like men to go off with [them] in the pickup trucks and go to somebody's house where there were nothing but men and a few older boys and talk about men's business. Especially since there seemed to be some danger in it and it was a secret from everybody" (262). For teenagers, it seemed just a game at the time, but Dallas reflects, years later,

I think it was a game to some of them [the adult men], too. They did it like they did the football and baseball, because it was what they were expected to do. And then it turned into something else and some of them were bewildered and ashamed. But their daddies had said: This is true. Do this. And how could they turn their backs and shame their daddies and call them sinners and criminals? They had to go on. (279)

Dallas isn't thinking about black-white relations at the time, any more than some of the men are; instead, he is trying to distinguish himself as a young male to impress Phoebe, going to meetings and carrying guns, thinking, "she'd know I was a man if she could see me now" (273). White male power—the need to be seen as strong and to dominate women and minorities—lies at the center of these Klan activities.

Then, as Dallas spies with his brother and father on the black Mercy Seat Church from up on a hill, he sees a car, on its way to the church, driven by the black Sam Daniels—and next to him, the beautiful, white Phoebe in the front passenger seat. Years later, Dallas tells Alan McLaurin, the protagonist of the novel and another of Phoebe's young admirers,

I saw him and then her through the sights of the gun and I didn't even see the wife in the back. To me it was the two of them alone together. . . .

"Look at that," Lindsay Lee said, whispering right in my ear. "She *touched* him. Look!"

I squeezed down.

I must have meant to do it. I didn't mean to do it. . . . The windshield exploded, glass flashing in the air, and it was like looking at a flock of birds through the scope, very close and very far away. . . . Everything was over before I knew what I had done. The car was at the bottom of the ravine. (281-82)

In a matter of seconds, Phoebe is dead, her throat cut by flying glass, and Sam Daniels's wife, Timmie, has burned to death in the backseat of their car.

Since that time, Dallas has carried the burden of his guilt with him—first off to Vietnam where he continued to kill and to feel racial hatred for "gooks" and "slopes" (75, 258), then back home where he married Lorene, asking her

to help me carry [the guilt] because we were married and I [gave] her all I had which included that. . . . [After their child was born] I told her that I knew what I was like, that I knew my soul was treacherous and full of rage and hate, that I could do terrible things—even to my own boy or maybe to her—and it was then that we decided I would have to go and make it right with the people I had wronged, or I would never come through. And so I'm telling, everything, everything, because that's the only way. (283)

Dallas's attempt to end his own cycle of violent action ironically triggers violence in the pacifist Alan McLaurin. A conscientious objector who performed public service at home rather than fight in Vietnam, Alan suddenly turns on Dallas and attempts to kill him for destroying his beloved cousin Phoebe years before. Now a sensitive, aspiring writer, Alan must face his own capacity for hatred and violence; he is no longer able to believe that he is morally pure. Alan concludes, "I knocked off being pure the day I strangled Dallas" (295), acknowledging his own participation in Mississippi's violent regional history and his own need for personal, spiritual redemption.

While Alan McLaurin and Dallas Boykin try to atone for their violence and rise above the cultural influences that have shaped them, ending cycles of white male competition, dominance, and hatred, other men in the writings of contemporary white southern women authors are shown succumbing to their feelings of insecurity and rage, venting anger upon the women and children in their lives (as Dallas Boykin worries he will begin to do) and growing more and more violent as their fears increase. In Jayne Anne Phillips's *Machine Dreams* (1984) and Martha

Stephens's *Children of the World* (1994), husbands and fathers take little comfort in their traditional, hierarchical superiority as white males, for there are always other men who are more successful than they are and who constantly remind them of their comparative inadequacies as role models and providers. In *Machine Dreams*, Jean tells her daughter, Danner, how her rich father's lumber business had failed, the Depression had descended upon the family, and her mother had used her resourcefulness, canning and sewing for the family, providing a little income for them all by selling milk, cream, butter, and cheese. Jean remembers her father's anger and despair growing into insanity, recalling,

My father got worse as time went on. . . . One autumn we were burning trash on the hill. He picked up a pitchfork of blazing leaves and chased Mother around the fire. After that we had to have him put away. A couple of weeks later, a guard knocked him down and that was all. I was fourteen. . . . We both felt such relief. We'd been ashamed to send him there, but we'd gotten afraid of him and had no money for anything better. I didn't know until he was gone what a shadow he'd cast. (7-8)

Now Jean's own husband Mitch has become ill-tempered and abusive as his insecurities have increased along with his family responsibilities, age, and financial worries. Selling large construction machines after the sale of the family business, Mitch "earn[ed] less and less" each year. As her husband contributed less, Jean reminds Danner of how she had "had to earn more and more. All those extension classes and summer courses to get the master's, almost a doctorate, then insisting we put that house [that Mitch had designed and built] on the market and move into town when you kids were in high school. . . . I couldn't take it anymore, struggling on his ground" (164). As Jean becomes more independent and outspoken, Mitch grows more angry and insecure. Jean recalls one quarrel where she locked herself in the bathroom, reminding Danner of how Mitch had yelled,

"You'd better stay the hell in there." . . . There was silence except for his voice. I imagined you and Billy in your rooms, listening. I heard you open your door ever so quietly and knew you were afraid. I told him clearly, "I don't have to stay anywhere. There are laws to protect me from men like you." The words came out of my mouth as though I'd had them in my mind all along. Later I wondered if I'd heard my mother say them to my father. (164)

Although Jean earns enough to send Danner and Billy to college, the family collapses as Jean and Mitch finally get divorced.

Billy completes the family dissolution by following in his father's footsteps (Mitch was in WWII), going off to war, fascinated as always by large machines such as those his father used to sell and the airplanes he watched and admired throughout his youth, going to Vietnam at nineteen years of age, never to return. Billy sacrifices his own life, as the culture has asked him to do, in order to become a man, which he now will never be able to do, while Danner survives by living on her own in California, equating family life with pain and marriage with the degradation of women—as afraid of being victimized by traditional female roles as Billy was by male roles in Vietnam. She concludes that her "parents are my country, my divided country [while Billy's was Vietnam]. By going to California, I'd made it to the far frontiers, but I'd never leave my country. I never will" (324). Human relationships remain difficult for Danner, even on the outskirts of her "country"—a victim of domestic battle as much as her brother Billy was of the war in Vietnam.[1]

In Martha Stephens's *Children of the World*, the protagonist, Margaret, holds her family together despite the violence of her husband's rages at her and his bewilderment over his children's rejection of him—especially his pacifist son's refusal to follow him (unlike Billy in Phillips's *Machine Dreams*) from WWII into Vietnam. In this novel, again, family offers little refuge but becomes, instead, the very battle-front Margaret must struggle to survive. We first encounter Leonard's rage in Stephens's novel the night before Margaret, his wife, goes to work to help send her children to college (although we soon learn that these attacks have been going on since the first year of their marriage). Margaret remembers,

then his anger was on him like a beast. . . . it covered and trapped him, and when he whirled around to her, his face was gorged and bloated with flushed rage, almost crazed, and his arm shot out, one finger fixing her like a gun. "If-you-leave-this-house-tomorrow-I'll-kill-you-don't-you-think-I won't!" She was a god-damned whore, he said, and always would be. Then he ranted on in a high rapid rant, like an auctioneer's or a preacher's. . . .

. . . she could only hiss and whisper. "Devil! You devil! You know what you said! You know! We talked about it and you said—" She was still in the hall, and just before he pitched forward and raised his hand to slap her face . . . she was able to close, with the hand behind her back, the door to where the children were sleeping. (12-13)

For Margaret, "the stage of hopeful bride" (91) would be the shortest stage of her life, to be followed by years of trying to cope with her husband's anger, fear, and domination of her life.

In her first year of marriage, Margaret's illusions about her future happiness are shattered; she becomes aware of

her new husband's tone of voice sharper by a hair each day, yes by a whole collection of words, acts and gestures which slowly paid out a current of what had been, in this husband, carefully pent-up rage, against what she could hardly guess, but which she knew, somehow, even at the time, had nothing to do with her and so was completely beyond her doing anything whatever about it. (88)

Leonard is afraid of life, of failure, of ending up as helpless and defeated as his own father has been made to feel: first, at the bedside of a dying ten-year-old daughter; then, before the boarded-up, Depression-doomed, shell of his once prosperous store; and, finally, on the front stoop of his little ice house, sitting year round, attempting to support his family through five-cents-a-block ice sales. By the time Leonard Barker realizes that his life will not repeat that of his father, and his rage begins to subside after the children are safely grown and he is "no longer afraid to open the mail, take out his bank statement; his wife with her own decent job, her little paycheck mostly her own now, with children out of school" (151), Margaret finds that Leonard's earlier mood-swings "had already defeated her, plunged her too deep in her lake of gloom for her to ever quite rise free again, breathe normal air" (154). Melancholy and confused, a woman relying on pills to help cope with feelings of depression and despair, Margaret wonders "whether women like herself were not obsolete. Were women different today or was everything just the same? Her whole marriage rose up in great flashing contours—and she almost wished people could study it and learn from it. *Little girls . . . women and men all over the world! . . . learn from us if you can*" (93).

Yet Margaret acknowledges that even before her marriage she had already been "dream-robbed"(155) by her childhood experiences. As the daughter of a retarded mother who gave birth, after Margaret, to three retarded children, Margaret begins life with the knowledge of "a dark, peculiar thing . . . that at the very core of things something was badly wrong. (Poor planning somewhere, that was for sure.)" (169). There is a rage in Margaret herself, a rage that is turned inward upon herself in the form of depression, not outward, as Leonard's has been, upon her, over the plight of her helpless family.[2] Margaret cannot believe in a loving God, the fairness of societal structures, the goodness of patriarchal arrangements, admitting her own anger at the unjust ways of the world she lives in:

Perhaps the trouble had been that her pity for them [her mother and siblings in Jacksonville, Florida], her fear for them, her fierce anger that they should have been as they were, had to be put up alongside another anger—the two of them mixed in like fire with fire, these two angers flaming, feeding each other forever: her rage, that is, that almost no one should care for them, that their own people [her maternal Grandmother and Grandfather Culp] should leave them, like Hansel and Gretel, to die in the forest, should not take them and love them and give them all they had and forgive them for what they were . . . and that all these angers, this compound of angers, would not behave (any more than Leonard's would) and went wildly astray sometimes. (167)

Margaret does not know what to do with her feelings—especially her hostility to members of her own family—over the mistreatment and indifference shown those most victimized by life.

It is ironic that it is a woman, Margaret's own beloved, yet hated Grandmother Culp—a strong, hardworking, upright, and successful owner of a dairy farm—who comes in the novel to represent patriarchal, capitalist values (as have Scarlett O'Hara and Dorinda Oakley, before her). Grandmother Culp reveals all that is wrong with the family, the church, the social and legal systems of Waycross, Georgia, and of American society. Although Grandmother Culp has taken Margaret in, finished raising her, and instilled in her a lifelong love of order and cleanliness, she has also turned her back on her retarded daughter, Margaret's mother, after she has eloped with Margaret's father. Grandmother Culp seems an enemy, the representative of

all proper people, complacent and secure, with X's scrawled on their shiny gates (No Stopping Here), all people all over the world that are above *other* people, and eat while others hunger, and drink while they thirst; people in houses of blind rippled glass, where the sun rides in on bursting beautiful waves but trouble does not, so that if you try to look outside there is nothing to see but light itself, a splendid sea of glorious glass, though people in distress may be standing in your yard. (201)

Margaret's anger, and resultant depression, over the injustices within her own family and the world at large—the way the helpless, dependent children and wounded victims of life's unfair arrangements are ignored by their "betters"—continues to be fed daily through her sobering work as a secretary in a juvenile court where she watches as the runaway children and impoverished families of Waycross, Georgia, suffer blow upon blow, defeat after defeat, ensuring their continuing "inferiority" and misery.

It is with mixed emotions that Margaret approaches the task of mothering her own children, for she is overwhelmed by the neediness of children everywhere, the neediness of humanity, in general. She remembers that

when Ruth was born she began a stage which was in itself one of amazing happiness—the stage of loving mama . . . and perhaps her emotion for Ruth was all the more fierce because of her terrible knowledge, perhaps she was prepared by that to have a rending pity for all little girls. . . . that had believed, or felt, that someone somewhere in the universe was protecting them and planning for them, knew what they wanted and needed and was getting it ready all the time, getting someone—The Someone—ready, growing him in another house on another street, to be chosen by her when the time came, grooming and training him for her to choose him. . . . Then, when the one-to-be-chosen had been chosen, boy for girl and girl for boy, daddy for mommy: then the fundamental miscalculation made known. The horror—the absurd horror of it! (88-89)

Margaret's own "miscalculation" in marriage remains a lifelong mystery she has never been able to solve. Her childhood trust in male protection, in the fairness of patriarchal society, seems to have betrayed her into a lifetime of depression and despair.

In *Children of the World*, men and women remain locked in their separate spheres of pain and anger, unable either to do much to help each other or ease the world's suffering. Margaret's boss, Jim (a judge), bears his own family travails as silently and as sadly as Margaret has herself, the two of them morosely passing in and out of the same office each day without feeling able to help the other—or the suffering souls who come through the judicial process they oversee. Margaret's Grandfather Culp drinks himself to death in a shed outside her Grandmother Culp's clean, orderly house where human distress has been made an unseemly, unwelcome presence. And Margaret's own father steadfastly trudges back and forth each day between the houses of two retarded women, marrying one, having four children by her, then divorcing and marrying another who is pregnant, drawn to each out of sympathy with her unfair suffering, taking each on as a legal obligation condemning him to "financial ruin and lifelong penury" (362), unable to explain his "betrayal" of his first family to his normal daughter Margaret (who runs away to Grandmother Culp's), fleeing himself to the peace and solitude of his tiny store each day after he has shaved the beards of his two grown sons, tidied up both slovenly houses, and helped feed the remaining six people left after Margaret has escaped—five of them retarded. Striving to help them, Margaret's father has nevertheless complicated their lives by multiplying their numbers; despite his efforts, his retarded wives and offspring remain always apart from him in their own childish worlds, out of reach and, ultimately, on their own upon his death. Margaret, too, in her own life with Leonard, as in her relationship with her "betraying" father and her helpless relations in Jacksonville, finds herself mentally "feeling along a wall for a door, pressing herself against the wall, feeling and feeling up and down, all over, for a door. Of course there was no door, but that did not keep her from feeling for it, in her mind, again and again" (15). Looking for some means of escape all her life, Margaret remains trapped in her marriage, her house, her job, her melancholy family past. She cannot find any door that might lead to her release.

Ancient, dark, family shadows continue to spread gloom over protagonists' lives in Jill McCorkle's *Tending to Virginia* (1987) and Lee Smith's *Black Mountain Breakdown* (1980). Twenty-eight-year-old Virginia Suzanne Turner Ballard (Ginny Sue), suffering a difficult pregnancy away from home in *Tending to Virginia*, longs for "Gram and Lena and her mother," desiring to return to the "solid" foundation of her past despite the many changes, the aging and dying, the buying and selling, that have taken place in her family and her town (18). In the course of the novel, she returns home, finds herself sheltered from a vicious storm in her grandmother's house, and is surrounded and comforted by all the women of her family. In just a matter of hours, however, Ginny Sue not only learns all of their desperate secrets, she reveals, as well, the darkness at the heart of her own "solid" family experience.

In her grandmother's living room, Ginny Sue listens to Great Aunt Lena Pearson express her longing for her deceased husband, Roy Carter, and the child she could never have (and professed not to want). Emily Pearson, Ginny Sue's beloved grandmother and Lena's sister, also mourns the husband she has loved and lost, James Roberts, as well as her son, David Roberts, who has died in war, remembering her anguish as she watched her son and husband fight over David's desire to go to war, feeling as if the two men had "roped her legs and taken off in different directions," tearing her body apart with their quarreling (146). Her daughter Hannah (Ginny Sue's mother) also remembers the hardships of marriage, saying

I was feeling homesick and I was starting to realize that I was never going to live in New York and be a fashion designer like Lena had always said I could be. I realized that I was never going to be a housewife and sip coffee and chat. No, I was going to work; I was going to send my children to school with keys around their necks. (275)

Early in her marriage, Hannah learns to accept that her life will be no "fairy tale" (273); she loses both her brother and her father; realizes that her husband's income will not be adequate to support their family; understands that her aspirations for a career will never be met; and finds herself "out-of-step" with other women who choose work according to the dictates of popular fashion rather than those of economic necessity.

But all of these female sufferings and disappointments pale in comparison to the family misery and horror revealed along another branch of the family tree—one that has spread its blight throughout the lives of several women, including Ginny Sue herself. Ginny Sue confesses that, when she was young, her Uncle Raymond Sinclair, dressed in a dark mask and gloves, scared her and threatened to kill her if she ever told her family. Ginny Sue admits,

He told me that I'd look nice in a tomb. . . . He said he could just see me wrapped up in a pure white sheet, my body oiled and perfumed, and he made me tell him that he was the king, that he was beautiful and that I worshipped him, and he said that I better never tell that I said all of those things to him because everyone would hate me, that [Aunt Madge] and Cindy [her cousin] would hate me. (242)

Raymond tells Ginny Sue that he has fed birds, killed them, and wrapped them in clean sheets, warning her, "You are like a little bird. . . . Oh, you'll never fly away. . . . I'll wrap you in a sheet" (286). When Ginny Sue's Aunt Madge returns home that afternoon, Uncle Raymond warns the terrified girl,

"If you ever tell anyone," he says . . .[a] hairbrush in his hand as he slaps his open palm. "Then I will take you. Don't think you can hide, you can't. I'll make you worship me, bathe my feet in oils, dry my feet with your hair and then I'll wrap you in a sheet until you can't breathe." (287)

At last, Ginny's mother, Hannah, understands her daughter's childhood fear of the dark, "all those times you were so scared, times you thought there was a man in the closet" (244).

The life of Cindy, Raymond's daughter, has been even more damaged by her father's insanity than her cousin Ginny Sue's. Cindy has lost Charles Snipes, a husband she has loved and the father of her child, trying to please her insatiable, crazed father with whom, in her youth, she had played a special "game," Catherine, Queen in the Tomb (243). Cindy trusted that her father had, as he said, "[given] her all that he had that was good. 'Take what you can get,' he told her. 'Get all that you can get and take it [to the tomb] with you'" (126). Cindy's need for worldly goods is so great that Charles Snipes leaves her, explaining, "I'll never be able to satisfy you. . . . I'm a plumber, okay? . . . I asked you not to ask your daddy for money. I told you we didn't have to have a new car, that stereo, the TV. . . . No, no, you need more. . . . You and your dad need more" (233).

Cindy's father has destroyed her marriage in other ways, as well. Raymond Sinclair had shown his adolescent daughter pictures of nude bodies, telling her,

"It's healthy to have [sexual] feelings, healthy to think of things that make you feel this way." . . . And Charles Snipes had made her feel that way, way back. But whenever he did, she thought of the pictures, heard her father's voice. It was like her father was always watching her; she never got to have just Charles, all by himself, and that's what she wanted. (248)

Now Cindy acknowledges what, in her lifelong defense of her father, she could never admit before:

"It's his [her father's] fault I lost Charles. . . . Why did he do that to me?" she screams and holds onto her mama's [Madge's] tightly clenched legs, so tight. . . . "I thought he loved me. He always told me how he was the one that loved me and you never seemed to. You never seemed to love me."
"Oh but I did," Madge says and squats beside her. "I did and I do. He was so sick, Cindy." Madge swallows hard. "I think he did love you. You are probably the one person he loved, but he was sick." (248)

Raymond's actions have separated mother from daughter and driven each to hide his insanity from the rest of the family and the world.

Madge's life has been ruined by her marriage to Raymond, a man who used his authority and power to terrorize her, a man she was afraid either to oppose or expose, even when to do so might have been to save them all. Madge has been badly frightened after Raymond tells her, "'The Egyptians believed that life went on. They took it all with them, valuables, food. Some of them had their wives put in the tomb.' He looked at her and she felt her spine freeze, a split second of fear that she knew he saw before she responded" (213). It is only when Raymond's plans have all been carried out and, as Madge confesses to the surrounding women in Emily's storm-blackened living room, she has killed him as he has ordered her to do, that Madge realizes Raymond had duped her into believing him as much as he had led Cindy to believe she was the only one with whom he ever played his special "game."

Only after Raymond's death does Madge come to understand fully the nature of her husband's insanity:

There was a concrete like a vault, a room, a picture of a pyramid on one wall, a TV stand that she had never seen before with that brand new widescreen color set, books, and a huge metal grate off to one side of the grave that she knew was meant to cover the top, to seal the tomb. It sent a chill through her body to watch them lower that casket onto a small bedframe, her [once beloved] Raymond, that [later crazy] Raymond, both gone. And again, there was that slight shiver when she realized that there was no room for her, no way for that seal to be broken once the concrete was poured over the top. He had never intended for her to be with him. (215)

Terrified of Raymond, and afraid of revealing his terrible secret to others, Madge carries out her husband's bizarre orders until the end, trapped inside the insanity that has become her home and family.

Yet, for all of Madge's secrecy, Raymond's madness has not escaped public notice. Madge's aunt Lena announces, even before Ginny Sue's and Madge's revelations, "He was crazy. . . . Roy [her deceased husband] said he knew that man was crazy as hell when we saw him there atop the hardware store acting like a woman" in what Raymond's daughter Cindy continues to defend as a "Chevrolet promotion" (216). But Lena has never talked to Madge about her suspicions, nor have any of the other women in the family tried to help Madge and Cindy. And Ginny Sue's grandmother has kept her granddaughter's secret about Raymond to herself all along, saying nothing to Madge, Hannah, Lena, or anyone else about the incident. In fact, Madge blames her marriage to Raymond on the inability of the family women to communicate with each other. Because she and her mother never talked and shared their experiences, she concludes, "You know my mama had a sad life, too. . . . God only knows how sad. She never talked to me about anything except how to sew something. Maybe if she had talked to me, I would have been different. Maybe I wouldn't have been so taken with Raymond and what he had to offer me" (249).

Now the family women have gathered together, at long last, on the stormy afternoon of Ginny Sue's return, confessing their deepest sorrows and fears, giving out advice to the youngest in their midst—Ginny Sue and her cousin Cindy. Yet their advice is, as Hannah says, to stop wasting time talking about these matters and "get on with it" (270). They tell Ginny Sue to go back to her husband and marriage, just as they have done, for better and for worse, all their lives. Ginny Sue's grandmother adds her own counsel, "Yes, you always said you wanted to be like me. . . . And I always said, 'yes Sweets, I know, but you'll have to be more than me; the world will change'" (264). Gram agrees with the others that Ginny Sue should go back to Mark, prepare to move farther away from her family than any of the family women have ever gone before, have his baby, and create a home of her own, however hard it may be for her; she will need to accommodate to modern life and be "more" than the women before her.

The message of *Tending to Virginia*, however, is not progressive but regressive, a message not of promise but of resignation. Women must be prepared, as mothers and wives, to be on their own, adapt to change, and endure the consequences of their own choices, becoming more isolated and, at the same time, more resourceful than ever before. Although they cannot go back to the past, as Gram counsels Ginny Sue, there seems to be nothing but the past as they prepare to marry, follow husbands through life, have babies, and tend houses, repeating the sorrowful, unfulfilling, even terrifying patterns of women before them. "I'll always be with you," Ginny Sue tells Mark upon her return home (312)—even after she has heard what such promises of loyalty and faithfulness have entailed for women in her own family. It would seem that all the female talk in the world cannot prevent the cycle of white female isolation and dependence, fear and submission, from continuing on into the future.

The message of Lee Smith's *Black Mountain Breakdown* is even more discouraging than that of McCorkle's *Tending to Virginia*. The novel reveals how sensitive women have been overwhelmed by their own historical powerlessness—as Dorothy Hill concludes, "crucified . . . through [their] failure of development. There is no way for Crystal [the novel's protagonist] to develop, no way for her to grow. She has tried every community-validated path to female identity and all end in paralysis" (49). At the end of the novel, the beautiful, fragile Crystal Spangler "paralyzes herself" (237), lying motionless on the bed of the room where she has spent her childhood, tended by two practical nurses, unable to find any viable means of expressing her own desires and selfhood. Her only way of rejecting the self-abnegating scripts that have been written for her seems this final, self-induced break with the outer world.

And yet, even then, Crystal is overcome, surrounded by townspeople who absorb her final act of defiance and defeat into their everyday lives. We are told,

she just lies there. Everybody in town takes a fancy to it. Crystal's old uncle Garnett comes and sits with her. . . . read[ing] the Bible to her, although there is no telling if she can hear it or not. [Crystal's old friend] Agnes's mama goes up and sits with her, and Susie and Neva, and other ladies in town. People often

bring congealed salads to Lorene because once Neva told somebody in the
beauty shop that Crystal seems to like them. Crystal can eat, but she has to be
fed. . . . She's no trouble lying there. After a while [her mother] Lorene and [her
stepfather] Odell grow accustomed to it. . . . Agnes goes over there often. . . .
[and] is glad [Crystal] came home. . . . It rests Agnes, sitting in that room, it's so
peaceful there. (238-39)

Women who seemingly have pushed forward in their own lives, such as
Lorene and Agnes, are as accepting of Crystal's regression into infancy
as are their more backward female friends.

In truth, we find that Lorene and Agnes have always endorsed the
status quo, including the traditional place of women in society. Agnes
may remain a single, "modern" woman, running several businesses herself, but she has always conformed to town mores and disapproved of
Crystal's desperate attempts to find a way out of the trap of her femininity. Agnes has believed all along "that if Crystal had married [her high
school boyfriend] Roger Lee the first time he asked her, if she hadn't
gotten all that education and fallen in with hippies, she could be having
intimate luncheons for people in Washington [as Roger Lee's wife] right
now" (239). Crystal's mother, Lorene, has also endorsed cultural norms,
accepting her own lot in life when her husband Grant drinks himself to
death, never complaining about her marriage, leaving her husband in the
front room and "mov[ing] to the back of the house. . . . tak[ing] pride in
the fact that she has never said a word against him to anyone, has never
mentioned his drinking to anybody" (14). Later, Lorene marries Grant's
half-brother Odell Peacock, although she thinks he "isn't smart" (20),
becoming Odell's partner and a successful businesswoman, yet continuing to emphasize her roles as homemaker, wife and mother.

Lorene prepares her daughter, Crystal, for a traditional woman's
life—one ending in marriage and motherhood, taking care of a house
and a man, a life like her own but more conventionally feminine even
than hers has been. The means to this end will be Crystal's beauty, and
Lorene encourages her daughter to take part in beauty contests, "her
heart so full and her head so full of plans for the future. Oh, Lorene can
see it all: the Miss Buchanan County Contest, the Miss Claytor Lake
Contest, the UMW's Miss Bituminous Coal Contest—everything seems
within reach. Maybe, even—who knows?—Miss Virginia!" (110).
Lorene wants Crystal to surrender her own desires, to become the bride
of the very culture that denies her her selfhood, in order to achieve community recognition and prizes.

While Crystal's father nourishes his daughter's creativity and sensitivity, in contrast to Lorene's endorsement of Crystal's physical being,

her ornamental functions in society, he, too, contributes to Crystal's defeat. After Grant's family mine has failed (Lorene's later success proves that Grant need only have waited to turn a profit on it), he begins to drink, entombing himself in the parlor of his home. There he creates "another world almost. Here where Grant stays, even the air seems denser and different somehow. It smells like old smoke, like liquor, like Grant himself, yet the combination is not unpleasant really and Crystal loves it" (14). Crystal is drawn to her father's willed self-destruction and isolation—so drawn that she repeats this pattern in her own self-paralysis at the end of the novel.

Much as Crystal loves her father and is drawn to him, Grant plays with her like a spider with a fly—as in the poem he reads her. He "grins at her, a surprisingly incongruous mischievous grin in his sick wrecked face," reciting to her even while Crystal sobs, " 'No, no!' . . . 'Don't do that one, don't do that one, Daddy!' . . . 'Oh, oh,' Crystal says, but it's hard to tell by the tone of her voice whether she's delighted or upset—intense emotion all unfocused—and her usually dreaming face is wholly alive" (17). Caught like a fly in Grant's web, Crystal becomes distraught over her father's death, searching again and again for a man who will mesmerize her and lure her once more into the realm of his morbid despair, as Jerold Kukafka will do until the day he "hung himself dead from an exposed pipe in the bathroom . . . and Crystal found him with his tongue hanging out and all black in the face" (161). This is the second time Crystal has discovered the dead body of a man she loves; her father's is the first. She is drawn to men who not only wish to destroy themselves but traumatize the women they leave behind (as did Raymond Sinclair in McCorkle's *Tending to Virginia*).

Family and gender work together to govern Crystal's fate in other terrible ways, as well. Immediately before Grant's death, her retarded Uncle Devere has raped her—something Crystal has denied and buried deep inside since the day it happened. One evening when she calls Devere to dinner, Crystal's gentle uncle suddenly pushes her to the floor of the tool shed and pulls off her clothes:

Devere is hurting her. She knows, of course, where the hurt is, but for some reason it seems to be traveling up her whole body into her shoulders and then pinpointing itself somewhere up at the very top of her head, like somebody driving in a nail up there. Her face is pressed into Devere's flannel shirt and she can't breathe much . . . Crystal never moves and soon it's over. Devere rolls off and gets right up, zips his pants, gets the wrench from the work table and hangs it up in the place on the pegboard where it's supposed to go. . . . Now things are in order again and . . . he turns to go. His deepset eyes, those Spangler eyes, don't seem to see her at all. Now his face is calm and smooth again, like a wide far field. He doesn't know, she sees. He doesn't know anything about it. (229-30)

Crystal is no more visible to Devere than she has been to her own mother and father—seen by all of them only in terms of her beauty and femininity.

Later, when Crystal has been hunted down and captured by another "innocent," yet determined, man—her first boyfriend, Roger Lee Combs—has been held in place and used by him for his personal fulfillment and ultimate political gain, Crystal remembers the physical rape she endured as a girl and connects it with her present pain—her inability to sleep, her "precarious" mental state, her intense "zoom lens" responses, and her sense of being caught up in a play instead of her own real, everyday life [220 221]). Roger Lee has come back to Black Rock for her, announcing what everyone else believes, as well, "This is not any kind of life for a woman like you, Crystal. . . . A woman like you needs a man. You need your own home, children, a position in the community. You need love. I want to make you happy, Crystal. I can do it if you'll give me a chance. It's all I've ever wanted, all my life" (209). Crystal gives in, recognizing her defeat, knowing that "Roger is inevitable. He has always been inevitable, but she hasn't always known it. . . . It's so comforting, really, to have somebody again to tell her what to do" (212). Crystal fulfills her part in the conventional drama, becoming again the fly for the spider, the victim for the rapist, the beloved for the lover, ultimately unseen and unimportant in herself. Wearily, Crystal concludes, at last, "Roger is the hero, always was. But she is out of the book" (234)—removing herself completely from the margins of the pages to leave the story intact and complete, untouched by her withdrawal, as she has known it would be. As Dorothy Combs Hill has shown, "two themes are inextricably linked [in Smith's *Black Mountain Breakdown*]: the difficulty of self-definition for women in a culture that hinges their self-definition on passivity and the necessity of self-expression for survival, for connection to the inner self" (46). Men and women, elders and peers, friends and family, have all conspired against Crystal Spangler to ensure her conformity and self-negation. Lee Smith reveals that Crystal's self-paralysis is a mere formal acknowledgment of what she has allowed her family and community to do to her in the name of love and care.

Paralleling Tyler: Making Adult Choices

In work after work, contemporary white southern women writers reveal the horror of female dependence and passivity—of grown women trapped in nightmare houses of the past where they have been unable to lead full lives, grow into mature adulthood, move out from under male rule, or make their own contributions to the larger world. Increasingly, however, white southern female protagonists recognize, as do Anne Tyler's, that they have had choices, even if the lives they continue to lead remain limited, fearful, and incomplete—that these are lives they have willed, as much as Crystal Spangler has induced her own catatonic state at the end of Smith's *Black Mountain Breakdown*. They alone are responsible for their lives; they alone must take control and make thoughtful choices.

As Corinne, the protagonist of Ellen Douglas's *A Lifetime Burning* (1982), admits, "But why should I cast myself in the ancient female part of victim of men's plots and passions?" (20). Even though her ancestor—the great-grandmother of her husband, and third cousin, George—may have committed suicide due to multiple pregnancies and miscarriages, abuse by her husband, and/or rejection by her father, Corinne, now sixty-two, realizes that she has had more choices than the foremothers who proceeded her. Corinne has wanted all five of her children, helped them grow into their adult lives, and entered a profession of her own as a literature professor, which long ago could have supported her through divorce from her physician husband. If she feels that "terrible irremediable reservations between men and women . . . [feelings] that we must be different species" (181) have come between herself and her husband George, driving them each into (possibly fantasized) homosexual affairs, Corinne acknowledges that she contributed to the dissolution of her marriage by simply playing out the conventional roles of wife and mother rather than by trying to find self-expression through her work and marriage:

But now, looking back, I have to say this. I set it up. I consented to it. I arranged the continuing life that invited him to rape and permitted me to hate. I drew him close and opened my legs and stared over his shoulder into the darkness—all in the name of stable family life and what was best for the children. (182)

Corinne has chosen to remain a subordinant in her marriage, living a traditional life and playing out conventional social roles—growing more and more tormented as she does so by the world of real relationships, of full human possibilities, she and George have squandered between them. By not insisting on her personhood within the marriage, she has lived two lives simultaneously—one real and one false—resulting in her present mental instability.

A few other protagonists who have chosen to marry and lead traditional lives have used their conventional roles more successfully than Douglas's Corinne, finding self-expression, personal fulfillment, and self-growth in the process. In Bobbie Ann Mason's *Spence and Lila* (1988), Lila loses a breast to cancer, faces the approach of death, only to look back with satisfaction on a life in which "she and [her husband] Spence have spent a lifetime growing things together" (143). Abandoned by her father and married to Spence before she turned eighteen, Lila has led a limited life in partnership with her husband—helping on their farm, raising three children, working in a clothing factory to provide extras for the family, and traveling to see a little of the world before she becomes ill. Nevertheless, she feels valued by her family for her individuality, resiliency, wit, and strength, finding continued pleasure in the company of her husband and children, as they do in hers, and in the daily world "stirring with aroused possibility" (176) they share together.

In Kaye Gibbons's *A Virtuous Woman* (1989), another protagonist, Ruby Stokes, dies at forty-five of lung cancer, and yet she feels her life has been fulfilled through her second marriage to a gentle, kind man twenty years her senior. After a violent first marriage to John Woodrow (who ends up being killed at an early age), Ruby regains her strength and self-respect through Jack Stokes's love, taking pride in her role as his wife, saying, "but you ought to see the way I've kept this house and cooked for Jack. I'm sorry to say that I might not have much in my life to be proud of, but I'm surely pleased with myself every time I see bread rise, and it rises every time" (73). Ruby has not fled back to her well-to-do parents after the disastrous end of her first marriage but has continued to build her own life and win the respect of all who know her as a woman of courage, a woman of "grace" (147), the wife of a simple tenant farmer. It is the life she has chosen for herself—and continues to choose when she and Jack turn down her third of her parents' property (land they have not earned themselves) upon her parents' deaths.

In Bobbie Ann Mason's *Feather Crowns* (1993), Christianna Wilburn Wheeler, also, can look back on her farm life at her husband's side without regret. Unlike her sister-in-law, Amanda, who hangs herself in despair over a loveless marriage, Christianna has known the respect and care of her husband, James, a man who has been her companion and friend through difficult times, "a good man. . . . the thoughtfulest man" (454) she has ever known. She and James grow and learn together, sharing the loss of their quintuplets (whose births have been called "the eighth wonder of the world" [149] by American newspapers), raising three remaining children together, working side by side in the tobacco fields, and losing their faith in God as they come to a shared realization of the harshness of life—the extent of human suffering and human culpability in an unjust universe (451).

The experience of having quintuplets, then losing them, has taught Christianna not to seek approval from a fickle public, as ravenous for the spectacle of her babies dead as they were for them alive. She feels stronger than she did before. Christianna reflects on her own hardening into a stubborn independence after the deaths of the quintuplets: "But I was so changed I fit in even less than I did before. I felt like I could endure anything after what I'd been through. I felt like I could do anything and that I never had to explain myself. It made me plumb sassy" (448). Christianna has become a survivor—enduring the deaths of her best friend and sister-in-law, Amanda, her companion-husband, James, one of her sons in war, and the quintuplets—a woman who has learned to think and act independently, despite the conventional appearance of her life, who never again feels a need "to explain [herself]" and gain community approval (448).

The protagonists of many contemporary novels by southern white women find that they have choices, can grow and heal themselves, gaining their independence in a variety of ways. In Jill McCorkle's novels, *The Cheer Leader* (1984) and *Ferris Beach* (1990), young women are shown learning from their own experience and the experiences of other women. Jo Spencer of *The Cheer Leader* undergoes a nervous breakdown after her disastrous love affair with a daring, callous, older boy, Red Williams, yet at the end of the novel she has undergone therapy, is in graduate school, and is moving forward, if tentatively, with her own life. While her aspirations remain conventional ones (marriage, home, children) and she is still wary of intimacy's potential loss and pain, she anticipates her future, knowing that she has "many choices to make. Clearly I am not an 'I Love Lucy' nor am I a 'That Girl.' *The Feminine Mystique* says that you don't have to be an either/or and I am convinced that this is true, that there is a safe inbetween" (264). No longer the "good" southern girl of her youth, or the wild, headstrong adventurer she became, Jo has learned something about who she is and what she needs. She feels comforted by the knowledge that she is growing in her understanding of herself, and she seems unafraid of life's possibilities as she "mov[es], slide[es], chang[es]" (266). She feels confident now that "there is a choice to make, a chance to take" (267), looking forward to the life that she can begin to fashion through more thoughtful, careful decision-making than she exerted in the past.

In Jill McCorkle's *Ferris Beach*, as well, the protagonist, Katie Burns, learns about life from watching what happens to other women. She longs for a different mother—one who is young, sexual, exciting—

and is attracted to her Aunt Angela, as well as her friend Misty's mother, Mo Rhodes, as role models and surrogate mothers. Yet Mo Rhodes abandons Misty and her family, as well as Katie, running off with another man, dying along with him and her small infant in a car accident immediately afterwards. Angela, too, proves an unwise choice as a role model —divorced several times, with a penchant, Katie finds, for men who abuse her. Angela is honest when she advises her young niece to be more sensible about life than she has been, saying, "We all want a fairy tale, Kitty. . . . Nobody wants the truth. But sooner or later you learn that there are no fairy tales; there is no glamorous mother hidden on a faraway island, no prince on a white horse, no treasure chest full of jewels" (334). Katie learns yet another lesson about female life as she watches, from her hiding place in a tree where she has been spying on her boyfriend Merle Hucks's house, her attractive classmate Perry Loomis being gang-raped by the violent Dexter Hucks and his older friends.

In the wake of multiple warnings in the persons of Perry Loomis, Angela Burns, and Mo Rhodes about the dangers of female sexuality, the failure of her alternative female role models, and her beloved father's death, Katie Burns realigns herself with her mother, concluding at last, "I *was* my mother's daughter" (341). She understands at the end that her mother has worked to create a fulfilling life, making wise choices—ones that have involved personal courage, a sense of adventure, mature commitment to others, as well as some self-sacrifice—to obtain what she has wanted in life. At last Katie understands the love her "mismatched" parents, her uptight northern mother and her laid-back southern father, had for one another, asking her mother, "You really did love him, didn't you?" (342). Her mother replies, "You think I'd choose a life of grits and black-eyed peas and summers so hot I could have a damned heat stroke for nothing?" (342). With her husband dead, Katie's mother decides to stay in the South, continuing on her own the satisfying life she has created for herself there. Katie finds she has been given a "second chance" to learn from her mother's independence and strength (342), become more cautious about sexual involvement than she has been with Merle Hucks, and create a good life through wise choices she will make for herself from "a whole world of possibilities spinning around her" (343).

In Ellen Gilchrist's *I Cannot Get You Close Enough* (1990), the message is a similar one. Helen Hand thinks,

Only yesterday, *only yesterday* a woman's body was completely at the mercy of nature. If she married or was fucked then she was impregnated until she died. A few women were able to withstand repeated pregnancies before they died. Some women lived to be forty or fifty years old. An occasional woman lived to be seventy or ninety. I guess those women were widowed or lucky or ugly. (385-86)

But now, Helen thinks, women have choices. We see the variety of those choices in the diverse women of this three-part novel.

Midlife women in *I Cannot Get You Close Enough* wrestle with earlier choices while continuing to shape their lives through their ongoing decisions. Helen Hand, who has been devoted to family, has become "sick of" her life and her children's "parasite" use of her over the years (386). Now, in midlife, she chooses to leave her former life in Charlotte behind to go to Chicago, live with her professor-lover, and be the literary executor of her deceased sister, Anna Hand. Lydia, Helen's friend, is an artist who, like the writer Anna Hand, believes "my work is my life. I take the world and create art from it. Ideas born of sadness or jealousy or rage, who knows what. A rage to order" (264). Lydia has had four abortions, choosing each time to put her art first, but finally, and painfully, she has learned not to let anyone "get too close [because] I might really fall in love. I don't do that anymore. I don't care how good it feels at first. The aftermath is death and more than death, a hole I don't want to have to crawl out of again" (365). Lydia wants to create beauty through paintings she can leave behind for the world, as Anna Hand has left behind her writing—both of them rejecting the life of their friend Crystal, a woman Lydia believes to be "the prototype of all the southern women I had ever known, worn out from dreaming of perfect worlds, perfect lives, perfect lovers, husbands, children, friends" (250) she can never have.[3]

Anna and Helen Hand's two young nieces, Jessie and Olivia, make their respective choices, too. Olivia pursues her education, determined to be a successful science writer, while Jessie chooses to have a baby. If Jessie's life will be difficult, it is the one she has determined for herself. She says, "I did what I wanted to. I wanted to have the baby and now I'm having it. I won't do it again" (388). Unsure of her future, Jessie plans to leave Charlotte and live with her sister, Olivia, fashioning a new life of her own:

[Jessie's young husband] King hates me now. He hates the way I look and he doesn't like to go out with me. That's okay. As soon as I get my baby I'll be out of here. I'll get some money from Grandmother and go live in New York. I'll get an apartment like the one Aunt Anna had and get a job or something up there. . . . [Olivia] wants to get to New York too. So, in two more months. I can wait. I wonder what it's going to be. I want it to be a girl. I'm sick of men. (387)

Having chosen to have her baby, Jessie will need to grow up quickly, learn from her past experiences, and struggle to provide a good life for herself and her child. It will not be an easy life—but it is the one she has, against all advice, chosen for herself, the one she must build upon for her future—learning from her mistakes, as Lydia and Helen are still doing in midlife.

In Beverly Lowry's *The Perfect Sonya* (1987), the protagonist Pauline Terry also finds that unexpected pregnancy, "too pat and old-fashioned a plot device to take seriously" (146), changes the course of her life. Sexually abused by her father, Pauline has sought good daddies in her relationships with men: in her four-year marriage to an older man, Michael Caproselli—who becomes her drama instructor and mentor; then, in her brief affair with her sixty-year-old college professor, author, and uncle, Will Hand. It is the latter relationship that results in pregnancy, her decision to get an abortion, and a subsequent divorce from her husband, Michael. Michael has wanted to keep the baby, believing it is his, but Pauline argues,

"Michael, we agreed," she said with great deliberation. "No children."

. . . "Now that it's happened"—he shrugged his shoulders—"how can we not? It's destiny, Pauline. Fate. I hope it's a girl. We can call her Destiny Caproselli."

. . . "Michael," she said. "I'm not having this baby." Her voice wavered a bit, but she felt strong. For once she knew what she wanted. If she could have reached up inside and pulled the baby out with her hands, she'd have done it then and there. (159-60)

After the divorce, Michael moves to California, remarries, and has a child; Will Hand marries again; Pauline's closest actor friends move to California; her New York neighborhood is being destroyed for condominiums; and Pauline is in long-term therapy with psychiatrist Russell Loving. Her choice to have an abortion—something that "she knew . . . she wanted"—has helped, seemingly, only to isolate and demoralize her.

Yet, like the Sonya she plays in Chekhov's *Uncle Vanya*, Pauline is a survivor. She learns that she is more resilient than she has believed, that her Uncle Will has been right about her. When she has told him, "I can't play suicides or victims. It's hard for audiences to think I can't handle misfortune's every arrow and sling. I have this appearance on-stage of strength and survival," Will has replied, "And in life." When Pauline insists, "Sometimes it's a mask," Will assures her once more of her own strength of character, "You wear it well," he says (108). On

Pauline's return to Texas to visit Will again, she rejects his sexual advances, this time telling him that she loves him but needs him as her family, not her lover. She prepares to return home to audition for a new part in her stalled acting career, feeling "proud of herself. Really proud" (238). At last she has been able to differentiate her need for a good father from her need for a lover. While she has suffered, she has learned from her experience and maintained control of her life. Pauline has said "no" to Michael and to Will both, refusing merely to please men—something she has learned to do early in life, and continued to do to earn money as an underwater swimmer in a tank for gawking men at the Shipwreck Inn, as well as in her sexual relationships (96). Now Pauline continues to chart her own course through life's choppy waters, with some help from her psychiatrist, Russell Loving, gaining confidence in her own judgment and strength as she does so.

Contemporary white southern heroines learn that they do have choices—sometimes too many choices—some that are clearly better than others. Some choices are self-destructive, some conventional, and some daring and adventurous. A few protagonists learn to become more cautious as a result of their experiences—while others learn to take risks. But what they almost always seem to need—for their own self-development—is distance from their family and community pasts. As Lucinda MacKethan explains in *Daughters of Time*,

Women novelists of the last several generations have shaped stories about women characters who begin their quests from the position of patriarchally defined daughter, yet who proceed to discover creative power beyond traditional roles. Breaking away from parental or communal expectations creates a rupture for these women characters, not only between themselves and their families, but within themselves. Descent into self-doubt, experiences of separation from family and from self, lead to discoveries that enable these women to identify within themselves the source of their creativity. . . . [Theirs is a] search for wholeness. (66-67)

When contemporary women fail to make the effort to discover their own identities—or when they do so only belatedly and haphazardly—they are shown as failing themselves and those they love.

The novels of Lee Smith are filled with warnings of what happens when women fail to achieve wholeness in their lives. As we have seen, Crystal Spangler paralyzes herself in *Black Mountain Breakdown*. The beautiful, "golden" Dory Cantrell of *Oral History* (1983) puts her head on a railroad track and is beheaded by a train when love has disappointed her. Dory's daughter Pearl also dies, after bearing a child conceived in a futile attempt to find joy in her life. Pearl has run off with one of her young high school students—only to realize the impossibility of a relationship between them—returning in shame to her upholsterer husband, the community she has defied, and an early death by childbirth. And in *The Devil's Dream* (1992), Rose Annie Bailey has a nervous breakdown after her father, R.C., runs her childhood friend and lover, Johnny Rainette, away from Grassy Branch. Unhappy in her subsequent marriage to the "modern-day saint" Buddy Rush (129), Rose Annie finally abandons her husband and two children to go off with Johnny, now a well-known country singer called Black Jack Johnny Raines. But it is too late. Wild Johnny has become addicted to alcohol and drugs and is unable to stop his self-destructive behavior, hurting Rose Annie, now, as well as himself. Rose Annie ends up killing Johnny and living out the rest of her life in a state prison.

Smith's heroines cannot find their way by going back into the past (like Rose Annie) or remaining locked in it (like Dory). They must move forward in their own lives, accepting that what has gone before remains a quicksand trap in which they can become easily mired and perish if they turn back and try to regain their footing. This is the lesson the young college student Jennifer learns in *Oral History* when she comes to Appalachia to interview her "grandparents," Ora Mae and Little Luther, to learn about her family history. The truth eludes her, although the reader finds out that Jennifer's real grandparents have been the ill-fated Dory and her upperclass lover Burlage—not Ora Mae and Little Luther, as she believes—her parents, the unhappy Pearl and her upholsterer husband. Jennifer has begun her visit believing "these people are so sweet, so simple, so kind . . . not backward at all" (4), but she ends it in tears, "scared" and confused (287), heading "off down the holler like a streak, crying and crying and wiping her eyes with the back of her hand" (290).

In rejecting her Appalachian past, Jennifer concludes that these mountain relatives are different from herself, "still liv[ing] so close to the land, all of them. Some things may seem modern, like the van, but they're not, not really. They are really very primitive people, resembling nothing so much as some sort of early tribe. Crude jokes and animal instincts—it's the other side of the pastoral coin" (290-91). Jennifer is, of course, deluding herself about the differences between herself and her Cantrell relatives, as well as about the disjunctions she finds between her own story and those she has heard. Yet, by distancing herself from her Appalachian heritage, Jennifer is able to move on with her own life: marrying her professor, Dr. Bernie Ripman, after she graduates from college and going to Chicago, "never [to] see any of [her Appalachian relatives] again" (291). If it is true, as her Aunt Sally has warned her stepsister Pearl, "Honey, there's no new life" (270), it is also true that the strong survivor, Sally, would, in all likelihood, have been no more use to Jennifer than she was to Jennifer's mother, Pearl: "'I'm going to have a baby,' Pearl said, 'like you.' *Not like me*, [Sally] wanted to scream. Not like me at all, you fool, no one is ever alike, I thought, don't say that" (272). Smith's heroines must find their own ways and listen to their own inner voices if they are to be strong and creative in shaping their lives. They can neither imitate the past nor learn very much from it—although they are surrounded by those who will continue to profess its importance while exploiting, romanticizing, and trivializing it for their own advantage.[4]

When ghosts of the past intrude on the present, Lee Smith's heroines find it best to lay them quietly aside. In *Family Linen* (1985), another family's sorrowful, bloody past reappears—only to disappear again without resolving the mystery of the family murder or providing solutions to ongoing family problems. Yet the novel's comedy embraces the "messiness" of family, past and present (12, 28)—celebrating family continuity in a loosely structured form familiar to readers of Anne Tyler. While it is true that the bones of a murdered Jewell Rife (Miss Elizabeth's first husband) probably are those lying at the bottom of the long-closed homestead well, it is also true that Miss Elizabeth's house can be renovated into a comfortable new home for her daughter Myrtle and Myrtle's husband Don; the well can be turned into a delightful swimming pool; and the family can enjoy it all without fear of further hauntings.

Families need to embrace difficulty and complexity if they are to survive. For instance, in *Family Linen* Myrtle believes her marriage has been "made in heaven" (37), but we also learn that her marital bliss has included a recent affair with Gary, the exterminator, as well as the long-standing, twenty-year relationship of her husband, Don, with her sister Candy. As Dorothy Combs Hill explains,

Yet this admittedly adulterous affair—with its potential to so damage a family—is, in this novel of reconciliation, almost an affirmation of family solidarity. Candy does not so much seem to be betraying her sister as filling in for what her sister cannot be. The affair is not tawdry or decadent; it is as deep and committed as a marriage, marked overall by mutual respect. Candy understands both Don's need to remain a family man and her own need for solitude and independence. (98)

It is the strong, resourceful Candy who most typifies the spirit of *Family Linen*—and of Smith's several survivor heroines throughout her novels.

As Hill says, "Candy has generosity of spirit. Nonjudgmental, she accepts her own feelings and those of others" (99), becoming a heroine Lee Smith has called a "well-integrated person . . . who lives successfully and works out her ideas and her aesthetics. She's very much her own person and the shaping force within the family, within the community" (qtd. in Lodge 110). Tolerance of difference, of human "sin" and neediness, as typified by Candy, can enable the family to survive and the community to flourish.

In *Family Linen*, Miss Elizabeth's four daughters form a vibrant, varied sisterhood—although it would appear that one daughter, Candy, is really Elizabeth's sister Fay's child by Jewell Rife; that the retarded sister, Fay, has murdered Elizabeth's abusive husband, Jewell; and that Elizabeth has helped to shield Fay and raise Candy as her own child. Each of these present-day sisters is as different from the others as was their ladylike mother, Elizabeth, from her sisters Nettie and Fay: the uptight Sybill who strives to be "in control of every minute of her life" (5); the cliché-prone, conventional Myrtle; the warmhearted, nonconformist Candy; and the searching intellectual Lacy. While some of the sisters have evolved more than others, Candy most of all, diversity and tolerance in this novel become strengths needed for the family to survive the damage of the past and the uncertainty of the present. Each woman has her own needs to fulfill; each has her own problems; and each faces the messiness of her own life with an eye to shaping a better future. As Miss Elizabeth's sister, Nettie, has found, "you do what you have to" (239) to make your own life. Yet Nettie has found, as well, that the more you are willing to fly in the face of family and community opinion, as both she and Candy have done, the more successful you will be in making your life a satisfying one. In her early marriage to Marvin Sizemore, Nettie has felt "the most lonesome I ever was" (238). When she decides to cast that life aside, she is ostracized by both her family and her town. Nevertheless, years later, she reflects complacently, "So you see how it is. If anybody's passing judgment, I've not got a leg to stand on, I've not got a thing to say. I left one good decent man, and married another woman's husband [Millard Cline], and don't regret any of it, to this day" (239). Since Millard's death, Nettie has continued to lead her deviant life, taking in young boys to raise and help her run her gas station, a woman thought to be as strange as the retarded sister Fay whom Nettie takes care of. Having first lived for herself, Nettie finds she now can live for others and give them the help they require.

In Lee Smith's *Fair and Tender Ladies* (1988) and *The Devil's Dream* (1992), other women who have achieved self-fulfillment find themselves able to reach out and care for others. In *Fair and Tender*

Ladies, Ivy Rowe discovers that being "ruint" through pregnancy out of wedlock has made her free. As she prepares to leave her home in Majestic, Virginia, she writes her sister Silvaney,

I feel strong. I feel good, and I have to say I am excited to leave, for you know I have always wanted to travel. . . . I think my baby is excited too. I think I can feel her moving. And this is another thing. I know she is a little girl. I will raise her so good up on Diamond Mountain where no body will know her mother is your ruint sister. (125)

In Ivy Rowe, Smith unites the sensual with the maternal, the individual with the family, creating a character who "refuses the prescriptions of patriarchy—shame, self-disgust—by staying close to her mountain roots, her womanly life" (Dorothy Hill 111). After her daughter, Joli, is born, Ivy marries Oakley Fox and gives birth to twin sons, Billie and Danny Ray, and two daughters, LuIda and Maudy. Yet she does not want to become a woman like her mother has been, "burdened by all her cares" (120), worn down by her love for her sick husband and her needy children, a woman Ivy describes as "not pretty no more but [who] crys all the time" (16). When Ivy herself threatens to disappear "into the easy darkness" of family life, losing all sense of herself and "feeling old" like her mother (208, 209), she runs off with Honey Breeding—a man who "*is* me, and I am him. . . . I felt I had got a part of myself back that I had lost without even knowing it was gone. Honey had given me back my very soul" (230, 232). Honey Breeding reconnects Ivy with the imaginative, poetic side of herself—the side she also expresses in her letters to her institutionalized sister Silvaney. Ivy believes she had no choice but to go off with Honey, concluding, "Say what you will, and I don't care what anybody said then or might say now, it could not have happened otherwise. I had to do it. I had to have him" (230). Most importantly, through her brief affair with Honey Breeding, Ivy comes to realize, "I could of climbed up here by myself, anytime! But I had not. . . . That is for boys [she had always thought]" (232). Now she can find the way to the mountain heights, and the heights of her own soul, by herself.

Yet when her daughter LuIda dies in her absence, Ivy feels overcome by guilt. It is Geneva Hunt who reminds Ivy:

"Ivy, don't be ridiculous. You are not the first woman in the world to run off with a man nor will you be the last. . . ."

"I am a scandal," I told Geneva.

". . . I used to be a scandal myself," Geneva said. "Now I'm an institution." She winked at me.

Even sad as I was then, I had to laugh. Geneva is 70 if she's a day, and still up to no good. (244-45)

Ivy comes to feel that her renewal through Honey Breeding was not only necessary for herself but beneficial to others besides. The retarded Martha Gayheart, whom Ivy had taken in and cared for along with her own children, becomes more independent during Ivy's absence (eventually marrying, to everyone's surprise), and Ivy's own husband, Oakley Fox, has gained "[rather than been] hurt. . . . [Oakley] has been *new* for me ever since, some way, and me for him" (270).

Ivy raises Joli to become the successful writer she would like to have been herself, and she helps to raise Joli's son, David, after her eldest daughter's divorce in order to help Joli achieve her ambition. Ivy moves Joli forward, as Geneva Hunt has done for her, reminding Joli that she wasn't raised "to be a quitter," that she can make it on her own (with some help from Ivy with the boy, David), that Joli is no longer merely a daughter—she is "past the point where [she] could ever come back here and live"—but a fulfilling life awaits her if she "keep[s] on keeping on" (281). Ivy persists in getting on with her own life after the death of Oakley. She refuses to marry Curtis Bostick and return to West Virginia with him, writing to Joli, "I belong right here. . . . I've got things to do!" (283). From her mountain home, Ivy works to establish a settlement school and fights the Peabody Coal Company to protect her mountain environment. In her old age, she continues to live the life she has wanted, remembering at the end how "I walked in my body like a Queen" (317) and how that sensual and spiritual sense of self empowered her: she had "loved, and loved, and loved. I am fair wore out with it" (316) at last.

In Lee Smith's *The Devil's Dream*, it is Katie Cocker who is the artist-survivor of the family, the one who can reach out to others at the end of the novel from the wholeness of her own being. Katie has run away from home into the world her mother has warned her about, loving and losing, marrying and separating, bearing children, and carrying on a singing career through it all. She is not terrified by the female life of the songs she sings or the topsy-turvy life she leads, unlike her great-aunt Lizzie Bailey. Lizzie has been frightened by "the very notion of love . . . bringing to mind all the old ballads, which show love as a kind of sickness, or a temptation unto death, a temptation which destroys women, even as it destroyed Mamma. To me, 'falling in love' was like falling in death" (97). Unlike Lizzie Bailey, who leaves home to become a career nurse who turns down hopeful suitors, Katie Cocker continues to embrace life's fullness through her singing career and a series of romantic entanglements. Often no more sensible than the women in the songs she sings (victims of demon lovers) or the women in her own family (women such as Lizzie Bailey's mother, Nonnie, who ran off with "Dr." Harry Sharp from the traveling medicine show only to die by herself in a hotel fire, seeing the blue eyes of the husband she has betrayed but loved, hearing the "cold singing" of his hell-fire church [79]), Katie Cocker survives through bouts of depression, addiction to alcohol and drugs, abandonment by her first husband, her daughter's crippling polio, and the sudden deaths of two husbands. Time after time, Katie pulls herself up, saying: "Katie, girl. . . . You can either lay in bed for the rest of your life, or you can get up and make something of yourself. It's up to you. You've got some more singing to do. Get up" (261).

Katie has a great capacity for love—but not for dependence on love. In her second marriage to Ralph Handy, we see Katie's ability to give of herself and also inspire a love equal to her own. She remembers one of her conversations with Ralph before his death:

> "Honey?" I said. "Will you love me when I'm old?" . . .
>
> "Katie-bird," Ralph said very solemn, feeling of my stomach [she is pregnant with their twins], "as God is my witness, I will love you when you're old. I will love you till the end of the world," he said.
>
> . . . I tried to explain. "The thing that kills me is, I just wish we were both real young right now, honey, and had our whole lives ahead of us. . . ."
>
> Good old Ralph. He'd bring me back down to earth every time. "But you can't do it, sugar," he said then. "It don't work that way. The only way you can go is straight ahead, full-tilt boogie. There ain't no other way." So that's the way we went, Ralph and me, and it was fine. (290)

After Ralph is killed in a head-on collision in their traveling van, Katie stumbles a bit but continues "straight ahead" on. She reviews her singing career, remembering,

> I had been a dumb hick Raindrop with Virgie, I had been a honky-tonk angel with Wayne Ricketts [her first husband], I had been a California pop singer with Tom Barksdale, I had been a good country woman with [her second husband] Ralph. For the first time in my professional life, I didn't have an image. I was alone again. (299)

And yet, in reviewing her past and working to shape her future, finding herself on her own once more, Katie realizes that she embraces all of the images and voices of her past—that she is as versatile and creative as her entire Grassy Branch singing family has been. Confident of herself once

more, Katie reaches out to the family she has left behind to find fulfillment in her own life. She brings all of them together again to celebrate
what they have shared—their love for music and their respective talents—by creating an album together. Katie Cocker reconnects with a
family she fled, a mother who stifled her, and a painful, confusing past,
determining to live her life and experience her selfhood as fully as possible. Her independence has provided her with a reservoir of strength and
love.

The protagonists of other contemporary white southern women
writers follow a similar pattern: escape from family; reconnection with
home; continuing independence. In Lisa Alther's comic novel *Kinflicks*
(1975), Ginny Babcock has left her family in Hullsport, Tennessee, to
assume

a dizzying succession of disguises—a black cardigan buttoned up the back and
a too-tight straight skirt and Clem Cloyd's red silk Korean windbreaker when
she left home for college in Boston; a smart tweed suit and horn-rim Ben
Franklin glasses and a severe bun after a year at Worthley; wheat jeans and a
black turtleneck and Goliath sandals after she became Eddie Holzer's lover and
dropped out of Worthley; a red Stark's Bog Volunteer Fire Department
Women's Auxiliary blazer after her marriage to Ira Bliss. (16)

With her father dead and her marriage to Ira in ruins, the "protean
daughter" (17) returns home one last time to sit at the bedside of her
dying mother, knowing that she has failed both to find a satisfying, lasting identity for herself or one that would please her mother: "all
attempted roles to date had been disasters in her mother's eyes, Ginny
knew. Wife to Ira, mother to Wendy—this her mother approved of. But it
was all over. Guilt" (169).

Now Ginny is surprised to find her own life of little importance to
her mother; Mrs. Babcock has concerns and needs of her own as she
approaches death. Ginny finds herself disoriented, no longer able to
define herself in relation to her mother's wishes. She realizes that

almost everything she had done to date had been either in emulation of, or in
reaction against, this powerful nonpal of a woman, or her equally influential
husband. . . . Ginny had no idea how her parents might better have occupied
themselves in life, but there had to be other ways for adults to amuse themselves
than by irreparably molding the young minds placed in their charge. (150)

On the verge of despair, questioning the value of all she has been and
done, acknowledging her continued dependence on her mother and

father throughout her "independent" life, Ginny is amazed to find herself *free*.

Bewildered and frightened, Ginny asks her mother what she should do. Mrs. Babcock replies, "I don't know what you should do, Ginny. . . . You must do as you think best" (430-31). Mrs. Babcock has given her daughter the gift of freedom—something Ginny has previously had to "take" and feel guilty about (170)—something, as well, that Mrs. Babcock's own mother had denied her daughter, insisting on the importance of "duty" to husband and children over the necessity of self-fulfillment (168-69). Ginny responds with grateful surprise, "[Her] eyes snapped open, as though she were Sleeping Beauty just kissed by the prince. . . . Was it possible that the generational spell had actually been broken? They smiled at each other, their delight mixed with distress" (431). Before she dies, Mrs. Babcock sells the family homestead as her "parting gift" to Ginny, saying, "every house should be sold before it's allowed to become a monument. The past, doted over, distorts the present"—giving Ginny her clock, instead, "to take with you wherever you decide to go" (501).

Ginny will not remain rooted in the house of the past. Instead, she has been released once more into the world—her mother's clock a reminder of all they have shared together, including the painful knowledge of their own mortality, as well as a symbol of the expanse of time Ginny now is free to shape as she pleases. As Katherine Payant explains,

At the same time Ginny comes to terms with her feelings of guilt, she realizes that the experimentation of the past ten years has been essential to her growth. Poised on the brink of her future, Ginny grapples with the frightening knowledge of her freedom. She has been caring for some baby birds who obviously represent herself and her mother; immediately before her mother's death, the last bird dies, killing itself by flying into a closed window, even though the window next to it was open. Unlike the bird, Ginny now sees the open window. After her mother's death, Ginny briefly contemplates suicide, a kind of existential crisis; but finally she embraces life, packs her things, and leaves Hullsport, "to go where [she] had no idea" (518). (40)

Freedom is not easy to win or to use. Ginny must work to shape a life worthy of the gift she has been given. Yet Alther's tone is positive, her outlook hopeful. Her heroine has shown great resourcefulness and resiliency in creating a life for herself all along. She will be capable of changing to meet the challenges ahead—no longer in defiance of her mother but with her mother's final blessing and love to strengthen her more.

In Lisa Alther's subsequent novels, her protagonists also learn, with Ginny Babcock, to adapt and grow: renouncing the past; then reconnecting with it; finally moving beyond it to create their independent lives. They are amazed to discover their own resiliency, as Caroline Kelley tells her therapist Hannah Burke in *Other Women* (1984): "I always thought it was a question of achieving some permanent state of tranquillity . . . but it's not. It's more like learning to surf. The waves keep rolling in, each different from the last, and you have to ride them, instead of getting pounded to bits" (376). While Caroline learns she cannot "control what happens," she finds she "can control [her] response to it" (309). The new lives she and other Alther heroines fashion for themselves may be incomplete and imperfect, one wave crashing after another, but they allow for personal freedom and growth, revitalization and renewal. In *Other Women*, for instance, Caroline realizes she has a number of choices for her future, deciding for the time being to live with her friend Diana in a difficult relationship while continuing to mother her two sons, confident in the knowledge that she has other options. In the later *Bedrock* (1990), Clea Shawn chooses to leave her husband of many years and two grown children whom she loves and to whom she continues to be bound, to move to the less-than-ideal village of Roches Ridge, Vermont, and begin a lesbian relationship with her artist friend, Elke. Clea does so, confident "that no pain was permanent, and no loss was real. That even though people treated each other abominably, even though they left, even though you let them go, even though you never laid eyes on them again, this fugue that linked you continued, whether you liked it or not" (341).

While some relationships are always beginning and others ending, Alther's protagonists discover that each one is part of life's complex "fugue." Personal choices affect everyone; they must be made thoughtfully and carefully. In the process of growing and changing, Alther's protagonists find themselves searching for ways to make life's rich musical pattern more harmonious and satisfying not only for themselves but for their societies at large. While human exploitation and degradation, sexism and racism, may continue, as Lisa Alther makes clear in her second novel *Original Sins* (1981), three of the special "Five" who have climbed the branches of the Castle Tree at the outset of her novel point to the next generation playing in its branches both with awareness of the need for societal change and the knowledge of their own sustained efforts to bring it about. While Emily Prince, Raymond Tatro, and Donny Tatro have failed to alter gender, class, and race relationships in their own time, they have continued to develop personally and to work for social betterment. Emily has renounced her privileged southern past to engage in the sexual revolution of the 1960s and 1970s, joining feminist groups and working for gay rights in New York City. Raymond Tatro, white son of a mill foreman, becomes politicized in the North, returning south to try to organize labor in his hometown cotton mills. Unsuccessful in this venture, he begins futile attempts to encourage his Kentucky coal mining relatives to cling to a simple, antimaterialist past. And Donny Tatro (Raymond's distant relative) engages in Civil Rights activities, attending Black Panther meetings and engaging in voter registration drives. Their failures are many, and their gains few, but Alther makes clear there is no hope without determined efforts such as theirs. Social change is work that, as Raymond Tatro is in danger of forgetting, "required patience. Tomatoes didn't ripen overnight. Bread took three hours to rise. Soup stock had to simmer all day" (489). Donny, Emily, and Raymond must persist for the benefit of the generation to follow. In Alther's *Five Minutes in Heaven* (1995), Jude's grandfather also attempts to help a younger generation. When Jude's grandmother protests her husband's "horrible [WWI] war stories" as unfit for a little girl, Jude's grandfather argues, "She needs to know what she's up against. I wish I had known. . . . She's a human being. We're all in this mess together. That's the only thing that makes it bearable" (37). Awakened early to life's sorrows through her grandfather's stories and the death of her mother, Jude finds her own life is also one of continual loss and pain—with her best friend Molly's death following that of her mother; her lover Anna's death coming on the heels of the murder of her longtime friend and male lover, Sandy. Jude finds she has "a gift for [suffering]. I've done it all my life" (370). However, after a bout of suicidal despair in Paris, Jude also discovers that her capacity for love, as well as for sorrow, ultimately affirms life, remaining a positive force she can carry within her. Alther demands that her heroines (and her readers) relinguish their romantic dreams of love and life and face up to reality. The optimism of her fiction, if hard won, remains powerful. Her protagonists grow and change, attempting to improve life; while they endure much failure and loss, they persevere in fighting human prejudice and social injustice against gays, blacks, women, the impoverished, and the exploited. They are stronger than they have believed; to their own surprise, as well as the incredulity of others, they choose not only to survive but to struggle for a better life.

In Mary Lee Settle's *The Killing Ground* (1982), Hannah McKarkle is another protagonist who has had to face up to human suffering and fight for individual freedom—for herself and others. Her parents believed that they owned their children, as their ancestors before them had owned slaves, being white southern aristocrats in whom the "ownership of people" seems to have become inbred (339). Hannah has escaped to New York, leaving her veteran brother Johnny at home to carry on a wastrel existence encouraged by his mother and ignored by his father. As police officer Toey tells Hannah,

I tell you something. [Your mother] *liked* Johnny's drinking like that. She *liked* it. That way he stayed guilty and he stayed home. When I'd take him home her face would melt with affection like butter and she'd take him over. It was obscene. If she could have carried him upstairs like a little baby she would have. (224-25)

Johnny is encouraged to remain irresponsible and childish, hating his own weak dependency and his class privilege, grateful when a poor, distant relative kills him and ends his burdensome life. Now it is Hannah who is wanted to fill the lack at home—her mother saying, "[W]e all think it best that you give up your apartment in New York and come back home where you belong. . . . where you are needed" (337). Her father refuses to continue her allowance so that she will have no alternative but to return home. Hannah must resist both of her parents—but, mostly, she must resist herself: "It was not only that those two people, poised there forever in my mind on the muted flowers of the sofa, took for granted they had the right to make decisions for other human beings, but that I had to fight my way out of the sin of taking it for granted, too" (358).

Leaving her powerful parents and the Virginia community they have influenced in order "to save my soul" (358), Hannah pays the price of her disloyalty: She is cut off from her father's money throughout his life and then is left "her share [of his estate] in trust to her children if any. Well, she was forty years old when he died and there still weren't any" (23). Despite her virtual disinheritance, Hannah knows that she has had early and continuing privilege through her family's position, "that people like me are never poor" (366) due to their advantaged beginnings. She grows spiritually through writing, teaching, and traveling, marrying only when she feels she has made a home inside herself, "carried . . . within . . . protected, like a Bedouin" (367). Hannah knows that she is different from the aristocratic southern women she has left behind

[with] their dangerous satisfactions. They are, in one of the bloodiest centuries of the Christian era, women to whom nothing has happened that is not personal. Aging, dry, and complicated girls, they still call each other girls, weathered by years, unchanged. . . . They are the prisoners of the welfare of their parents, their husbands, the habits of their privilege. (9)

Hannah is unlike her aging hometown contemporaries in her sense of self, the scope of her world, the gravity of her concerns. She is vital, independent, committed to change in her writing and her life while her contemporaries have remained "girls," staying behind to become irrelevant, isolated, withering "prisoners" of the past.

The old guard is dying out, its power already challenged by women like Hannah and Hannah's Aunt Althea—who has freed Johnny's killer from jail and established him in a business of his own, recognizing both the accidental nature of his crime and the long-standing injustices that have led to his anger at Johnny's social class privilege. Further, on her brief return home to give a speech in 1978, Hannah comes to feel hope for the children of the modern South:

I was watching a new breed of child, maybe as mistaken as we had been, but at least unafraid of the fathers. Beyond the long knives of the sixties revolution, these children of the next decade had been granted adulthood as a right. It is the only lasting result of revolution I know, when a dream of one generation becomes a right of the next. (382)

With the dissolution of southern patriarchy comes adult privilege and responsibility for all. The few can no longer keep the many dependent, encouraging their childishness, irresponsibility, anger, and resentment, which have led to Johnny McKarkle's tragic death. Hannah believes that "our children had been born to clean . . . away" their fathers' "arrogance and lack of care for each other" (384). When these sons and daughters assume the rights of full adult choice and their responsibilities for the welfare of others, Hannah predicts that the South, the nation, and the world alike will benefit.

Nancy Finch in Doris Betts's *Heading West* (1981) must also wrest full adult life from a domineering, yet dependent, mother and the obligations of her family life. Nancy admits that "nothing of [her] life except a few tepid love affairs had taken place unseen by her family" (14), yet she is unable to break away (like Tyler's Charlotte Emory in *Earthly Possessions*) until she is kidnapped by a man who calls himself Dwight Anderson. Librarian Nancy believes that her life story can be summarized to read, "Unsatisfactory Conditions, from which she was being abducted by an Unsatisfactory Kidnapper" (31). She finds that her life experience has been so limited that she admits that seeing Texas and Arizona made "the thought that rescuers might arrive any minute . . . not as pleasing as it should have been" (64). Nancy begins to feel that "[she] was dumb not to [escape from home] sooner" (169)—understanding that her family were "lifetime victims . . . [who had become] skillful at the tyrannies of martyrdom," keeping her in thrall to them all these years (23-24). Ironically, after a lifetime of sacrificing herself on their behalf, Nancy finds that her family has thrived in her absence. Her sister Faye has managed to assist her mother and brother from time to time, finding that the health of both has improved in Nancy's absence, and her mother has dipped into a nest egg Nancy didn't even know existed to buy an answering machine and a new color television for herself and her retarded son, Beckham.

While Nancy still values unselfishness and responsibility to others, she realizes that her life at home has made her so dissatisfied that she has had little time to think of others: "Yet I've been living a home life that must have looked unselfish to others—and I hated it," that "it wasn't unselfish if you were primarily thinking of your own reactions" (126). She sees how dissatisfaction can build to create the kind of unhealthy obsession her kidnapper has had with his family. Despite his "independent," outlaw life, Dwight Anderson has never freed himself from thoughts of the past, the terrible anger and resentments of his youth. Nancy escapes both Dwight and her family's own hold on her, at the same time. Returning home, Nancy helps her family make arrangements for her final leave-taking, feeling at last "more tender toward her family than [she had] in years" (350) as she prepares to marry Hunt, a man she met in Arizona after her escape from Dwight. Hunt tells Nancy he is glad that she has "stopped blaming [her] family for so much" (357) and has taken responsibility for fulfilling her own needs and making a life of her own. At the end of the novel, Nancy watches as her mother and retarded brother sit in front of their new television with "an identical expression of what Nancy would have called happiness. . . . They did not notice the smile she gave them, but she did not mind" (359). Once more, in this novel, self-fulfillment makes love for others possible.

Just as Nancy Finch must be forced into creating an independent life for herself, so, too, are a number of younger protagonists thrust into self-development at much earlier ages. Molly Bolt of Rita Mae Brown's *Rubyfruit Jungle* (1973) never feels that she belongs. As her mother continually reminds her, she has been adopted and has no blood relations. She grows up feeling different from others, an outsider:

I had never thought I had much in common with anybody. I had no mother, no father, no roots. No biological similarities called sisters and brothers. And for a future I didn't want a split-level home with a station wagon, pastel refrigerator, and a houseful of blonde children evenly spaced through the years. . . . I didn't even want a husband or any man for that matter. I wanted to go my own way.

That's all I think I ever wanted, to go my own way and maybe find some love here and there. (88)

Her cousin Leroy warns Molly, "[Y]ou're headin' for a hard life. You say you're gonna be a doctor or something great. Then you say you ain't gettin' married. You have to do some of the things everybody does or people don't like you" (36). Her mother, Carrie, also scolds her daughter, complaining to her husband, Carl:

[S]he don't act natural. It ain't right for a girl to be running all around with the boys at all hours. She climbs trees, takes cars apart, and worse, she tells them what to do and they listen to her. She don't want to learn none of the things she has to know to get a husband. Smart as she is, a woman can't get on in this world without a husband. (39)

Molly Bolt is, in fact, in for a hard life, as she has been told: expulsion for homosexuality from the University of Florida; sleeping in an abandoned car, then in a roach-infested apartment in New York; serving ice cream and hamburgers at The Flick in order to pay her rent and college tuition at New York University; majoring in the male-dominated field of film directing and being ostracized by her fellow students and male department head.

Yet Molly becomes stronger through her experiences, feeling kinship with others who are social outcasts and minorities. "Since I don't know who my real folks are maybe they're colored [she has argued to her mother in her youth]. Maybe it's all right for me to go in those bathrooms. . . . I don't care what the hell I am. And I ain't staying away from people because they look different" (59). She values her black friends Cal and Holly in New York. And she comes to understand that she has learned not only how to be strong and independent by fighting with her mother but has gained empathy with the poor and a growing awareness of American social class differences through her mother. She comes to understand, despite her mother's harsh and cruel words to her in childhood, that she has gained something from her: "Carrie wasn't fooled by show and she regarded most of the world around her as a show for the rich at the expense of the poor" (95). Because of Carrie's influence, Molly turns down archeologist Chryssa Hart's offer to "pay my way through film school, if only [Molly would agree to be her mistress]" (167). Molly's family inheritance has been "poor pride," enabling her to deconstruct Chryssa's interest in her and reject the rich woman's offer to "buy me the way she goes and buys a winter coat or a Gucci handbag" (168). Molly determines that she will continue on her own, in poverty, retaining her proud independence and succeeding on her own to complete her degree and make movies, "real movies about real people and about the way the shit comes down. Now if I don't get the money to do that until I'm fifty, then that's the way it is" (174).

For her senior project, Molly returns home to Florida to film her mother:

Carrie, Carrie whose politics are to the right of Genghis Khan. Who believes that if the good Lord wanted us to live together he'd have made us all one color. Who believes a woman is only as good as the man she's with. And I love her. Even when I hated her, I loved her. . . . maybe underneath her crabshell of prejudice and fear there's a human being that's loving. (242)

Molly Bolt overcomes the barriers of poverty and social difference, forgives her mother and others who have been cruel to her, and celebrates her lesbian identity and the pleasures of life. She creates a film that values Carrie's strength of character, interpersonal love between a mother and daughter, and human survival in the face of pain and hardship—their shared experience as well as that of so many others:

And the projects began. The one that drew the most applause was a gang rape on an imaginary Martian landscape with half the cast dressed as Martians, the other half, as humans. All the men mumbled about what a profound racial statement it was. The "chicks" gasped.

My film was last on the list and by the time we got to it some of the audience had already left. There was Carrie speeding away in her rocking chair looking straight at the camera and being herself. No quick cuts to steals from Kenneth Anger, no tinfoil balls dropping out of the sky to represent nuclear hail—just Carrie talking about her life, the world today, and the price of meat. (243-44)

Molly will continue to face intolerance, rejection and hate, but she has learned from her experiences. She faces the future with hope and determination: "One way or another I'll make those movies and I don't feel like having to fight until I'm fifty. But if it does take that long then watch out world because I'm going to be the hottest fifty-year-old this side of the Mississippi" (246). Rita Mae Brown's Molly Bolt has experienced many obstacles in life but she remains invigorated by her struggles and undaunted as she faces the future.

Ellen in Kaye Gibbons's *Ellen Foster* (1987) is another adolescent strengthened by early battles with family and poverty. At eleven she loses her mother, whose heart has been weakened by "romantic fever"

(3)—an appropriate term in view of her disastrous marriage. When her mother finally despairs, taking an overdose of sleeping pills, Ellen is not allowed to seek help. Left motherless and alone with a man she regards as a "monster" (18) and "a mistake for a person" (58), Ellen later admits that "when I was little I would think of ways to kill my daddy" (1). While her father goes off to drink every day, eating his meals at the local dinette, leaving his daughter on her own, Ellen fends for herself. She goes to school, pays all their bills with money she takes from her father's monthly payments for land he has sold his brothers, and fixes her own meals: "I found the best deal was the plate froze with food already on it. A meat, two vegetables, and a dab of dessert" (30). When her father begins to make sexual advances, calling Ellen by her mother's name, she escapes to her black friend Starletta's family who provide her with a warm coat, a safe bed, food, and company.

Ellen knows that she cannot continue to impose on Starletta's family, that she needs a more permanent refuge from her father. When her Aunt Betsy tells her she can take her only for a weekend, Ellen talks to her art teacher at school about her situation; the teacher promptly decides to take her home where Ellen lives blissfully free of fear and want with her new mother and father. However, a judge decrees that Ellen must return to live with her own blood relatives, causing Ellen to wonder helplessly "what . . . you do when the judge talks about the family [as] society's cornerstone but you know yours was never a Roman pillar but is and always has been crumbly old brick?" (66). Family again proves disastrous for Ellen when her "mama's mama" takes her in yet can only feel hatred toward Ellen for having her father's eyes and letting her mother die. She forces Ellen to work in the cotton fields all summer for room and board. There Ellen learns about true family connectedness and human compassion once more, not from her own people or her own race, but again from blacks who work in the fields, especially storytelling Mavis. Ellen realizes that her grandmother's exploitation of blacks is far worse than the abuse she herself endures at her grandmother's hands—and begins to understand that a generous, kindhearted people has long suffered at the hands of whites, such as her cruel grandmother, who consider themselves "betters."

When she has been freed from her own enslavement by her grandmother's death, Ellen goes one last time to a relative's to live—her Aunt Nadine's and cousin Dora's—knowing in advance the quality of the "love" she can expect to find there. From the outset, she prepares to find a real home for herself—one where Christmas will not mean Ellen's receiving a simple pack of paper while she watches Dora open package after package. She has seen the "Foster" family at Nadine's church and determined to join them (although she does not realize that they are called "Foster" only because the daughters are all foster children). When Nadine tells Ellen to leave, "that she didn't want me to begin with. That Betsy didn't want me either" (131), Ellen appears on "Mrs. Foster's" doorstep explaining, "I figured since you already had some girls about my size that you might be able to squeeze me in. I planned to come on New Year's but here I am today [Christmas Day]" (138).

Ellen Foster is a survivor who sustains life's blows, learning how to protect herself and become more self-sufficient with each difficulty. She refuses to see herself as a victim but maintains her pride and self-respect throughout—qualities nourished by her "new family." When they go to church together, Ellen feels that "we are somebody because my new mama gets part of the collection money every week. That goes for our support, our food and clothes. You go in that church and act genuine. . . . Worse could happen than for you to sit for a hour. You could be where you came from" (66). True family may have failed Ellen, but she has faith in herself and in the home she has chosen for her own. Rather than dwelling on the abuses of her family past, Ellen reflects, "[I]f I think about my life . . . I can see how lucky I am" (140). She invites her friend Starletta to visit with her foster family, desiring to repay a debt that she knows can never be repaid. "I came a long way to get here but when you think about it real hard you will see that old Starletta came even farther. . . . And all this time I thought I had the hardest row to hoe. That will always amaze me" (146). Ellen's early knowledge of life's hardships has not only prepared her for the future but deepened her respect for her fellow survivors—the ongoing courage, dignity, and compassion with which they have taught her to meet life.[5]

Samantha Hughes in Bobbie Ann Mason's *In Country* (1985) has just graduated from high school in Hopewell, Kentucky, but she, too, has known the loss of a parent and family dissolution in her life. Fred Hobson points out that "family to seventeen-year-old Sam in *In Country* is Hawkeye and Colonel Blake and the other characters on M*A*S*H, and community is those other people out there who also see and believe in M*A*S*H" (12). With her father killed in Vietnam, her mother remarried and settled in Lexington, Kentucky, with a husband and new baby, and her housemate Uncle Emmett psychologically damaged by the Vietnam war and afraid to commit to work, relationships, or family, Sam has learned to cope on her own and lead an independent life.

Yet she wants to connect with the family she has been denied—especially her dead father and his Vietnam experience. While her Uncle Emmett warns her, "You can't learn from the past. The main thing you learn from history is that you can't learn from history. That's what history *is*" (226), and Sam's mother has fled the past to begin a new life of her own, Sam remains preoccupied by personal loss (and the country's military one). In seeking to understand the losses of the Vietnam war and the male experience of her father Dwayne, Samantha is actually, we find, preparing for her own future. She is seeking a way out of the traditional female role that has ensnared her pregnant and about-to-be-married friend Dawn, as well as Sam's own mother, who is starting on her second marriage and second round of motherhood. In the course of the novel, Sam breaks up with her boyfriend Lonnie, decides to enter the University of Kentucky in the fall, and prepares to leave Hopewell and her Uncle Emmett to live with her mother in Lexington, Kentucky. As Ellen Blais explains,

Ultimately, Sam's preoccupation with her dead father and the Vietnam War brings her out of Hopewell on a path toward the University of Kentucky and provides her with emotional experiences that suggest she may also be able to reconcile her male and female aspects and resolve her ambivalence about gender. Her decision to attend the University of Kentucky rather than remain in Hopewell, working at the Burger Boy and taking care of Emmett, indicates she will probably be able to do this without slipping into conventional feminine roles. (113)

Samantha advises her friend Dawn to have an abortion, as she herself would do, coming to realize the enormity of such a female decision and its connection with the male experience of her father, her Uncle Emmett, and the Vietnam veterans she knows: "soldiers murdered babies. But women did too. They ripped their own unborn babies out of themselves and flushed them away, squirming and bloody" (215). Further, as Ellen Blais points out, "in coming to accept Dwayne's dealing out and suffering death, Sam accepts her own complicity in war, violence, and death itself, her own mortality as well as America's 'mortality' [through] . . . military defeat" (116). Impurity and loss are inevitable parts of life, Samantha finds. She has "lost" her father, a traditional family life, the complete attention of her mother, and her youthful innocence—but she has gained the maturity she needs for survival and decision-making in the future.

Another thoughtful seventeen-year-old heroine obsessed by loss is Lucille Odom of Josephine Humphreys's *Rich in Love* (1987). When Lucille's mother leaves her twenty-seven-year-old marriage, "betray-[ing]" (in Lucille's eyes) her youngest daughter and her entire family (1), disappearing "to start a second life" (18), Lucille loses the sense of her family as more safe and secure than those of her friends:

These [other] families let themselves in for it. All around me I saw the American family blowing apart, as described in *Psychology Today*. The American family needed to hold itself more closely, I thought. Like mine. We were a hermit family. We had each other and we had our house, and nothing could touch us. (15)

When her "hermit family" begins to fall apart, Lucille is so upset that she misses her exams and her high school graduation, feeling that her mother has failed them all: "a family without a mother is vulnerable. She left us sitting ducks. If she had stayed, I believe we would have been all right" (24). Now Lucille's father has become depressed and confused, while her sister Rae has returned home with her new husband, Billy McQueen. Rae is pregnant with the baby Billy tricked her into conceiving in order to make her "his" forever (231) and bewildered by the changes in her life and her tumultuous feelings. Lucille finds both her family life and her own life far more difficult than they had ever seemed before—and love more complex (as in Billy McQueen's act of love making Rae pregnant (231))—than she had known it could be.

While Lucille feels "rich in love [her love for others and theirs for her]" (146), she finds, too, that others make enormous demands upon that love, such as her boyfriend, Wayne Frobiness. She begins to understand the pain of loving:

Sometimes I felt a strong urge to quit loving my father. Just quit, the way you can go down to a bank and draw out your life's savings. It was a kind of love that tuckered me out while returning no great reward, and maybe that is how it's meant to be, so that sooner or later a child will realize love is more wisely invested elsewhere than in a parent. (77)

Gradually Lucille begins to understand the limits of love—that it was possible, as her mother has told her, for her parents to have "carried love to its conclusion" (205). With Rae grown and Lucille self-sufficient, a girl who hadn't "needed [her mother] for anything since the sixth grade. . . . You wanted to take care of yourself, and you succeeded, too" (204), Lucille's mother had found her life at a standstill:

Nothing was ever new. Nothing! I don't mean it was [your father's] fault, his fears were not his fault, they came from the Depression and his mother and father—but he wanted to protect everything. That was his goal. To protect me, the children, the house, even the dogs. And from what, I wanted to know! From the world. But people should not be protected from the world, Lucille, it cripples them. Look at me. I am unfit for the world, and I always loved the world. I loved travel and politics and art. . . . I was crazy for the world, at one time. (204-05)

Now, at forty-nine, Lucille's mother begins to "'recuperate'" (209) by "get[ting] away from . . . the whole package, the house, everything. The family. Let me get away from it, I've been in it so long, Lucille. We did it for so long!"—reentering the world through her little job and small house, finding that her former husband, too, "is already improving. He was in a rut, and now I can hear in his voice on the phone that he's excited about new things . . . taking up new interests," even beginning a relationship with another woman (210). Amidst "all this troubled love" (258)—of her parents, Rae and Billy, her high school friends and their relationships—Lucille begins to find her self.

Lucille awakens and realizes, "I was nothing but myself, I was simple and . . . unscathed, yes" (258). She has survived the break-up of her parents' marriage. Eventually her father remarries; her sister Rae moves with Billy and their new baby into a small house of their own; Lucille moves in with her mother; and the family homestead is sold. Lucille discovers that "though I once believed I could not live without that house, the ease with which I gave it up was almost frightening" (260). No longer trapped in the house of her family past, Lucille concludes:

Our family is not what it was, but we are all gravitating back into family lives of one sort and another. . . . [Once] "family" meant people in a house together. But that was in a language so far back that all its words are gone, a language we can only imagine. (260)

Unlike Danner of Phillips's *Machine Dreams,* Lucille Odom embraces her new and more far-flung, flexible, modern family—as well as her growing independence as she prepares to go to college, telling her little niece Phoebe, "I don't think I will marry. . . . I'm not afraid to live alone. . . . But who knows what will happen?" (261). Lucille has been liberated from the concept of the traditional, patriarchal family, thanks to her mother's courage in renewing a life gone stale. She finds that the enduring "family" is one that is loosely structured and flexible—able to endure betrayal, departure, growth, and renewal—its love more elastic and far-reaching than she had ever imagined. Lucille has matured, gaining a sense of her own needs as ones apart from those of her family. She is ready for life's complexity, which her family now mirrors—learning from her "adventuress" mother (192) how to grow and change, love and let go, roam free and remain centered, at the same time.

Paralleling Godwin: Creating New Communities

In Humphreys's *Rich in Love*, as in so many of the works we have looked at, care for others is shown to grow along with care for self. Over and over, female protagonists who have learned to respect themselves, as in the mature novels of Gail Godwin, are shown to be more capable of giving to others than they have ever been before. Those who have succeeded most in their own self-development (Candy and Nettie in Smith's *Family Linen*; Ivy Rowe in *Fair and Tender Ladies*; Emily Prince in Alther's *Original Sins*; or Hannah McKarkle and her Aunt Althea in Settle's *The Killing Ground*) become forces for the betterment of their communities, as well. These mature and independent women work to achieve the social justice Margaret in Stephens's *Children of the World* and Ellen in Gibbons's *Ellen Foster* hunger to know—a justice Margaret and Ellen have found thwarted by their own grandmothers, women who have failed to understand that "to work well for your own ends is not enough . . . not as long as people are suffering" (*Children of the World* 77). Kaye Gibbons in *A Cure for Dreams* (1991) and *Charms for the Easy Life* (1993) offers us grandmothers who can be both loved and respected by their daughters and granddaughters—women who have found that they cannot separate their own development and well-being from that of their community and the world in which they live.

The grandmother of Gibbons's *A Cure for Dreams* is a precursor of the more powerful one who follows in *Charms for the Easy Life*. In the former novel, the grandmother takes responsibility for women and children up and down her Milk Farm Road community—paying for the burial of a boy killed in a cotton baler on her husband's farm (when her husband won't pay); taking up a collection for groceries for an abandoned woman and her many children; getting her friend Amanda back on her feet after her husband's death has thrust her into grief and poverty; and lending a helping hand wherever desertion, disease, destitution, and death seem to have acquired the upper hand. When her daughter objects to going into one home with her mother to make holes in the walls (for pegs on which one family can learn to help itself by hanging its clothes and straightening up its messy environment), her mother pronounces, "Anytime somebody's not looking after themselves it becomes your business" (97). Satisfied with her own life journey from "the bottom rung" in Bell County, Kentucky, to "Queen Bee" bustling about on her Milk Farm Road in Virginia (100), determined to restore order and justice wherever she can, the grandmother of *A Cure for Dreams* finds her own self-sufficiency strenghtened by the self-sufficiency of others, her well-being enhanced by their achievements and success. Her admiring daughter recalls for her own daughter, "Mr. Roosevelt's programs were very helpful [during the Depression], but I'm sure he never realized how much women like my mother were doing to help him pick up after Mr. Hoover" (64).

Charlie Kate, the grandmother of Gibbons's *Charms for the Easy Life*, is another Depression-era grandmother—a woman Judith Beth Cohen believes "might well become the most memorable older woman in twentieth-century literature" (24). In Raleigh, North Carolina, Charlie Kate becomes well-known as an unlicensed physician who uses a combination of herbal remedies and modern science to heal the derelict and the wealthy, the aged and the young, the malnourished and the overfed, alike. She "provides sex education for every child, sends a deserving boy to medical school, frees a woman's hand from a wringer, forces a bumbling doctor to retire, and heals the hermit son of a witch and a warlock"—a woman who does not "accept the reality [of life but instead works to] . . . alter it" (Cohen 24). When her granddaughter Margaret discovers Charlie Kate's body, she finds physical proof, as well, of her grandmother's fulfillment in life: "she hadn't purged. She had always said all she needed to say, and so there were no secret longings, no secret wishes and desires that had never been spoken" (254). Charlie Kate has shown her daughter and granddaughter that the secrets of people's lives, their inner happiness or frustration, can be detected in the condition of the bodies they leave behind.

Charlie Kate has passed on to her daughter, Sophia, and her granddaughter, Margaret, all her insights into and remedies for life's problems, including the charm for "the easy-life" given her by a black man she has saved from lynching. Charlie Kate tells Margaret to pass on this special rabbit's foot to her betrothed with a message, "Tell him it works, depending on your definition of easy" (231). Having taught her daughter and granddaughter that there is no "easy life"—that life is to be lived fully and its challenges (its leprosy and warts) met head on—she has also shown that life does become easier when it is embraced fully. Charlie Kate, an abandoned wife herself, a woman whose twin sister and many other family members have committed suicide, lives and dies without self-pity or resentment. She has fulfilled her dreams—and the needs of her community—as much as her intelligence and skill have allowed, working towards the realization of her goals all along. She watches with pride as her granddaughter, no "giddy girl from the country club set," acquires knowledge and "audacity to match" her future husband's, encouraging Margaret to enter medical school, fulfill her own potential, and follow in her grandmother's footsteps (rather than simply plunging in the immediate into having a family of her own) (183).

Barbara Kingsolver also depicts strong women who work for their communities with growing confidence in themselves and their visions for a better world. In *Animal Dreams* (1990), Codi Noline loses her sister, Hallie, in Nicaragua where she has been trying to help people grow more plentiful and resilient crops, followed by the death of her Alzheimers-disoriented physician father. But she finds an unexpected community in her small hometown of Grace, Arizona, when she returns to look after her father. Unlike Crystal Spangler of *Black Mountain Breakdown*, Codi finds ultimate meaning in returning home and teaching in the local highschool: "I've about decided that's the main thing that separates happy people from the other people: the feeling that you're a practical item, with a use, like a sweater or a socket wrench" (334). Codi not only alerts her science students to local environmental problems, teaching them "to be custodians of the earth" (332), but she finds a sisterhood of concerned and determined women in the local "Stitch and Bitch club" which confronts the Black Mountain Mining Company on the consequences of its seventy years of local operation. Codi acquires new "family," as well, in her Apache lover, Loyd, and her resourceful friend Emelina, plus all of their assorted relatives—deciding to stay in Grace and have Loyd's baby (not abort it as she has in high school), fashioning her "soul" out of daily work and dreams of improving her community (334).

In *The Bean Trees* (1988), Taylor Greer discovers home and family, as well, by leaving her mother in Pittman County, Kentucky, and journeying west to Tuczon, Arizona. As she moves west, she finds that "when I'd crossed into Rocky Mountain Time, I had set my watch back two hours and got thrown into the future. . . . Pittman was twenty years behind the nation in practically every way you can think of, except the rate of teenage pregnancies" (47). Yet her western future includes a Cherokee child thrust upon her by an insistent aunt who is trying to protect the small girl from further sexual abuse by a boyfriend. Taylor protests, "If I wanted a baby I would have stayed in Kentucky. . . . I could have had babies coming out my ears by now" (18), but Turtle (as Taylor calls her) needs Taylor's love and care to come out of her shell and grow strong. Taylor accepts responsibility for Turtle's well-being, acting as mother to her new daughter—formerly just another bruised and unwanted child.

When they arrive in Tuczon, Arizona, Taylor happens upon more new family members, as well: Mattie, her boss at the Jesus Is Lord Used Tire store, and Lou Ann Ruiz and her son, Dwayne Ray, from whom she rents a room. When Lou Ann begins to take on the role of a traditional wife, watching Turtle and Dwayne Ray while Taylor goes to work, cooking and cleaning for them, Taylor protests, "It's not like we're a *family*, for Christ's sake. You've got your own life to live, and I've got mine. You don't have to do all this stuff for me. . . . I never even *had* an old man, why would I want to end up acting like one?" (85). Nevertheless, Taylor finds that Lou Ann and Dwayne Ray, her boss, Mattie, her elderly neighbors Edna Poppy and Virgie Mae Valentine Parsons, all have joined her mother to become "family"—as have the Guatemalan refugees Estevan and Esperanza, whom she helps find a "safe house" in Oklahoma, as well (183). Like the wisteria "bean tree" Turtle loves, thriving in poor soil with "a whole invisible system for helping out the plant that you'd never guess was there. . . . The way Edna has Virgie, and Virgie has Edna, and Sandi [another of Taylor's friends] has Central Station [childcare], and everybody has Mattie" (227-28), Taylor and Turtle find that they have a large extended "family" to nourish and support them.

That extended family is broadened even further in Kingsolver's *Pigs in Heaven* (1993) when Taylor and Turtle discover yet another community as their support system. When Cherokee lawyer Annawake Fourkiller challenges Turtle's "adoption," pointing out that under the Indian Child Welfare Act, Turtle rightfully belongs to the Cherokee Nation, Taylor must learn another lesson about family: that family can be even more inclusive than that she has fashioned for Turtle and herself in Tuczon, Arizona. She discovers that Turtle can be nourished and supported by a "family" located in two different states, composed of people of many different backgrounds, and learns that her own love and care for Turtle can be enhanced, not threatened, by the care of the Cherokee Nation for one of its own.

In fact, Taylor learns that the "contracted" nuclear family is insufficient on its own (284). When she tries to take care of Turtle by herself, escaping Annawake Fourkiller's legal challenge by taking Turtle to Las Vegas and Seattle, Taylor not only runs out of money but, due to her ignorance of Native American milk-intolerance, weakens Turtle's health. Taylor admits that she has needed to acknowledge the existence of extended family in their lives all along:

I *think* of [her boyfriend] Jax and Lou Ann and Dwayne Ray, and of course you [Alice, her mother], and Mattie, my boss at the tire store, all those people as my family. But when you never put a name on things, you're just accepting that it's okay for people to leave when they feel like it. (328)

Taylor, Turtle, and Taylor's mother Alice find in the Cherokee Nation an impoverished society which, nonetheless, takes responsiblity for nurturing all its people (even when individuals such as Turtle's Cherokee abuser fail to do so). They find adolescent boys who show respect for their elders (222) and a "town lunatic" beloved by her people. As Annawake Fourkiller explains to Alice,

"One time in law school we were discussing the concept of so-called irresponsible dependents. That a ward of society can't be a true citizen. I wanted to stand up and tell the class about [crazy] Boma and the bottle tree. That there's another way of looking at it. . . . Just that you could love your crazy people, even admire them, instead of resenting that they're not self-sufficient." (231)

Taylor finds that the Cherokee Nation is important to Turtle's full physical and psychological development, learning that her own love will be respected and strengthened through a "joint custody" arrangement whereby Turtle will live with her grandfather in the Cherokee Nation in the summer and with Taylor in Tuczon the rest of the year.

In the fiction of Fannie Flagg, as well, relatedness is not exclusive but inclusive—not a mere function of the nuclear family but what bonds neighbors, friends, co-workers, even chance acquaintances and passersby. In *Daisy Fay and the Miracle Man* (1981), originally titled *Coming Attractions*, the eleven-year-old protagonist, Daisy Fay, records in her diary a series of events that leads inevitably to the dissolution of her parents' marriage. Rather than becoming self-pitying and afraid of life as a result of her parents' separation and divorce, however, Daisy is shown as developing strength of character, insight into others' hurt and pain, and care for the members of her community. She learns from the mistakes of her mother who writes to her, "I married your daddy because I thought he would take care of me, but he couldn't. Now I find I can barely take care of myself. Try to be more like Grandmother. Don't depend on anyone" (188). Far from depending on her parents, the resourceful, independent Daisy takes on adulthood early, learning from her mother's mistakes while attempting to protect her irresponsible, alcoholic father—even as she enjoys taking part in his zany, get-rich-quick schemes. She covers for her father, confessing to a crime she did not commit: "I am responsible for burning down the malt shop. I did it by mistake, so don't try and take the insurance money away from Daddy. It wasn't enough anyway" (134).

Yet, even when helping her father and participating in his money-making plans, Daisy rises above his selfishness and manipulation of others to reveal her basic human decency. Pretending to have drowned and returned from the dead at a community revival, in order to collect money for her father and his friends, Daisy admits that she got carried away with myself and forgot my planned speech. I started talking about how wrong it was to catch fish that they weren't going to eat and leave them on the pier to die and that catfish have souls and I had seen a lot of them in heaven and it was evil to kill them. I went on about how wrong it was to be mean to colored people and especially little children and albinos. I had a lot to say that night about meanness no matter what form it took. (179)

Daisy befriends many social outsiders in Shell Beach, Mississippi, including: a gay priest, a black funeral director-saloon keeper, an albino black woman, a gay costume designer, a young classmate abused by her father, a young man with elephantiasis, and a local columnist/Junior Debutantes leader institutionalized by her husband for insanity.

Becoming an odd-jobber and sometime-actress at the local amateur theater during her last year of high school, Daisy is encouraged by her friends there to enter the Miss Mississippi contest for a scholarship to study acting at the American Academy of the Arts in Manhatten. When her father squanders the money Daisy has saved to enter the contest, her friends and repentant father come to her support, throwing a "This Is Your Life" party and raising not only the money she needs for the trip but also free dentistry to repair two chipped teeth; ten free Dale Carnegie lessons; a complete leather-bound set of Shakespeare's works; a white evening gown; and Samsonite luggage for the competition. When Daisy wins the title and the scholarship, once more it is as a result of communal effort on the part of her extended and supportive "family." Working behind the scenes, they rig microphones, unplug organs, and grease batons to give Daisy a decidedly unfair advantage. Daisy realizes that her final triumph is not her own—but the work of many who love her and whom she has loved in return. With her mother dead and her father more alcoholic, womanizing, and irresponsible than ever, Daisy concludes, "Here I thought I didn't have any family, but all these people were out there pulling for me. . . . I do know I owe a lot of people a lot of things and I promise I won't come back until I'm somebody. And I won't" (318; 320). Daisy's commitment and love extend beyond the nuclear family to the entire community of relations, friends, acquaintances, and neighbors she has cared for and who have given her support throughout her life.

In Flagg's second novel, *Fried Green Tomatoes at the Whistle Stop Cafe* (1987), the community of Whistle Stop, Alabama, sustains and enriches human life even after it has ceased to exist as a physical reality. At the heart of the novel is the story of forty-eight-year-old Evelyn Couch, a woman who finds that she has become "lost somewhere along

the way" (40) until she meets Mrs. Cleo (Virginia "Ninny") Threadgoode while visiting her mother-in-law at the Rose Terrace Nursing
Home in Birmingham, Alabama. Listening each week to stories about
the Threadgoode family who adopted Ninny; the love affair between
Idgie Threadgoode and Ruth Jamison; the Whistle Stop Cafe Ruth and
Idgie ran; the black family—Big George Peavey, his wife, Onzell, and
his mother, Sipsey—who did all the cooking at the cafe; as well as the
many neighbors, friends, railroad customers, and drifters who came to
eat there while in Whistle Stop, Evelyn finds "the only time she wasn't
angry and the only time she could find peace was when she was with
Mrs. Threadgoode and when she would visit Whistle Stop at night in her
mind" (291).

Having been a "good girl" all her life, Evelyn feels betrayed to find,

so in the long run, it didn't matter at all if you had been good or not. The girls in
high school who had "gone all the way" had not wound up living in back alleys
in shame and disgrace, like she thought they would; they wound up happily or
unhappily married, just like the rest of them. So all that struggle to stay pure,
the fear of being touched, the fear of driving a boy mad with passion by any
gesture, and the ultimate fear—getting pregnant—all that wasted energy was for
nothing. (42)

Not only does Evelyn Couch find care and understanding in the company of Ninny Threadgoode, she also discovers models for female self-
development and courage in the stories Ninny tells about Sipsey, Eva
Bates, Essie Rue Threadgoode, and especially Ruth Jamison and Idgie
Threadgoode.

Ruth has had the courage to leave her abusive husband Frank Bennett, bear his child alone, live and work side-by-side with her female
lover, Idgie, in the unforgiving South of the 1920s. But Whistle Stop is
special in its tolerance of diversity, its compassion and care for all of
humanity. And Ruth and Idgie are not only accepted into this community
but accept others, in return. Opening their cafe on the eve of the Depression, Ruth and Idgie provide food day after day to as many people as
possible:

all the railroad people ate there, colored and white alike. . . . Of course, a lot of
people didn't like the idea of [Idgie] selling food to the coloreds, and she got
into some trouble doing it, but she said that nobody was gonna tell her what she
could and could not do. . . . she stood right up to the Ku Klux Klan all by herself, and wouldn't let them stop her. (51)

In the face of Klan threats, Ruth and Idgie "both knew they had to make a decision about what to do. And they did. After that day, the only thing that changed was on the menu that hung on the back door [for black customers]; everything was a nickel or a dime cheaper. They figured fair was fair" (55). Years later, Ruth and Idgie's "son" Stump Threadgoode reveals another act of bravery on the part of his "Aunt" Idgie Threadgoode. He discloses that it was Idgie herself who had hopped trains and thrown food to hungry blacks along the way as the Depression hero Railroad Bill: "I suddenly figured out why I'd seen [Idgie] and old Grady Kilgore, the railroad detective, always whispering. He'd been the one who was tipping her off about the train schedules. . . . it had been my Aunt Idgie jumping them trains, all along" (332). In addition, Idgie and Ruth have taken in tramps such as Smokey Lonesome Phillips throughout the Depression, giving them shelter and food, respect and care, to see them through hard times. As Ninny Threadgoode recalls over fifty years later, "[I]f it hadn't been for Ruth and Idgie, [Smokey Lonesome] might have starved to death" (134-35). Further, Idgie rescues Ruth's son, Stump, when his arm is severed by a train, gets him to the hospital, teaches him to use one arm better than most people use two, and helps him see his handicap as an advantage. And again, Idgie stands trial with Big George Peavey for the murder of Frank Bennett—one they did not commit—in order to protect the elderly Sipsey. They are rescued by Idgie's old enemy, the Reverend Scroggins, along with "Sister" Eva Bates, and a "congregation" of tramps "with fresh haircuts from Opal's Beauty Shop and borrowed clothes" (343), all of whom testify on a bogus Bible that Idgie Threadgoode and Big George Peavey had spent three days and three nights at a revival at the time of the murder. Idgie "was floored by the whole thing for quite a time. . . . 'You know, I've been thinking. I don't know what's worse—going to jail or having to be nice to the preacher for the rest of my life'" (344). Whistle Stop knows, however, and is grateful to have Idgie back. Religious and nonreligious, rich and poor, black and white, gay and straight, respectable and nonrespectable, unite to help one another and minimize life's sufferings in Whistle Stop.

As Evelyn Couch sits week after week listening to Ninny Threadgoode's stories about Whistle Stop, she begins to find the courage she needs to change her life:

She began to see herself as a woman with half her life still ahead of her. Her friend [Ninny] really believed she was capable of selling Mary Kay cosmetics. Nobody had ever believed she could do anything before, or had faith in her;

least of all, Evelyn herself. . . . she began to see herself as thin and happy—behind the wheel of a pink Cadillac. (359)

Evelyn accomplishes her goals, carrying on life where Ninny left off at eighty-six, selling cosmetics and driving a Cadillac, remembering Ninny while cooking the recipes and cherishing the photographs Ninny left her from "a little knockabout place . . . that brought so many people together" (386). Keeping one photograph of Mrs. Ninny Threadgoode herself on a living room table, Evelyn acknowledges Ninny as her spiritual mother and Whistle Stop as her spiritual home.

So, too, the aged Idgie remembers the past, placing jars of wild honey and love notes on Ruth Jamison's grave in Whistle Stop. Yet she continues on, passing along care and hope to a new generation, as Ninny has done with Evelyn. Selling wild honey at a roadside stand in Florida, Idgie tells young Patsy Neal how special she is—that eight-year-old Patsy is her "one millionth customer this month" and deserves a jar of honey free. "And listen, Patsy," Idgie adds, "if you ever get anywhere around these parts again, you be sure and look me up, y'hear?" (395). *Fried Green Tomatoes at the Whistle Stop Cafe* is a novel about female empowerment, community love, zest for life, and hope for the future. Fannie Flagg suggests that Whistle Stop will continue to exist wherever young and old, male and female, black and white, poor and rich, heterosexual and homosexual, come together to take pleasure in each other's company and interact with love and care.

Rita Mae Brown has created another comic world where justice and goodness prevail—where women love and care for one another; stand up to, even kill (as Sipsey has Frank Bennett in *Fried Green Tomatoes*) evil and powerful men; a world where fair-minded, fun-loving people unite for the betterment of their community and pleasure in life. Runnymede is Brown's utopia of extended family, neighbors, and friends, a place similar to Fannie Flagg's Whistle Stop, Alabama, or Shell Beach, Mississippi—a little town on the border between Pennsylvania and Maryland, North and South, modernity and antiquarianism, a place where exhilarating, daily skirmishes may occur, but a truce has been declared on full-fledged, all-encompassing, open warfare. In *Six of One* (1978) and its sequel *Bingo* (1988), the Hunsenmeir sisters, Julia (Juts) and Louise (Wheezie); Juts's daughter, Nicole (Nickel); the grandmother Cora; and respective husbands, lovers, employers, neighbors, and friends, all overcome their differences to enjoy life and give human warmth and support to one another. In *Six of One*, Nickel grows up in the company of strong women—an only child constantly reminded that she is adopted (like Molly Bolt in *Rubyfruit Jungle* and Rita Mae Brown herself[6]), a child who learns from her "family" and friends, both rich and poor, well-educated and illiterate, homosexual and heterosexual, religious and irreverent, to love life, value herself, fight with, and for, those she loves and causes she believes in, above all, enjoying life.

If Nicole is a strong, confident, well-educated journalist, leading a fulfilled and independent life, comfortable and open about her lesbian lifestyle, she cannot take credit for this herself. Like Fannie Flagg's Daisy Fay in *Daisy Fay and the Miracle Man* or Evelyn, Ninny, Ruth, and Idgie in *Fried Green Tomatoes at the Whistle Stop Cafe,* Nickel has been the recipient of great care and intensive community support. As her grandmother, Cora, tells her in *Six of One*, when Nickel says she wants to grow up to be like her grandmother's best friend and employer Celeste Chalfonte—on whose birthday she was born: "[P]eople are like snowflakes. No two alike. You be you. That would please Celeste and that would please me. . . . And as for you. You go as far as you can in this life, but don't you forget where you came from" (321). Nickel is her own person—but she is also a Runnymedean, loved by its inhabitants, those still living and many who are dead, shaped by its past struggles and present tensions, and nurtured by Runnymede's many pleasures. She is herself—but Runnymede is part of Nickel's special makeup.

Six of One covers the years between 1909 and 1980, moving back and forth between the past and present, from one narrative perspective to another. It examines the lives and friendships of three Vassar friends, Celeste Chalfonte, Fannie Jump Creighton, and Fairy Thatcher, a friendship that extends far beyond their mere sexual or ideological differences. All three are courageous; all devote themselves to causes for the betterment of humanity; all are passionate in their love lives and in their personal loyalties. Fairy loses her life as a political activist in Europe; Fannie "rais[ed] hell . . . tak[ing] on the whole world [in Runnymede]. Any little thing that Fannie thinks ought to be corrected gets corrected" (307-08) until she dies at one hundred years of age; and Celeste provides for the education of her housekeeper, Cora's, daughter Louise, and grandchild, Nicole; battles for woman's suffrage, the rights of women, and causes of human justice, standing up to, and finally killing, the unscrupulous town patriarch, Brutus Rife. Celeste faces Brutus for the last time, feeling "disgust for the rest of us for allowing [bullies such as Brutus Rife] to flourish unmolested" (121). She tells him:

You probably killed Hans Zepp many years ago. You certainly ordered Aimes Rankin out of this world. You purchase congressmen like cigars. You hold I don't know how many second mortgages and foreclose with a missed payment. You buy what you can and who you can. Anyone who resists is run into the ground. (120)

Celeste becomes Antigone to Brutus's Creon, acting in the interest of "simple morality and simple responsibility" (121) to rid Runnymede of its evil "monarch" so that goodness and care can grow.

These strong women use their power to produce a better, more democratic, community, taking on the forces of evil to create a place where love can flourish over hate, where tolerance can overcome (and even delight in) human difference. Celeste accepts that her female lover, Ramelle, has a love affair with Curtis Chalfonte, Celeste's brother, rejoicing in becoming the "parent" of Ramelle and Curtis's daughter, Spottiswood (as Idgie "parents" Ruth's son, Stump, in *Fried Green Tomatoes*). Celeste also seeks human warmth and wisdom from her illiterate friend and housekeeper, Cora, helping Cora raise her spirited and rivalrous daughters, Louise and Julia, on Bumblebee Hill—where all the townspeople gather to celebrate life's pleasures, including the occasion of Spottiswood's birth. The novel ends with Nicole returning to Runnymede to buy and remodel her grandmother Cora's house on Bumblebee Hill. In the company of her mother, Juts, and her Aunt Wheezie, Nickel celebrates her rich female heritage:

She felt lifted, inspired. She suddenly trusted the future. She had always trusted herself, but now she trusted the future. Hearing the comments, catcalls and laughter from the ground, she knew in her heart she could trust the future because those two women had given it to her. She opened her arms wide like a bird and gathered the sunlight. "Don't fall up there!" Juts yelled. Crying with happiness, Nickel replied, "Everything is possible. Pass the word." (336)

Being an orphan has given Nickel an advantage in life, she finds. She delights in her Hunsenmeir "family" heritage while understanding, at the same time, that relationship is something we all share. She remodels her grandmother's house on Bumblebee Hill, building on her past to create a house for the future, made possible by many, dead and alive, and open to all.

Community is not a given, however. It must be continually renewed and nourished. In *Bingo*, Nicole Hunsenmeir fights to preserve the Runnymede she loves, a place that "nourish[es] [its] eccentrics" and "operate[s] on the principle that boredom corrupts" (130). She battles to buy the town newspaper for which she writes upon the retirement of its owner, Charles Falkenroth, not only because she feels "ready for more responsibility, for more power in my community" (142), but because she believes the old-fashioned way the newspaper operates is the best way for the town's well-being:

I don't believe in putting people out of work just so you can have new machines. . . . I'd die before I'd fire Arnie and the guys in the back room. So there's an easier way to print a paper. Is it more fun? Does it serve the community any better? What we've got is plenty good enough and as time goes by people can visit us the way they visit Williamsburg. (169)

She argues further concerning the interrelationship between the newspaper and the community,

A newspaper is more than a business. It's a community resource. If we don't guard that resource, the press will soon become indistinguishable from General Motors or any other industry. We're the lifeblood of a free country. No press, no democracy. Profit is secondary to that function. (256)

Nicole carries on in the tradition of Celeste Chalfonte, Fannie Jump Creighton, and Fairy Thatcher, "imagin[ing] [herself] the center of a large family" (339) and fighting for that family's survival. She works for the preservation of the best of Runnymede's past, as well as to move herself and other townspeople forward in human understanding and tolerance of difference.

And Nicole starts and finishes the struggle for growth and human improvement with herself. In breaking off her affair with her best friend Regina's husband, Jackson Frost, she argues that her own individual desires cannot take precedence over the good of Runnymede:

We each need to find a suitable mate who will not only love us but protect us and help us become productive, useful members of our community. . . . The community absolutely must know who is straight, who is gay, who is married, and who is single. . . . coming out is not an issue of individual liberty; it is a matter of community responsibility. Communities must have truth and trust. Not understanding that sexual information is crucial to our building communities is going to weaken the community as well as harm the individual. (327)

Nickel is lesbian, Jackson is married to Regina, and community trust, as well as a long-term friendship, has been violated by Nickel and Jackson. Nickel argues for human care and commitment to one another on both a professional and a personal level: "Homosexual or heterosexual, black or white, man or woman, we suffered, we cried, we bled. . . . What mattered was, could we give one another comfort and perhaps even laughter? Could we make this journey of life with some tolerance and grace? Could we grasp the simple, splendid truth that we are all part of one another?" (328-29). Nickel concludes that the love we share with one another makes us human: "It's the only force that might possibly save our pitiful race" (330). She will go on loving Jackson, but not continue her affair with him, and apologize to Regina for betraying the trust they shared. She relishes mothering the twins Jackson has given her, but knows that they will not belong to her alone but to Runnymede itself: to Jackson, as biological father and godfather; to Mr. Pierre, who marries Nickel to become the child's gay, but legal, father; to Regina, as Jackson's wife and Nickel's best friend, and second mother to the twins; to Diz Rife, as second godfather; to their grandmother Juts and great-aunt Wheezie, as well as to the many others who gather together on Bumblebee Hill to celebrate the twins' birth and donate their bingo winnings to help Nickel buy the town newspaper. As Nickel discovers, "People don't have to sleep together to be a family. They only have to love one another" (480).

The more inclusive, rather than exclusive, love and family become, the greater the gain for individual women and their societies in the works of Rita Mae Brown and many other of her white southern female contemporaries—from Lee Smith to Kaye Gibbons, Bobbie Ann Mason to Josephine Humphreys, Doris Betts to Lisa Alther. These novelists reveal that white southern women must not only free themselves from houses of the past—but from outworn concepts of "family," "love," "selflessness" in their lives. By developing their individual skills and resources, they find that they are more able to reach out and make lasting contributions to the lives of others. The more fully they have grown, the more loving and useful they become—not just to "their own" blood relatives but to their communities at large. Those who have developed the most (Gibbons's Charlie Kate, Brown's Nickel Hunsenmeir, Flagg's Idgie Threadgoode, or Kingsolver's Taylor Greer) have understood that the house they keep belongs to everyone. It is the house of the future they honor—and the adult challenge of working to make life possible and worthwhile for all.

6

Conclusions

Even the most loving and admiring of late twentieth-century southern daughters, Harper Lee in *To Kill a Mockingbird* (1960), finds herself exposing the failures at the heart of white southern patriarchy and the southern family romance. While *To Kill a Mockingbird* pays tribute to the good father (Atticus Finch), placing him in opposition to the bad father (Robert E. Lee Ewell), the novel also reveals the inability of the good white father either to uphold law and order or safeguard the lives of those in his care (the black man Tom Robinson and Atticus's own children, Jem and Scout).

Doris Betts tells us that "Harper Lee, like her fictional [Scout], watched proudly from a courtroom balcony the jury speeches of her lawyer father" ("Daughters" 265). Yet we find that Scout's respected and beloved father (like Harper Lee's own father?) can't deliver the justice to which he dedicates his life: Tom Robinson ends up dead and Scout and Jem are attacked by Bob Ewell. Defenseless "mockingbirds" in the novel, such as Scout, Jem, Tom Robinson, and Boo Radley, find that they not only must watch out for each other but even combat or protect those stronger than themselves. Jem and Scout come to the rescue of their father and break up a lynching party that intends to fight Atticus Finch in order to lynch Tom Robinson, while the neighborhood recluse, Boo Radley, kills Bob Ewell to protect Jem and Scout from an enemy who strikes back at them rather than at their prominent father.

Having lost his case to establish Tom Robinson's innocence, Atticus Finch nevertheless "assured [his children] that nothing would happen to Tom Robinson until the higher court reviewed his case" (231)—but Tom Robinson is shot trying to escape a system in which he has no faith, dying before justice can be brought about (if, indeed, it could have been brought about in the case of a black man accused of raping a white girl in Depression-worn Maycomb, Alabama). Atticus also reassures Jem and Scout by saying, "We don't have anything to fear from Bob Ewell," with the result that they "were not afraid" (231). Thus, it is fortunate that they have the retiring Boo Radley, mistreated by his own father and sensitive to the mishaps of patriarchy, to watch over them and protect them while Atticus remains oblivious to the danger to which he has exposed his children. Fathers—even good ones—cannot assure family security and social justice, Harper Lee—perhaps unwittingly—reveals. Patriarchy's dependents must empower themselves for their own well-being, as well as that of society as a whole. The subtext of *To Kill a Mockingbird* suggests that patriarchy, even in its most well-intentioned form, cannot help failing. Social justice must be everyone's responsibility; the many, women and men, black and white, can never allow themselves to be dependent on the powerful few, whether good or bad.

Increasingly, as we have seen in contemporary novels by southern white women, heroines have come to terms with the powerlessness, absence, or death of their fathers, turning away from traditional roles as dependent daughters to establish more fully responsible adult lives of their own. More and more, they have sought to empower themselves by turning away from daughterhood and other related forms of nuclear family entrapment to find a focus outside their immediate family units. Ginny in Alther's *Kinflicks* flees north to embark on a series of relationships with men and women, hoping to free herself from her family past and the obligations of daughterhood. When she settles into marriage with Vermont-born-and-bred Ira Bliss, she suddenly finds herself repeating her mother's family entrapment, this time in the roles of northern wife and mother—necessitating another new struggle to escape suffocation and find a more meaningful role for herself in society. On the other hand, Charlotte in Tyler's *Earthly Possessions* runs away from marriage only to find that marriage itself *is* for her the adventure—one that provides her with ample opportunity to fulfill her own needs while relating to family outsiders who benefit from her skills, including the "stranger" who is her husband. Similarly, Nancy in Betts's *Heading West*, Hannah in Settle's *The Killing Ground*, and Muriel in Tyler's *The Accidental Tourist* find that marriage need neither be an extension of dependent daughterhood nor a threat to their personal autonomy. On the contrary, they find that they can marry without risk, having already achieved a sense of themselves through their life experiences, coming to recognize their own personal strengths and social skills outside their families before bonding with men from backgrounds different from their own. Other Tyler heroines—Emily in *Morgan's Passing*, Justine in *Searching for Caleb*, and Elizabeth (Gillespie) in *The Clock Winder*—find the challenges of marriage (to men who remain strangers through all the vows of love) a bracing restorative that returns them to a sense of their individual difference, strength, and personhood in communities that require their unique talents.

Other heroines of contemporary white southern women's novels find that they must turn away from husbands and male lovers to follow in the paths of older women who can help them shape their lives— women who themselves seem to have achieved a successful transition from submissive daughterhood to confident, adult womanhood, whether outside or within marriage. Occasionally it is their own mothers who offer them models of female development, as in McCorkle's *Ferris Beach*, Kingsolver's *Pigs in Heaven*, Brown's *Six of One* and *Bingo*, or Godwin's *A Mother and Two Daughters*. Sometimes, it is their grandmothers, as in Gibbons's *Charms for the Easy Life* and *A Cure for Dreams*. At other times, the female influence can be a stepmother (Shivers's *Here To Get My Baby Out of Jail*), a foster mother (Gibbons's *Ellen Foster*), or a mother-in-law (Tyler's *Celestial Navigation*). Most often, women who are family outsiders influence the maturation of southern heroines, as seen in Alther's *Bedrock, Original Sins, Other Women*, and *Five Minutes in Heaven*, Betts's *Heading West*, Flagg's *Fried Green Tomatoes at the Whistle Stop Cafe*, Godwin's *Father Melancholy's Daughter, The Finishing School*, and *The Good Husband*, or Kingsolver's *The Bean Trees* and *Animal Dreams*. Female employers, neighbors, therapists, chance acquaintances, family foes—all are shown making an impact on women who search for new ways to lead their lives. Even older women whose lives have been ones of struggle, family entrapment, or personal frustration themselves can have a positive influence on the lives of younger women with whom they come into contact. Female strength, resilience, adaptability, and sensitivity inspire southern heroines to move forward in their lives towards greater self-expression and responsibility of their own.

Black women, especially, are shown inspiring white southern heroines with their courage, assertiveness, and will to live. While African-American southern women writers portray black women from the inside, exploring the pain and vulnerability of their heroines (Sherley Ann Williams of a Dessa Rose, for instance, or Toni Cade Bambara of Velma Henry in *The Salt Eaters* [1981]), and examine the arduous path of self-development for black heroines (such as Alice Walker's Meridian in the novel of the same name or Celie in *The Color Purple*), in the fiction of their southern white female contemporaries, black women are most often viewed from the outside only. Usually white female writers portray African-American women , as Barbara Christian has said, as "servant[s] . . . rival[s] . . . [and] wise indefatigable adviser[s]" (33), stereotypes African-American women authors challenge, "attempt[ing] to define and express our totality rather than being defined by others, . . . present[ing] many styles of life, many different ways of approaching the issues that confront [us] as blacks, as women, as individual selves" (159, 183). Occasionally southern white heroines are shown penetrating the exterior defenses of black women in novels by white southern women writers. Emily Prince in Alther's *Original Sins,* for example, "studied [her family housekeeper] Ruby's face and saw it as a mask of deceit. Goddam it, you've just sat there all these years, gumming your tobacco and grinning and saying, 'We be just fine.' When you've actually been cold and sick and hungry and scared and resentful and contemptuous. For God's sake, why didn't you say so? She glared at Ruby" (254).

For the most part, however, black women are shown in the novels of contemporary southern white writers as strong, confident, and complete in themselves—with all weaknesses, all neediness, safely tucked away, hidden from sight. In Shivers's *Here To Get My Baby Out of Jail,* for example, when Roxy realizes that Aaron has murdered her husband and finds herself on the run with him, she thinks "of strong black women walking straight and proud with baskets of laundry, fresh and clean, balanced on their heads, their clean but ragged children running around their feet, while on a porch a series of men lay drunk" (109). She begins "to feel a little strength come to me" (109) as she prepares herself to face the humiliation, hostility, and hurt that await her return home, learning to stand up for herself and take care of her daughter, Baby, on her own, to stand as "straight and proud" as the black women she has watched endure life's miseries and struggles. In Humphreys's *Rich in Love,* black Rhody Poole helps Lucille Odom's mother escape from her marriage and helps Lucille turn loss into a positive force in her life. Lucille finds Rhody "formidable, because she understood human foibles and rose above them" (74). Rhody teaches Lucille to see her mother as "an adventuress" (192), explaining, "I am like your mother. Marriage does not agree with me. One reason your mother befriended me all these years . . . was we are two peas in a pod. You could believe we were sisters if not for the skin color" (194). Rhody has extended the support of her sisterhood to Lucille's mother and to Lucille herself, helping each in turn become more independent and "formidable" in her own right. In Gibbons's *Ellen Foster,* as well, Ellen "learn[s] everything old Mavis had to teach [her]" (76). Working out in the fields at Mavis's side, Ellen "toughened up good" (77), learning from Mavis how to survive mistreatment, poverty, and degradation at the hands of Ellen's grandmother and still remain strong, dignified, and loving in spite of her pain. Lydia Strickland in Godwin's *A Mother and Two Daughters* also learns from a "'formidable'" black woman, Renee Peverell-Watson—first as a student in Harvard-trained Renee's sociology class at the University of North Carolina and, later, as she watches Renee become a lawyer with "a real cause" in her fight against racial injustice (554). And Fannie Flagg's Daisy Fay in *Daisy Fay and the Miracle Man* relies on saloon keeper and funeral director Peachy Wigham, who is black, not only for maggots with which to frighten snobby Kay Bob Benson but as someone she can turn to for help and advice in every major crisis in her life. It is Peachy she relies on—Peachy she trusts—to have the right answers and not tell her secrets to anyone else.

Even when the relationship between black and white women in the South is shown as difficult and troubled, as in Ellen Douglas's novel *Can't Quit You, Baby* (1988), the two "lives [are portrayed as] . . . so entangled that you can never separate them" (215). Black Tweet, at the end of her life, may admit to her white employer Cornelia, "You ain't got *sense* enough to know I hated you. I hate you all my life, before I ever know you. . . . Every day, every hour of my entire life from the day I'm born" (254), but then she "reaches out, touches Cornelia's hand" and sings the words of a Willie Dixon song, "Oh, I love you, baby, but I sure do hate your ways. . . . I say, I love you, darlin, but I hate your treacherous low down ways" (255, 256). After her husband's death, the "sheltered" white Cornelia goes to New York to a friend's apartment to learn to survive on her own, relying on Tweet's spiritual presence to take her safely through New York's strange and threatening streets, endeavoring to become as "cautious, foresighted . . . [and able] to stand on my own feet" as Tweet became at a very young age through the guidance of her grandfather (11, 17). When Cornelia returns home, she finds Tweet near death; she nurses her and helps her regain her voice, listening and giving support as Tweet says, "No, no, no, to the surgery on her head" (249). Tweet's ability to say no, her courage in speaking her own mind, defending herself and healing herself in the midst of her struggle for life, are the continuing riches she bestows on Cornelia, whereas Cornelia has "given" Tweet only a gold barrette (after she finds Tweet has stolen it from her over-filled jewelry box long ago). Belatedly, Cornelia gives Tweet her sick-bed vigil, her acknowledgment of the value of Tweet's life stories and struggles to her own life journey, and recognition that the words Tweet sings are Tweet's way of continuing to try to communicate through her illness. Cornelia's delayed maturation depends on working to save Tweet's life—and repaying Tweet debts, which are long overdue.

This "Africanist presence," as Toni Morrison has called it, in Douglas's *Can't Quit You, Baby* and other contemporary novels by southern white women, attests to the truth of Morrison's central idea in *Playing in the Dark* (1992), that "black people ignite critical moments of discovery or change or emphasis" throughout white American literature (17, viii). In a number of the novels we have looked at, black women are shown as models for contemporary white southern heroines—models of women, married and unmarried, rich and poor, who have not only developed strong identities but, at the same time, retained their care for others. In two of her best works, *The Keepers of the House* and *Roadwalkers*, Shirley Ann Grau pays tribute to the remarkable spiritual strength she finds in black women, their endurance, independence, and care for others, in her portraits of the stately Margaret Carmichael and her "enchantresses," Mary and Nanda Woods. The ability of these three women to love is shown to be as powerful as their self-sufficiency (a seeming contradiction in terms), while their proud heritage remains inaccessible to the white women who are their social "superiors."

Critic Gayle Greene has lamented the individualistic tradition of American literature in general and of contemporary white women's literature, in particular, arguing, "Of American writers, only African-American women writers—coming out of a tradition which is preoccupied with the survival of a people, where the formation of self is resolved not in individualistic terms but by identification with black culture—convincingly portray the interdependence of individual life with community" (23). Greene argues that the fiction of Anne Tyler, Gail Godwin, Jill McCorkle, and Ellen Gilchrist, among that of other best-selling contemporary white women authors, "hardly acknowledges the world, let alone challenges it" (200) by comparison to that of African-American women writers. She is concerned by what she finds in the works of many of America's contemporary white women writers: "the privatization and depoliticization of their concerns, the sentimentalization of the family, the resignation to things as they are. . . . Most of these writers do not envision much possibility of change. . . . Far from opening up new possibilities, postfeminist fiction tends to nostalgia" (200). Writer and critic Carolyn Heilbrun agrees, opining: "Yet, for the rare Toni Morrison portrait [of a woman], we have many more like [Mrs. Emerson in Tyler's *The Clock Winder*] . . . portraits of women clinging to a life and conditions they have in fact outgrown, instead of launching off into another world" (128).

The criticisms of Carolyn Heilbrun and Gayle Greene are, in some ways, justified. Mrs. Emerson in Tyler's *The Clock Winder*, it is true, does not "launch off into another world." However, Elizabeth Abbott (Gillespie), the heroine of the novel, *does*—a world that, admittedly, remains private and limited, but one, nevertheless, which empowers her and connects her to people outside her own immediate family—taking her from North Carolina to Maryland, from personal inadequacy and powerlessness to competence and self-respect. In the Emerson's Baltimore household, Gillespie takes responsibility for her own life and those of others, rejecting daughterhood for adulthood, familiar territory for a new adventure. Before marrying Matthew Emerson and becoming a wife and mother, Gillespie becomes an indispensible, all-purpose, "handyman" on whom the Emerson family comes to rely—a quirky, androgynous figure whose self-confidence and strength grow stronger the further she travels from her judgmental father, her role as inadequate daughter, and her enclosure in the nuclear family cauldron. While Gillespie does not change society, she does change herself and the lives of several other persons besides. She learns that she can make things happen. While she cannot prevent bad things from occurring (as in Timothy Emerson's suicide), Gillespie can use her abilities to better her own life and those of others—even if she does not take those skills as far out into the world as we would wish her to do—or as Tyler herself explained to Clifford Ridley that Gillespie should (26).

The first steps of many southern white women heroines toward adult responsibility for themselves and others may seem small and inadequate, but they are shown as having the potential to lead to greater social responsibility and cultural change as these heroines gain confidence in themselves and their ability to affect the larger society in positive ways. A majority of contemporary American women writers, including those from the South, have opted for change. Despite her disappointment in white American women authors in general, Molly Hite in *The Other Side of the Story* contends that contemporary women's works "are *more* radical in their implications than the dominant modes of fictional experiment, and more radical precisely inasmuch as the context for innovation is a critique of a culture and a literary tradition apprehended as profoundly masculinist" (2). The realism of contemporary American white women's writing, Gayle Greene agrees, questions traditional social and sexual mores (22). In addition, Katherine Payant points to the impact of this literature on female readers: "Such fiction keeps the new ideas about women in circulation and helps women to expand and grow in their struggles with self and society" (221). Joanne Frye concurs that women's novels are radical, arguing that they "reassess experience toward the possible formation of new patterns. . . . readers become better prepared to develop new narrative constructions of their own experience (195, 200).

Women readers turn to contemporary women's fiction not for plot endings, nor for finality and resolution, but for the process of growth and the patterns of change the works depict. While many of the novels I have discussed do posit more flexible, open-ended forms of family, including the works of Anne Tyler and Gail Godwin, as we have seen, and contemporary white southern women writers in general seem to be struggling toward reformulations of self and community that recognize the interdependence of the individual and the larger world, their conclusions can, in fact, seem disappointingly tentative, contrived, and, at times, more than a little unbelievable. Some heroines, such as Gillespie in Tyler's *The Clock Winder*, move from one family situation to another without moving out into the world beyond to affect change in the larger society. Other women who do go out to play more responsible roles in their communities lead lives that seem disconnected from the everyday problems of readers' own lives. Women go to college, become doctors, and have brothers who become computer analysts and time-efficiency experts, in families that are barely coping; we do not see how these feats are accomplished in Tyler's *Dinner at the Homesick Restaurant* and *Saint Maybe*, for instance. Other protagonists remain poised on the brink of successful careers while the hard work, personal sacrifice, and humiliation they most certainly will need to undergo in the process of becoming Episopalian priests, acclaimed actressess, and public health physicians are left undramatized (Gibbons's *Charms for the Easy Life*, Flagg's *Daisy Fay and the Miracle Man*, and Godwin's *Father Melancholy's Daughter*). New fairy-tale endings replace old ones as heroines find themselves, whether in trailer courts or on Indian reservations, in worlds "rich with possibilities" (Tyler's *Morgan's Passing*; Kingsolver's *Pigs in Heaven* and *Animal Dreams*; McCorkle's *The Cheer Leader* and *Ferris Beach*; Humphreys's *Rich in Love*; and Brown's *Six of One*). Yet the richness here has been redirected from the coffers of the fathers to the psyches of the southern heroines themselves. It is they who have been awakened to the possibilities of life through their newfound strength and growth, their resiliency and adaptability, the abundance and diversity of their love and skill. They carry a new richness inside themselves and out into the world—even if their material circumstances have declined and their lives seem much more precarious and unstable than ever before.

Contemporary white southern women writers are clearly engaged in forging new myths to replace old ones—and as they do so, contemporary women readers for the most part appear willing to forgive the artifice, manipulation, and wish-fulfillment of the endings, perhaps knowing that the right ending doesn't and can't exist, at present—that the task we are undertaking together, as readers, writers, and heroines, is to work toward new and better endings for us all. As Judith Beth Cohen says of Gibbons's *Charms for the Easy Life*, contemporary white southern women writers are trying "to give us a deeper imaginative truth in [their] subversive vision of women's possibilites" that will allow us "to dream in a new vocabulary" (25). At this stage of contemporary women's writing, the processes of self-development, as well as of domestic and social change, matter most. Better families, communities, men and women will result, readers and writers seem to agree, from women's growth into full adulthood. For all her disappointment with contemporary white women's fiction, Gayle Greene concludes: "We may be sure, at any rate, that changes are in the making—as they were thirty years ago, as they always are—that are even now making a new beginning: that this last turn is not the last round, that processes are 'not yet finalized'" (222). It is this knowledge that buoys us up, gives us faith in the new myth-makers, their developing heroines, and the processes of change they envision.

It is important to remember that contemporary women writers are revisioning themselves, as well as their characters and societies. As Gail Godwin explains, "All my protagonists—slapstick, allegorical, disguised by gender, species, occupation, social class, or hardly disguised at all— are parts of myself" (qtd. in Sylvia Burack 75). Through their heroines, women writers such as Gail Godwin have been able, in the words of Patricia Spacks, to "dominate their own experience by imagining it, giving it form, writing about it" (413). As Carolyn Heilbrun suggests, as well, in "creating Kate Fansler and her quests, I was recreating myself. Women come to writing, I believe, simultaneously with self-creation" (117). Joan Schultz has noted that white southern women writers have had more difficulty, historically, in approaching their imaginative recreations than other American women writers. She says of their fiction, "To expect women who have not been encouraged to be goal-oriented and who have almost no positive models for alternative life patterns to be other than vague in their sense of what that 'something worth loving' is, is to demand too much" (104). More and more, however, white southern women writers seem to be creating characters who are willing to commit themselves to alternative life patterns; who are beginning to combine love of self with love for others; and who are able to create and build without needing simply to run away. They are beginning, like southern African-American women writers before them, to develop strong heroines who can love and lead, at the same time.

Women writers of the contemporary American South, as well as their counterparts in other parts of the nation, are revisioning the traditional family through their protagonists. In so doing, they have rejected what Robert Bellah and others in *Habits of the Heart* call America's historically embedded idea that "the family is the core of the private sphere, whose aim is not to link individuals to the public world but to avoid it as far as possible" (112). By propelling heroines forth into the world, or creating new and looser models of the family reflective of the diversity of the larger society, white women writers of the contemporary South strive to change the world inherited from their fathers. If, as Carolyn

Heilbrun has said, "There will be [new] narratives of female lives only when women no longer live their lives isolated in the houses and the stories of men" (47), that end is being accomplished in the novels of contemporary southern white women. Southern heroines may continue, at times, to live *with* men, but the houses they inhabit belong to them as much as to the men with whom they share the adventure—and often to quite a number of other people, as well.

White southern heroines are moving on, recognizing that only by assuming full adult responsibility for themselves and others can they change and improve their society. As historian Stephanie Coontz has said,

To handle social obligations and interdependency in the twenty-first century, we must abandon any illusion that we can or should revive some largely mythical traditional family. We need to invent new family traditions and find ways of reviving older community ones, not wallow in nostalgia for the past. . . . There are good grounds for hope that we can develop such new traditions, but only if we discard simplistic solutions based on romanticization of the past. (278)

This revisioning for the future is the work Tyler, Godwin, Kingsolver, Gibbons, Alther, Brown, Flagg, and many other white southern women writers we have looked at have taken upon themselves—imagining new roles for women, new family structures and new, more inclusive and tolerant, forms of community to replace those that are dying away as we enter the twenty-first century.

These white southern women writers and their heroines have discovered, as Gayle Greene has said, "Clearly, leaving home is not enough. Change requires more than moving out, resolution, or will: it requires a process of re-envisioning which allows an evolution and alteration of desire and consciousness, both protagonist's and reader's" (14). Contemporary white southern heroines are in the process of changing from seeing themselves as keepers of the house of the past to shapers of the house of the future. As they begin to take greater responsibility for themselves and their society, they are learning, as Dorothy Dinnerstein says,

What growing up means is embracing the responsibility for each other, and for nature and our place in it, which has from the outset been implicit in humanness and what we have all along denied and evaded. And *essential to this continued denial and evasion has been our use of gender—our use, that is, of the long-standing and widespread, prevailing forms of psychological symbiosis between women and men—to keep ourselves infantile.* ("Afterword" 298)

In renouncing an infantile, dependent, powerless past for a more full, creative adult future, contemporary white southern heroines have embarked on the difficult task of building new houses rather than decorating old ones; creating new models of the family rather than reconstituting the steamy cauldrons of the past; and working for justice themselves rather than merely watching from courtroom balconies.

In seeking change for themselves, they are helping to create new possibilities for us all. For, as Joanne Frye has shown, while appearing to be focused on the individual life, contemporary novels by white southern women writers are, in fact, about communal experience—the experience of the female protagonist within her fictional community and the transformative experience shared by the writer in league with her readers: "Through its individualism the novel opens onto a capacity to offer new narrative interpretations of the female individual, not as isolated and self-serving but as a strong and complex human being in social interaction with other human beings" (26). As female novelists concentrate on the growth and change of their individual protagonists, they not only place them in social contexts that respond to women's self-development but they engage their readers, as well, in a new understanding of the self—as we have seen in the novels of Anne Tyler and Gail Godwin—"as multiple and flexible, rather than unitary and fixed" (Frye 26). Contemporary female novelists "affirm [for readers] the possibility of social communication and of shared understanding" (Frye 27) between female reader and female author, creating a "sense of community in the new shared reality" (Frye 44) about the development and multiplicity of the female self, the need for women's personal growth and social leadership, and the reciprocity existing between self and others.

Rita Mae Brown makes the relationship between author and audience, fiction and reality, explicit in the Introduction to her novel *Bingo*. She speaks of, and to, the reader as a "co-creator" who "participate[s]" in the work and "forms a bond . . . [with the] author . . . akin to the bond between audience and performer in the theater" (9). She encourages her readers to develop their "creativity" and "imagination" by keeping a diary to record details of their lives to "give [them] some perspective and insight into [themselves] and [their] community. . . . [to enable them to] forge new solutions to old problems. . . . to step forward and contribute to a safe and sane future" (10-11). Rita Mae Brown clearly believes that readers and writers, fictional heroines and real-life ones, are engaged together in working to shape more independent and fulfilling lives and more responsible and life-affirming communities for the future.

These very acts of reading and writing about women's lives suggest the interconnection existing between authors and readers, their common "need to escape the confines of the purely personal: to find, in the acknowledgment of shared experiences, a confirmation or clarification of what has been culturally denied or trivialized," as Joanne Frye states (192). She suggests, further, that this strong connection between reader's lives and the literature they read can only lead to social change:

As the autonomous woman in literature becomes a shaping force for the autonomous woman in life, we can see in the novel a power beyond the "mirroring" of life, a power to open the eyes and understandings of its readers, a power to participate in cultural change. No longer trapped within stories of the past, women can learn—are learning—to create new stories for the future, to live new lives in the present. No longer forced by narrative expectation or cultural assumption to choose between femaleness and autonomy, women can begin to identify in their lived experiences the possibilities for altering the constraints on their lives, the possibilities for claiming human wholeness. (203)

Contemporary southern women writers, working to reclaim human wholeness for their protagonists, are exploring the potential of their own and readers' lives—for the future well-being of us all.

Notes

1. Introduction

1. Carol S. Manning, "The Real Beginning of the Southern Renaissance," 37-57, and Jan Cooper, "Zora Neale Hurston Was Always a Southerner Too," 57-73, in *The Female Tradition in Southern Literature,* ed. Carol S. Manning, point out that the Southern Renaissance has always been considered a white male movement. They seek to relocate the inception of this literary movement and to broaden its definition to include black writers (Cooper) and female writers (Cooper and Manning).

2. See Helen Fiddyment Levy, *Fiction of the Home Place: Jewett, Cather, Glasgow, Porter, Welty, and Naylor,* 97-131, for a discussion of how Glasgow's later works grow away from this "male model of competitive individualism" (29) and identification with the father to "acknowledge the claims of community" and the female sphere (24).

3. In an interview with Danny Miller in *Melus* 9.2 (1982), 83-98, Harriette Arnow remarked that she was amazed that one college student had seen "Gertie as Judas and all Gertie's neighbors as Judas—Judas before he gave back the thirty pieces of silver. I was surprised by that, but I always have surprises. . . . I was trying to show that all people in Gertie's eyes—or most—had something of Christ in them" (86). Thus, Arnow seems to view Gertie and her sacrifice in a positive way; however, the structure of her plot reveals that Gertie's submissiveness results in a weakened husband-wife relationship, the loss of her art, the death of a child, the betrayal of her eldest son, and the diminishment of her positive influence on her children as a role model. *The Dollmaker* resists such a simple, uncomplicated view of its protagonist and her story as Arnow gives here.

4. See Flannery O'Connor's "Letters to A" in *The Habit of Being*, ed. Sally Fitzgerald, especially that of August 24, 1956, 170. O'Connor's complex relationship with her mother, whom the mothers in her fiction resemble and with whom daughters are caught in love-hate conflicts, can be found in the letters of this volume, as well.

5. See Helen Fiddyment Levy, *Fiction of the Home Place*, 183-88, for a different reading of Miss Julia Mortimer as a woman representative of the "language of abstraction, of the citizen, of the father, of the legalistic optimists . . . [with] disregard [for] . . . human emotions and natural realities" (165).

213

6. In Sherley Anne Williams's *Dessa Rose,* the black heroine and her community guide a white plantation mistress, Miss Ruth Rufel, into discovering her own voice ("I don't want to live round slavery no more; I don't think I could without speaking up" [239]). Ruth protects Dessa Rose as her "friend" (239) and protests against Dessa's addressing her as "Miss'ess. . . . Miz' ": "My name Ruth. . . . I ain't your mistress" (255). At the end of the work Ruth has asserted her own independence, traveling north to live out her adult life in "some city didn't allow no slaves" (259), as Dessa puts it, refusing either to return to the protection of her family in Charleston or to continue her dependency on Dessa Rose and the other runaway slaves by accompanying them west. Ruth finds her freedom by watching Dessa Rose and her friends, learning to pattern her behavior on theirs, in a reversal of their ostensible mistress/slave, teacher/pupil, leader/follower roles.

2. Shirley Ann Grau's Keepers of the House

1. There is some critical disagreement about the quality of the marriage of William Howland and Margaret Carmichael. Pamela Parker believes that Margaret "finds love and devotion and personal satisfaction in her relationship with Will Howland" (141), and, "although she is somewhat submissive" to her husband, Will "grows to respect her and to act according to her wishes" (142). Eleanor Chiogioji defines theirs as "a relationship based on mutual respect, mutual support, and mutual understanding" (122). Yet Clair Schulz suggests that, even in the best of Grau's marriages (including this one), husbands and wives "live together, yet apart" (95). Margaret carries on her duties in the house and kitchen; William mends fences, tends cattle, and works outside. In front of both family and guests, Margaret continues to fulfill her role as William's "housekeeper"; the two seem comfortable in their master-servant roles. The one glimpse we have into their bedroom does little to assure us of Margaret's place in the relationship; on the night that Margaret first comes to him, "she seemed small and fragile again; and for the first time in his life he wanted to hit a woman. It was the bend of the neck that did it. It was so exposed and patient" (135). It is true that, behind the scenes, Margaret is able to assert herself in getting William to marry her and legalize the births of their children—extremely significant and consequential actions, to be sure. But, in every other way, Margaret acts out her part, conforming to community mores and demuring to the wishes of her husband, William Howland.

2. Grau has herself suggested that even that strength is part of the growing darkness, that "if there is a moral [in *The Keepers of the House*], it is the self-destructiveness of hatred." See Mary Campbell, "Miss Grau Eyes Her Novel," *New Orleans Times-Picayune,* June 27, 1965.

3. Eleanor Chiogioji points out that Margaret Carmichael seems "a pillar of strength" in the Howland household, "almost super-human, a perception that

is based on [the Howland family] (sometimes subconsciously) associating her with the Alberta of folk tales" (119). Pamela Parker suggests that Margaret is "a strong figure," "the most independent woman" and "the only true androgynous figure in the novel" (141, 142). While Margaret is a more independent and less destructive woman than Abigail, she, too, is shown as having remained dependent on men for her identity: first, on the blood of the white father she has never seen, telling the ghost of her great-grandmother, "I buried my blood with you. . . . I'm using only the other half now" (103); then, on William Howland who gives her a home and takes the place of the white father who has abandoned her. Will becomes a man without whom she finds she cannot live. When Margaret dies several years later, it is on the day of William Howland's death. Abigail is left to wonder "what it was like living for four years, not wanting to, only waiting for your hold to weaken so you could finish up and leave" (235).

3. Anne Tyler's "Homeless at Home"

1. In a letter to Maria Whitney (Spring 1883), Emily Dickinson includes a poem about her mother's death which ends with this stanza:

> Fashioning what she is,
> Fathoming what she was,
> We deem we dream—
> And that dissolves the days
> Through which existence strays
> Homeless at home.

Tyler's heroines, too, are responding to loss and change (cultural, as well as, often, the actual deaths of fathers) that also render them "homeless at home" (see *The Letters of Emily Dickinson*, ed. Thomas H. Johnson, vol. 3, 770-71).

2. See Nancy Chodorow, *The Reproduction of Mothering: Psychoanalysis and the Sociology of Gender*, and Dorothy Dinnerstein, *The Mermaid and the Minotaur* for psychological and sociological perspectives, respectively, on the consequences for children and for society of mother dominance and primary female nurturing in the home. Chodorow discusses the way in which male children close off from mothers and other female nurturers to protect their (male) selves, making intimacy difficult in their lives, while female children develop more amorphous ego boundaries, often creating difficulties for them in separating the self first from the mother (with whom they presumably share the same biological and social destiny) and then from others in their lives. See also Henry B. Biller, *Fathers and Families: Paternal Factors in Child Development*, an extended study of the role of the father in the family.

3. See Theresa Kanoza, "Mentors and Maternal Role Models: The Healthy Mean Between Extremes in Anne Tyler's Fiction" in Stephens 28-40, for discussion of the importance of female networking, especially the role of influential mothers-in-law, in the lives of many of Tyler's heroines.

4. Theresa Kanoza discusses Charlotte Emory's maturation in *Earthly Possessions*, looking at the role of her mother-in-law, Alberta Emory, in helping Charlotte define herself. See "Mentors and Maternal Role Models: The Healthy Mean Between Extremes in Anne Tyler's Fiction," in Stephens 32-36.

5. Anne Tyler has said of herself, "I write because I want more than one life. I insist on a wider selection. It's greed, plain and simple," in "Because I Want More Than One Life," in Petry 46. In an interview with Marguerite Michaels, "Anne Tyler, Writer 8:05 to 3:30," in Petry 40-45, she elaborated: "I want to live other lives. I've never quite believed that one chance is all I got. Writing is my way of making other chances. It's lucky I do it on paper. Probably I would be schizophrenic—and six times divorced—if I weren't writing. I would decide that I want to run off and join the circus and I would go. I hate to travel, but writing a novel is like taking a long trip. This way I can stay peacefully at home" (40).

4. Gail Godwin's Family Reconfigurations

1. See Gail Godwin's "Becoming a Writer" in Sternburg 231-57.

2. Sternburg 250-52.

3. Eudora Welty's *The Optimist's Daughter* deals with a similar theme, the need for a daughter to understand and move beyond her parents' lives and her family past. Welty's male "optimist" at the end turns away from life and gives in to death (becoming a "Father Melancholy" at the last). However, Welty's optimistic father has remarried, asserting the life principle, and rejected his former wife's despair in her years of illness (and her personhood in expressing thoughts and feelings that make him uncomfortable). Godwin's father (unlike Welty's) is melancholy, perhaps in unconscious recognition that his plot denies validity to his wife (who must leave him for a drama of her own) and his daughter (whom he tries to release from caring for him by sending her away to college and giving her some important advice on finding herself). Father Gower is trapped in a past not of his own making—one that relegates the female to a minor role (as in Welty's novel)—and one that he intuits must be changed (even if he resists female priests and the changing world around him).

4. See Jane Hill, *Gail Godwin*, 1-18, 102-35, on the autobiographical parallels between Godwin's own family and the southern family of this novel.

5. Other Contemporary Authors and Their Fictional Worlds

1. See Nick Hornby, *Contemporary American Fiction*, 116-24, for a discussion of Phillips's "twin themes of movement and stasis," the promise of "escape" that "offers no freedom (especially, perhaps, for women)" (120, 122), in her collection of stories *Black Tickets*—including "Blue Moon" about Danner, Billy, Jean and Mitch.

2. See Jean Baker Miller, *Toward a New Psychology of Women*, 122-23, on the relationship between female anger and powerlessness, masochistic behavior and victimization.

3. In *The Anna Papers* and *The Annunciation*, Ellen Gilchrist's midlife heroines, the writer Anna Hand and translator Amanda McCamey, look for ways to balance their care for others with their own creative and personal needs. They are able to reconnect with family in the course of their lives, but they do so on their own terms, from the fullness of their own independence. Before her death, Anna can say, "I have lived my life. I have not forgotten to be alive. I was glad to be here" (*Anna* 144). Amanda, too, affirms her own life even as she reaches out to others at the end of *The Annunciation*, "on my terms, my daughter, my son. My life leading to my lands forever and ever and ever, hallowed be my name, goddamit, my kingdom come, my will be done, Amen, so be it, Amanda" (353).

4. In *Oral History*, Lee Smith satirizes the exploitation of Appalachia for profit through Richard Burlage's memoirs with the LSU press; Almarine Cantrell's ski run on Black Rock Mountain; and "his grandest plan yet: Ghostland, the wildly successful theme park and recreation area (campground, motel, Olympic-size pool, waterslide and gift shop) in Hoot Owl Holler," where tourists can sit on the porch of "the old [Cantrell family] homeplace" and experience its ghosts for $4.50 apiece (291-92).

Josephine Humphreys in *Dreams of Sleep* also exposes southern (and northern) exploitation of the mythical South. Fred Hobson in *The Southern Writer in the Postmodern World* discusses Humphreys's portrayal of this "debasement" of the past through characters' imitative actions: Will Reese and Danny Cardozo's "poor imitation of a Southern gentleman" at the Old South Apartments (*Dreams* 166) and Ohioan Duncan Nesmith's crass commercial scheme, planning a pirate theme park for visitors to Charleston (Hobson 66-67).

5. See Doris Betts's discussion in "Daughters, Southerners, and Daisy," in Manning 259-77, of the parallels between the lives of Ellen in *Ellen Foster* and Kaye Gibbons herself, as well as between Ruby Stokes in *A Virtuous Woman* and Kaye's mother Shine, 262.

6. See Carol M. Ward, *Rita Mae Brown*, on Rita Mae Brown's early life, 1-3.

Works Cited

Aldridge, John W. *The American Novel and the Way We Live Now*. New York: Oxford UP, 1983.

Alther, Lisa. *Bedrock*. New York: Ballantine, 1990.

——. *Five Minutes in Heaven*. New York: Dutton-Penguin, 1995.

——. *Kinflicks*. 1975. New York: Signet, 1977.

——. *Original Sins*. New York: Knopf, 1981.

——. *Other Women*. New York: Signet, 1984.

Arnow, Harriette Simpson. *The Dollmaker*. 1954. New York: Avon, 1972.

Bambara, Toni Cade. *The Salt Eaters*. 1980. New York: Random House, 1981.

Bellah, Robert N., Richard Madsen, William M. Sullivan, Ann Swidler, and Steven M. Tipton. *Habits of the Heart: Individualism and Commitment in American Life*. New York: Harper, 1985.

Betts, Doris. "Daughters, Southerners, and Daisy." Manning 259-77.

——. "The Fiction of Anne Tyler." Prenshaw 23-39.

——. *Heading West*. New York: Knopf, 1981.

Biller, Henry B. *Fathers and Families: Paternal Factors in Child Development*. Westport: Greenwood, 1993.

Blais, Ellen. "Gender Issues in Bobbie Ann Mason's In Country." *South Atlantic Review* 56.2 (1991): 107-19.

Breslin, John B. Review of *A Mother and Two Daughters*. *America* 146.15 (1982): 305.

Brown, Rita Mae. *Bingo*. 1988. Thorndike, ME: Thorndike P, 1989.

——. *Rubyfruit Jungle*. 1973. New York: Bantam, 1988.

——. *Six of One*. 1978. New York: Bantam, 1984.

Brownstein, Rachel M. "Gail Godwin: The Odd Woman and Literary Feminism." Pearlman 173-92.

Burak, Sylvia K., ed. *The Writer's Handbook*. Boston: The Writer, 1988.

Campbell, Mary. "Miss Grau Eyes Her Novel." *New Orleans Times-Picayuene* 27 June 1965.

Carson, Barbara Harrell. "Complicate, Complicate: Anne Tyler's Moral Imperative." *Southern Quarterly* 31.1 (1992): 24-35.

Chiogioji, Eleanor Nobuko. *A Matter of Houses: Structural Unity in the Works of Shirley Ann Grau*. Diss. University of Maryland, 1981. Ann Arbor: UMI, 1993.

Chodorow, Nancy. *The Reproduction of Mothering: Psychoanalysis and the Sociology of Gender*. Berkeley: U of California P, 1978.

Chopin, Kate. *The Awakening.* 1899. Ed. Nancy A. Walker. Boston: St. Martin's, 1993.

Christian, Barbara. *Black Feminist Criticism: Perspectives on Black Women Writers.* New York: Pergamon, 1986.

Clinton, Catherine. *The Plantation Mistress: Woman's World in the Old South.* New York: Pantheon, 1982.

Cohen, Judith Beth. "Daughters of the South." *Women's Review of Books* 11.1 (1993): 24-25.

Coontz, Stephanie. *The Way We Never Were: American Families and the Nostalgia Trap.* New York: Harper, 1992.

Cooper, Jan. "Zora Neale Hurston Was Always a Southerner Too." Manning 57-73.

Dickinson, Emily. "Letter #815." *The Letters of Emily Dickinson.* 1958. Ed. Thomas H. Johnson. Vol. 3. Cambridge: Belknap-Harvard UP, 1970. 770-71.

Dinnerstein, Dorothy. "Afterword: Toward the Mobilization of Eros." *Face to Face: Fathers, Mothers, Masters, Monsters—Essays for a Nonsexist Future.* Ed. Meg McGavran Murray. Westport: Greenwood, 1983. 293-311.

——. *The Mermaid and the Minotaur.* New York: Harper, 1977.

Douglas, Ellen. *Can't Quit You, Baby.* 1988. New York: Penguin, 1989.

——. *A Lifetime Burning.* New York: Random House, 1982.

——. *The Rock Cried Out.* New York: Harcourt, 1979.

Faulkner, William. "Barn Burning." *The Short Story: Fifty Masterpieces.* Ed. Ellen Wynn. New York: St. Martin's, 1983. 419-37.

Fitzgerald, Sally, ed. *The Habit of Being.* New York: Farrar, 1979.

Flagg, Fannie. *Daisy Fay and the Miracle Man.* 1981 as *Coming Attractions.* New York: Warner, 1992.

——. *Fried Green Tomatoes at the Whistle Stop Cafe.* 1987. New York: McGraw-Hill, 1988.

Fox-Genovese, Elizabeth. "The New Female Literary Culture." *Antioch Review* 38.2 (1980): 193-217.

Friedman, Jean E. *The Enclosed Garden: Women and Community in the Evangelical South, 1830-1900.* Chapel Hill: U of North Carolina P, 1985.

Frye, Joanne S. *Living Stories, Telling Lives: Women and the Novel in Contemporary Experience.* Ann Arbor: U of Michigan P, 1986.

Gardiner, Judith Kegan. "On Female Identity and Writing by Women." *Critical Inquiry* 8.2 (1981): 347-63.

Gibbons, Kaye. *Charms for the Easy Life.* New York: Avon, 1993.

——. *A Cure for Dreams.* Chapel Hill: Algonquin, 1991.

——. *Ellen Foster.* Chapel Hill: Algonquin, 1987.

——. *A Virtuous Woman.* Chapel Hill: Algonquin, 1989.

Gibson, Mary Ellis. "Family as Fate: The Novels of Anne Tyler." Petry 165-75.

Gilbert, Sandra M., and Susan Gubar. *No Man's Land: The Place of the Woman Writer in the Twentieth Century.* Vol. 1. New Haven: Yale UP, 1988.

——. *No Man's Land: The Place of the Woman Writer in the Twentieth Century.* Vol. 2. New Haven: Yale UP, 1988.

Gilchrist, Ellen. *The Anna Papers.* Boston: Little, Brown, 1988.

——. *The Annunciation.* Boston and Toronto: Little, Brown, 1983.

——. *I Cannot Get You Close Enough: Three Novellas.* Boston: Little, Brown, 1990.

Glasgow, Ellen. *Barren Ground.* 1925. New York: Hill and Wang, 1980.

Godwin, Gail. "Becoming a Writer." Sternburg 231-57.

——. *Father Melancholy's Daughter.* New York: Morrow, 1991.

——. *The Finishing School.* 1984. New York: Viking, 1985.

——. *Glass People.* New York: Knopf, 1972.

——. *The Good Husband.* New York: Ballantine, 1994.

——. "Journals: 1982-1987." *Antaeus* (Fall 1988): 186-95.

——. *A Mother and Two Daughters.* New York: Viking, 1982.

——. *The Odd Women.* 1974. New York: Viking, 1987.

——. *The Perfectionists.* New York: Harper, 1970.

——. "The Southern Belle." *MS* July 1975: 49-52; 84-85.

——. *A Southern Family.* New York: Morrow, 1987.

——. "The Uses of Autobiography." Burak 71-75.

——. *Violet Clay.* New York: Knopf, 1978.

Grau, Shirley Ann. *The Condor Passes.* New York: Knopf, 1971.

——. *Evidence of Love.* New York: Knopf, 1977.

——. *The Hard Blue Sky.* New York: Knopf, 1958.

——. *The House on Coliseum Street.* New York: Knopf, 1961.

——. *The Keepers of the House.* New York: Knopf, 1969.

——. *Roadwalkers.* New York: Knopf, 1994.

Greene, Gayle. *Changing the Story: Feminist Fiction and the Tradition.* Bloomington: Indiana UP, 1991.

Harrison, Elizabeth Jane. *Female Pastoral: Women Writers Re-Visioning the American South.* Knoxville: U of Tennessee P, 1991.

Heilbrun, Carolyn G. *Writing A Woman's Life.* New York: Ballantine, 1988.

Heller, Dana A. *The Feminization of Quest-Romance: Radical Departures.* Austin: U of Texas P, 1990.

Hendin, Josephine. "Renovated Lives" [review of *A Mother and Two Daughters*]. *New York Times Book Review* 10 Jan. 1982: 3, 14.

Hill, Dorothy Combs. *Lee Smith.* New York: Twayne, 1992.

Hill, Jane. *Gail Godwin.* New York: Twayne, 1992.

Hite, Molly. *The Other Side of the Story: Structures and Strategies of Contemporary Feminist Narratives.* Ithaca: Cornell UP, 1989.

Hobson, Fred. *The Southern Writer in the Postmodern World.* Athens: U of Georgia P, 1991.

Hornby, Nick. *Contemporary American Fiction.* New York: St. Martin's, 1992.

Humphreys, Josephine. *Dreams of Sleep.* New York: Viking, 1984.

——. *Rich in Love.* New York: Viking, 1987.

Hurston, Zora Neale. *Their Eyes Were Watching God.* 1937. New York: Harper, 1990.

Jones, Anne G. "Home at Last, and Homesick Again: The Ten Novels of Anne Tyler." *Hollins Critic* 23.2 (1986): 1-14.

Jones, Anne Goodwyn. *Tomorrow Is Another Day: The Woman Writer in the South, 1859–1936.* Baton Rouge: Louisiana State UP, 1981.

Kanoza, Theresa. "Mentors and Maternal Role Models: The Healthy Mean Between Extremes in Anne Tyler's Fiction." C. Ralph Stephens 28-40.

King, Richard H. *A Southern Renaissance: The Cultural Awakening of the American South, 1930–1955.* New York: Oxford UP, 1980.

Kingsolver, Barbara. *Animal Dreams.* New York: Harper, 1990.

——. *The Bean Trees.* New York: Harper, 1988.

——. *Pigs in Heaven.* New York: Harper, 1993.

Kreyling, Michael. *Figures of the Hero in Southern Narrative.* Baton Rouge : Louisiana State UP, 1987.

Lawson, Lewis H. *Another Generation: Southern Fiction Since World War II.* Jackson: UP of Mississippi, 1984.

Lee, Dorothy. "Harriette Arnow's *Dollmaker*: A Journey to Awareness." *Critique* 20.2 (1978): 92-98.

Lee, Harper. *To Kill a Mockingbird.* Philadelphia: Lippincott, 1960.

Lerner, Gerda. *The Creation of Patriarchy.* New York: Oxford UP, 1986.

Levy, Helen Fiddyment. *Fiction of the Home Place: Jewett, Cather, Glasgow, Porter, Welty, and Naylor.* Jackson: UP of Mississippi, 1992.

Linton, Karin. *The Temporal Horizon: A Study of the Theme of Time in Anne Tyler's Major Novels.* Stockholm: Uppsala University-Almqvist and Wiksell, 1989.

Lodge, Michelle. "PW Interviews Lee Smith." *Publishers Weekly* 20 Sept. 1985: 110.

Lowry, Beverly. *The Perfect Sonya.* New York: Viking, 1987.

MacKethan, Lucinda H. *Daughters of Time: Creating Woman's Voice in Southern Story.* Athens: U of Georgia P, 1990.

Manning, Carol S., ed. *The Female Tradition in Southern Literature.* Urbana: U of Illinois P, 1993.

——. "The Real Beginning of the Southern Renaissance." Manning 37-57.

Mason, Bobbie Ann. *Feather Crowns.* New York: Harper, 1993.

——. *In Country.* 1985. New York: Harper, 1986.

——. *Spence and Lila.* New York: Harper, 1988.

McCorkle, Jill. *The Cheerleader.* 1984. New York: Penguin, 1986.

——. *Ferris Beach.* Chapel Hill: Algonquin, 1990.

——. *Tending to Virginia.* Chapel Hill: Algonquin, 1987.

McCullers, Carson. *The Ballad of the Sad Cafe and Other Stories.* 1951. New York: Bantam , 1986.

——. *The Heart Is a Lonely Hunter.* Boston: Houghton Mifflin, 1940.

——. *The Member of the Wedding.* Boston: Houghton Mifflin, 1946.

McMurtry, Larry. "Life in a Foreign Country. Review of The Accidental Tourist." Petry 132-37.

Meese, Elizabeth A. *Crossing the Double-Cross: The Practice of Feminist Criticism.* Chapel Hill: U of North Carolina P, 1986.

Michaels, Marguerite. "Anne Tyler, Writer 8:05 to 3:30." Petry 40-45.

Mickelson, Anne Z. "Gail Godwin: Order and Accommodation." *Reaching Out: Sensitivity and Order in Recent American Fiction By Women.* Metuchen: Scarecrow, 1979. 68-87.

Miller, Danny. "A Melus Interview with Harriette Arnow." *Melus* 9.2 (1982): 83-98.

Miller, Jean Baker. *Toward a New Psychology of Women.* Boston: Beacon, 1976.

Mitchell, Margaret. *Gone With the Wind.* 1936. Garden City, NY: International Collectors Library, 1964.

Morrison, Toni. Interview. *Black Women Writers at Work.* Ed. Claudia Tate. New York: Continuum, 1983.

——. *Playing in the Dark: Whiteness and the Literary Imagination.* 1992. New York: Vintage, 1993.

O'Connor, Flannery. *The Complete Stories.* New York: Farrar, 1979.

——. *The Habit of Being.* New York: Farrar, 1979.

Papadimas, Julie Persing. "America Tyler Style: Surrogate Families and Transiency." *Journal of American Culture* 15.3 (1992): 45-52.

Parker, Pamela Lorraine. *The Search for Autonomy in the Works of Kate Chopin, Ellen Glasgow, Carson McCullers, and Shirley Ann Grau.* Diss. Rice University, 1982. Ann Arbor: UMI, 1982.

Payant, Katherine B. *Becoming and Bonding: Contemporary Feminism and Popular Fiction by American Women Writers.* Westport: Greenwood, 1993.

Pearlman, Mickey, ed. *American Women Writing Fiction: Memory, Identity, Family, Space.* Lexington: UP of Kentucky, 1989.

——, ed. *Mother Puzzles: Daughters and Mothers in Contemporary American Literature.* Westport: Greenwood, 1989.

Petry, Alice Hall, ed. *Critical Essays on Anne Tyler.* New York: Hall, 1992.

Phillips, Jayne Anne. *Black Tickets.* New York: Penguin, 1988.

——. *Machine Dreams.* New York: Dutton, 1984.

Prenshaw, Peggy Whitman, ed. *Women Writers of the Contemporary South.* 1984. Jackson: UP of Mississippi, 1985.

Pyron, Darden Asbury. *Southern Daughter: The Life of Margaret Mitchell.* Oxford: Oxford UP, 1991.

Rhodes, Carolyn. "Gail Godwin and the Ideal of Southern Womanhood." Prenshaw 55-67.

Ridley, Clifford A. "Anne Tyler: A Sense of Reticence Balanced by 'Oh, Well, Why Not?'" Petry 24-28.

Roberts, Elizabeth Madox. *The Time of Man.* New York: Viking, 1926.

Robertson, Mary F. "Anne Tyler: Medusa Points and Contact Points." Petry 184-207.

Rogers, Kim Lacy. "A Mother's Story in a Daughter's Life: Gail Godwin's *A Southern Family.*" Pearlman 59-67.

Rowe, John Carlos. "The Economics of the Body in Kate Chopin's *The Awakening.*" *Kate Chopin Reconsidered: Beyond the Bayou.* Ed. Lynda S. Boren and Sara deSaussure Davis. Baton Rouge: Louisiana State UP, 1992. 117-42.

Runyon, Randolph. *The Taciturn Text: The Fiction of Robert Penn Warren.* Columbus: Ohio State UP, 1990.

Schlueter, Paul. *Shirley Ann Grau.* Boston: Twayne, 1981.

Schultz, Elizabeth. "Out of the Woods and into the World: A Study of Interracial Friendships Between Women in American Novels." *Conjuring: Black Women, Fiction, and Literary Tradition.* Ed. Marjorie Pryse and Hortense J. Spillers. Bloomington: Indiana UP, 1985. 67-85.

Schulz, Clair. "Recommended: Shirley Ann Grau." *English Journal* Feb. 1986: 95-96.

Schulz, Joan. "Orphaning as Resistance." Manning 89-110.

Scott, Anne Firor. *The Southern Lady: From Pedestal to Politics, 1830–1930.* Chicago: U of Chicago P, 1970.

Settle, Mary Lee. *The Killing Ground.* New York: Farrar, 1982.

Shelton, Frank W. "Anne Tyler's Houses." C. Ralph Stephens 40-47.

——. "The Necessary Balance: Distance and Sympathy in the Novels of Anne Tyler." Petry 175-84.

Shivers, Louise. *Here To Get My Baby Out of Jail.* New York: Fawcett, 1983.

Showalter, Elaine. "Tradition and the Female Talent: The Awakening as a Solitary Book." *The Awakening.* Ed. Nancy Walker. Boston and New York: Bedford-St. Martin's, 1993. 169-89.

Smith, Lee. *Black Mountain Breakdown.* New York: Ballantine, 1980.

——. *The Devil's Dream.* New York: Ballantine, 1992.

——. *Fair and Tender Ladies.* New York: Ballantine, 1988.

——. *Family Linen.* New York: Ballantine, 1985.

——. *Oral History.* New York: Ballantine, 1983.

Spacks, Patricia Meyer. *The Female Imagination*. New York: Knopf, 1975.

Stephens, C. Ralph. *The Fiction of Anne Tyler*. Jackson: UP of Mississippi, 1990.

Stephens, Martha. *Children of the World*. Dallas: Southern Methodist UP, 1994.

Sternburg, Janet, ed. *The Writer on Her Work: Contemporary Women Writers Reflect on Their Art and Situation*. New York: Norton, 1980.

Tobin, Patricia Drechsel. *Time and the Novel: The Genealogical Imperative*. Princeton: Princeton UP, 1978.

Town, Caren J. "Rewriting the Family During *Dinner at the Homesick Restaurant*." *Southern Quarterly* 31.1 (1992): 14-24.

Tyler, Anne. *The Accidental Tourist*. New York: Knopf, 1985.

——. "Because I Want More Than One Life." Petry 45-50.

——. *Breathing Lessons*. New York: Knopf, 1988.

——. *Celestial Navigation*. New York: Knopf, 1974.

——. *The Clock Winder*. New York: Knopf, 1972.

——. *Dinner at the Homesick Restaurant*. New York: Knopf, 1982.

——. *Earthly Possessions*. New York: Knopf, 1977.

——. *If Morning Ever Comes*. 1964. New York: Berkley, 1983.

——. *Ladder of Years*. New York: Knopf, 1995.

——. *Morgan's Passing*. New York: Knopf, 1980.

——. *Saint Maybe*. New York: Knopf, 1991.

——. *Searching for Caleb*. 1975. New York: Berkley, 1983.

——. *A Slipping-Down Life*. 1970. New York: Berkley, 1983.

——. *The Tin Can Tree*. 1965. New York: Berkley, 1983.

——. "Trying to Be Perfect. Review of *One-Eyed Cat* by Paula Fox." *New York Times Book Review* 11 Nov. 1984: 48.

Updike, John. "On Such a Beautiful Green Little Planet." Rev. of *Dinner at the Homesick Restaurant*." Petry 107-11.

Voelker, Joseph C. *Art and the Accidental in Anne Tyler*. Columbia: U of Missouri P, 1989.

Wagner, Joseph B. "Beck Tull: 'The Absent Presence' in *Dinner at the Homesick Restaurant*." C. Ralph Stephens 73-84.

Walker, Alice. *The Color Purple*. 1982. New York: Washington Square, 1983.

——. *In Search of Our Mothers' Gardens*. New York: Harcourt, 1983.

——. *Meridian*. New York: Harcourt, 1976.

Walker, Cheryl. "Feminist Literary Criticism and the Author." *Critical Inquiry* 16 (Spring 1990): 551-73.

Walsh, Kathleen. "Free Will and Determinism in Harriette Arnow's *The Dollmaker*." *South Atlantic Review* 49.4 (1984): 91-107.

Ward, Carol M. *Rita Mae Brown*. New York: Twayne, 1993.

Washington, Mary Helen. "Foreword." *Their Eyes Were Watching God*. By Zora Neale Hurston. New York: Harper, 1990. vii-xiv.

Welty, Eudora. *Delta Wedding.* 1945. New York: Harcourt,1946.

———. *The Golden Apples.* New York: Harcourt, 1949.

———. *Losing Battles.* 1970. New York: Vintage Books, 1978.

———. *One Writer's Beginnings.* Cambridge: Harvard UP, 1984.

———. *The Optimist's Daughter.* 1969. New York: Random House-Vintage, 1972.

———. *The Ponder Heart.* 1953. New York: Harcourt,1954.

———. *Thirteen Stories.* 1937. New York: Harcourt, 1977.

Westling, Louise. "Fathers and Daughters in Welty and O'Connor." Manning 110-25.

———. *Sacred Groves and Ravaged Gardens: The Fiction of Eudora Welty, Carson McCullers, and Flannery O'Connor.* Athens: U of Georgia P, 1985.

White, Isabelle. "Toward a Different Aesthetic: The Artist and Community in Harriette Arnow's *The Dollmaker.*" *Journal of Kentucky Studies* 9 (Sept. 1992): 130-38.

Williams, Sherley Ann. *Dessa Rose.* 1986. New York: Berkley, 1987.

Wyatt, Jean. *Reconstructing Desire: The Role of the Unconscious in Women's Reading and Writing.* Chapel Hill: U of North Carolina P, 1990.

Wyatt-Brown, Bertram. *Southern Honor: Ethics and Behavior in the Old South.* New York: Oxford UP, 1982.

Yardley, Jonathan. "Gail Godwin: A Novelist at the Height of Her Powers" [review of *A Mother and Two Daughters*]. *Book World—The Washington Post* 13 Dec. 1981: 3.

Index

227